Für
Herrn Gerhart Hauptmann
in Herzlichkeit und
Ergebenheit
Arnolt Bronnen

IN THE VALLEY

AND OTHER CAROLINA PLAYS

*Two hundred copies of this book have been
printed on special paper and issued in special bind-
ing, of which one hundred and sixty, numbered 1
to 160, and signed by the author, are for sale.*

IN THE VALLEY
AND
OTHER CAROLINA PLAYS

BY

PAUL GREEN

SAMUEL FRENCH

Incorporated 1898

THOS. R. EDWARDS, Managing Director

NEW YORK CITY :: :: MCMXXVIII

SAMUEL FRENCH, LTD. :: :: :: LONDON

TO

Frederick H. Koch

IN GRATEFUL APPRECIATION

CONTENTS

IN THE VALLEY

CHARACTERS

QUIVIENE LOCKLEY, *an old Negro boarding-house keeper.*
WILLIE LOCKLEY, *her youngish and feeble-minded husband.*
ZEB VANCE LOCKLEY, *her illegitimate son.*
MILLY WILSON, *a boarder and cook for the white-folks.*
BANTAM WILSON, *her husband, an ex-convict.*
TOM STERLING, *a boarder and bricklayer, Milly's sweetheart.*
ED UZZELL, *a laborer.*
LEVIN FARROW, *a laborer.*
SEENY GRAY, *a dishwasher.* } *Boarders with old* QUIVIENE
BAD-EYE SMITH, *a drayman.*
JOHN HENRY, *a stranger.*
TWO GUARDS.
SEVERAL CONVICTS.

TIME—*The present.*
PLACE—*At the edge of a college town in North Carolina, also on a road.*

IN THE VALLEY

In a little ravine or sort of valley close by the college town is part of a larger Negro settlement called Johnson's Gully. Of late years the more respecting inhabitants have restyled the place Johnstown. Here the laborers, many of whom have come from different parts of the state and from neighboring states for the building of the greater Institution, herd together, sleeping and eating as best they can. In the evenings you will find them laughing, singing, and sitting before the shacks with their girls, or walking out if the weather is fine towards the hilly fields that lie west of the town. Swarms of kinky-headed children shoot marbles or roll battered automobile tires along the crooked roads called streets. At times they stop and look on in awe as BELLE'S sweetheart from Raleigh comes cadillacking along in his flashy wire-wheeled Ford.

And the "sport" calls to a girl sitting in the yard with a man. She rises and goes with him. Her companion left alone growls wrathfully to himself and registers an oath on high that he too will ride like that some day, goddam he will. But he won't, for the crapshooters know his soul.

On the porch of old QUIVIENE LOCKLEY'S shack across the street sits EDDIE UZZELL, a man past fifty now, with his head bent despondently in his hand. BAD ED he had been called in the old Memphis days. Bootleg liquor, women and cards have caved him in. He looks out towards the west where the sun is setting behind the smokestacks of the cotton-mill and hums a song to himself about BRADY the rounder who broke the hearts of the women in Gawgy. He too was like that once. And remembering the gal in Winston-Salem and the three kids which once were his, he hits the side of his chair and

3

*spits softly in the yard. After such a life, swinging a pick
in a ditch for two bucks a day and all the manhood gone out
of you is a hell of a way to end. And then too them white
men stand around in their collars and tell you what to do
. . . Jesus . . . . The big-bugs come down from Durham
and Raleigh and the Lord knows where, rolling around in
their Packards and Franklins and Studebakers. They walk
about with the president and point with their canes . . . .
O God A'mighty. Spitting again, he gets up, takes a step
or two and then reseats himself with his head in his hand.
The sun goes down, other boarders come out of the house
and join him on the porch. They light their pipes and ciga-
rettes, they talk a bit now and then. The little valley fills
with dusk, and darkness rolls up to cover them. Now and
then a spurt of a match lights up a face, and the coal of a
smoker intermittently glows and subsides, like a dull firefly.
Silence comes over the sort of town, voices up and down the
streets grow softer, come less often. The boarders on* OLD
QUIVIENE'S *porch sit in long stretches of motionless silence.
Each grows busy with his thoughts of tomorrow and yester-
day, each withdrawing into the sanctuary of himself. . . .
Soon they will get up one by one, "see you all tomorrow,"
and mosey off to their bug-ridden beds in different parts of
the valley. . . . Ignorant and blind, valiant of the Lord!
. . . Then a soft voice tinkles in the darkness.* SEENY GRAY,
the bold-eyed dishwasher in a cafeteria uptown, asks if
MILLY *has been heard from lately.* OLD QUIVIENE *spits a
stream of snuff before her and answers, "Nun-unh." And
her thoughts like those of the others on the porch go back to
a night last winter when things went wrong. Nothing particular happened, but still things went wrong. It happens that
way sometimes, they all had said. In our words, matters get
tangled up, explosions occur like thunder and lightning in a
storm and then quiet comes again as after a rain. . . . Still
the twisted and torn cannot be straightened and eased when
the quiet does come. . . . "Poor* MILLY . . . . *Poor* TOM

STERLING . . . . *poor everybody."* AUNT QUIVIENE *said. Weather or not, things are not so nice in winter in this little town. Certain it is that the cold huddles these poor ones together indoors, and sickness makes the days and nights more difficult to bear. And at times things other than sickness break out among them as if an invisible and malignant devil were sicking them on to blood and murder. . . . Ask him afterwards why it happened and he will reply, "I dunno, suh . . . I went blind, crazy-mad all of a suddent." . . . "He called me a son of a bitch and no man kin do that and live. My mother was . . ." Nobody except the orthodox knows why, but still at times all goes wrong. It happened so one cold night last January there in* OLD QUIVIENE'S *place —at least the beginning of it.*

It is about seven o'clock in the evening and OLD QUIVIENE *is setting the supper for her boarders on a long rakish table in the rear of the room. She brings the dishes from a sort of lean-to a step lower at the back where a stove can be seen and where two or three men are washing up. A large tin heater almost red-hot with a roaring fire is near the right wall, a cot near it, a door opening out, and farther to the left of the room a wide ragged bed. At the foot of the bed and nearer the front a low door leads into another room. The men come in from the lean-to shed and sit down by the stove where two others are sitting.*

They snuggle down in their chairs humped over, warming themselves by the stove and saying nothing. The weariness of the day's labor is upon them and the warmth of the fire makes them drowsy. Presently there is a knock at the door to the right. LEVIN FARROW *raises his head up alertly.* LEVIN *is always alert. He is quick on the call and lives as if always expecting something or somebody.*

FARROW. Come in. [JOHN HENRY, *a heavy stolid man with a bluish soot-black crafty face, comes in. He wears a derby, a yellow overcoat and gloves, and carries a suitcase in his hand.*]

HENRY. [*Pleasantly.*] Good evening, everybody. [*The men around the stove raise their heads, stare at him a moment, and then return to their rest. Only* FARROW *remains watching him—and that attentively.*]

FARROW. How you come on?

HENRY. Tell me youg'n git meals here.

FARROW. Ax her in there.

OLD QUIVIENE. [*Coming in.*] Good evening, suh.

HENRY. Git meals here?

QUIVIENE. Make yourself at home.

HENRY. Can I git supper?

QUIVIENE. Won't be a speck of trouble.

HENRY. [*Taking off his overcoat showily and folding it carefully on his suitcase by the wall.*] How much?

QUIVIENE. We won't fall out over that, Mister—

HENRY. Never mind the name, grub taste the same. [*He lays his derby on his overcoat, slowly takes off his gloves, and sits down near the stove.* QUIVIENE *waits a moment and then returns to the kitchen.*]

FARROW. [*Smiling friendly.*] Cold out. [HENRY *turns sleekly about and stares at him patronizingly, saying never a word.* FARROW *raises the lid of the stove quite precisely and stirs the fire.*] Yes suh, cold and a snow maybe.

QUIVIENE. [*Calling from the shed.*] Willie, git me some stovewood. [WILLIE, *a slender Negro of about thirty with a childish face and cloudy eyes, stretches his hand vainly towards the warmth of the stove, grins mulishly at the men, hesitates and then goes out.*]

FARROW. [*Jollily.*] Hep, some husband!

HENRY. Brain's dead on him.

FARROW. How come, stranger?

HENRY. Just is.

FARROW. Sho'. Smart whah you come from, ain't they?

HENRY. Smart and sharp.

FARROW. How sharp?

HENRY. [*Coldly.*] So sharp they got p'ints on their fists like a needle. Stick 'em right through a man, git 'em wrong.

FARROW. Uh-uh. That Willie tied like a yard-dog, po' fool.

HENRY. Never knows it, 's all right.

FARROW. Sho'. [*Reaching over and slapping the bent figure beside him.*] Wake up, Bad-Eye, be roasting that face 'g'in the stove, don't mind.

BAD-EYE. [*Raising a gnarled face set with two crossed and bloodshot eyes.*] Lawd, sleepy and hongry!

FARROW. How many trunks you haul today?

BAD-EYE. Working on my truck all day.

FARROW. [*Hee-hawing.*] Truck! A bundle of scrap-arn tied together with strings.

BAD-EYE. Pullingest engine in de country. Go up any hill in high. Des' need tahs on it.

FARROW. Jesus Christ. Turn that face from me! . . . Better git you a pick and fall in the ditch with us. [*To the morose figure across the stove from him.*] Hadn't he, Eddie?

UZZELL. His business.

FARROW. [*Barking out imitatively.*] Dis heah's de Old Ninety-Seven, put yo' trunks into Center on time. [*Singing.*]

Making ninety miles a' hour,
Please suh, jest gi' her a
lil' mo' juice . . .

Hee—hee! Speed! That thing got speed. Pass everything on de road but a filling station. [BAD-EYE *fingers his jewsharp and looks piteously at* FARROW.]

HENRY. [*Sharply.*] Let him alone. Give us a piece with your harp. [BAD-EYE *turns his face upwards and begins plucking and humming.* FARROW *pulls his plug hat out of his pocket and passes it around, taking up imaginary pennies. Presently he tires of it and sits down with all the fun gone from his face.*]

FARROW. Supper 'bout ready, Aunt Quivie?

QUIVIENE. Be ready time the rest 'rives. [WILLIE *comes in and sits meekly by the stove.*]

FARROW. [*His fun turned to bitterness.*] Git yo' mammy her wood?

WILLIE. Ain't my mammy.

FARROW. What is she? [WILLIE *snickers and blinks at* FARROW.] Weaned you yit? [WILLIE *bursts into squeals of laughter.*] Damn! the old cow's been dry forty year. [*He bends his head between his hands and is silent, his face hardened with spitefulness. Now and then he stares brightly at* UZZELL *whose head is bowed on his breast.*]

BAD-EYE. Dem fish smell lak de new life.

WILLIE. Fish and oysters.

FARROW. [*Suddenly warm again and smiling.*] Fish and oysters for supper?

,WILLIE. [*Shyly.*] Surprise.

FARROW. What for? [*He sees* HENRY *smiling patronizingly at him.*] Oh, sho' . . . .

HENRY. [*Softly.*] Sho'?

FARROW. [*Mysteriously.*] Ne' mind.

HENRY. [*Brutally.*] Such a fool. He don't know. [FARROW *turns away.*] I tell you, birthday supper.

FARROW. [*Starting.*] Mebbe mine.. [*Subsiding.*] No, mine come in December. Yo'n?

HENRY. Her boy Zeb Vance. [WILLIE *nods jubilantly and then looks stealthily behind him.*]

FARROW. [*Perplexed.*] How come you know so much, stranger?

HENRY. I ain't stranger. My name's John Henry.

FARROW. [*Furtively teasing.*] Any kin to the John Henry was such a steel-driving fool?

HENRY. [*Cryptically.*] Mebbe the same man, but no fool.

FARROW. [*After a moment—astonished.*] Great goodness!

HENRY. [*Chuckling softly to himself.*] Yeh. [UZZELL *straightens up and looks at him with a show of interest.*]

FARROW. [*Cunningly.*] The same John Henry you say?

HENRY. Ain't said, but mebbe so.

FARROW. [*Triumphantly.*] Cain't be. He done daid. [*Singing.*]

> Dis heah de hammer killed John Henry,
> Killed him daid, boys, killed him daid.
> Busted de brains all outen my pardner,
> In de haid, boys, in de haid.

[WILLIE *slaps himself with joy and* BAD-EYE *pops his hands together, standing up to the music.* UZZELL *smiles a sort of writhing smile and punches the fire.* FARROW *rears back in a burst of exultant laughter.*]

HENRY. [*Singing impassively.*]

Heard mighty rumbling,
Heard mighty rumbling,
Heard mighty rumbling,
    Under de ground.
Must be John Henry turning round.

Nine-pound hammer
Nine-pound hammer,
Can't kill me,
    Well it can't kill me.
Nine pound hammer couldn't kill me.

[*As if listening.*]

Up on de mountains
    I hear John Henry crying . . .

FARROW. Foh Christ sake stop that!

HENRY. Easy as pie. [UZZELL *watches him with growing interest. His face before sagged and dead now seems alive.*]

FARROW. Who is you?

HENRY. John Henry and not Stranger.

FARROW. [*Soothingly.*] Sho'.

HENRY. Sho'.

FARROW. [*Going quickly over to the bed at the left.*] Hunh, po' things lie hyuh same as two little old men and look at you. [*The two children in the bed begin to whine.*] Uh-uh now!

QUIVIENE. [*Calling from the shed.*] Gi' 'em some bread from the table. [FARROW *gets some bread for them. Two pairs of tiny, clamorous black hands reach up above the cover and seize it.*]

UZZELL. What you doing here in Johnstown?

HENRY. [*Lighting a cigarette.*] Oh, figgering on a job mebbe.

UZZELL. [*Now smiling cryptically.*] Digging in or digging out?

HENRY. Since you ask, mebbe neither. [*With a touch of braggadocio confidence.*] Mebbe I'm waiting foh my partner. [FARROW *draws nearer, listening.*]

UZZELL. John Henry with a pardner?

HENRY. I said . . .

UZZELL. Maybe not.

HENRY. [*Singing.*] Busted de brains all outen my pardner . . .

UZZELL. Yo' business. [*He drops his head and says no more.*]

FARROW. [*Half to himself.*] Quare man. [BAD-EYE *falls asleep, perhaps dreaming about his truck and mountains of baggage.*]

HENRY. Think so?

FARROW. Hearing like a hawk.

HENRY. Them twins over there belong to Milly Wilson—anh?

FARROW. Yeh suh. [WILLIE *snickers and* HENRY *stretches out his legs expansively.*]

HENRY. Her husband name Bantam Wilson and he's on the road—anh?

FARROW. How do you know so much?

HENRY. And one of 'em got club feet, ain't he?

FARROW. 'Fore God!

[SEENY GRAY, *a young bold-eyed girl of twenty, is seen entering the shed at the rear. She begins washing her face and dolling herself up before a mirror that hangs on the wall, talking to* OLD QUIVIENE *the while.*]

HENRY. [*Pulling out a heavy gold watch.*] I ain't so smart. Other folks dead in the head. [*Snapping his head up so that*

FARROW *starts back*.] And I can prophecy the future too.

FARROW. Uh—uh! Not too fast, bo'.

HENRY. [*With a kind of threatening levelness*.] I can prophesy the future.

FARROW. Show me. (*After a moment*.) Tell me then sump'n about the gal back there.

HENRY. Sho', easy. Your gal, ain't she?

FARROW. *You* prophesying. What going to happen between us?

HENRY. Think you're gonna marry? But plenty trouble coming in between.

FARROW. Us done tied hard and fast, all 'cept the preacher.

HENRY. [*Whistling teasingly a moment*.] Ever had any fusses?

FARROW. Like two ripe apples.

HENRY. [*Staring at him with a touch of maliciousness*.] Huh—I see—going to have trouble tonight.

[BAD-EYE *sleeps away*, WILLIE *looks on with open mouth, now and then wiping his dripping chin with his sleeve.* UZZELL'S *face again seems live and full of interest*.]

FARROW. [*Cracking out the words in the open air*.] Heighp, Lord-a-mercy! Listen that fool talk and say nothing.

HENRY. [*A rasp in his voice*.] Talk but I ain't no fool. Tell you once . . .

FARROW. [*Soothingly*.] Sho', sho'.

HENRY. [*Raising his head with a kind of mystic gesture*.] I see in the future. [*Loudly, so that* BAD-EYE *starts up from his dreams*.]

> Fit for none . . .
> Fun for some,

Yea, I even see new tars on Bad-Eye's truck. [BAD-EYE *looks up in consternation, and* WILLIE *giggles with a mixture of squeal and shout.* UZZELL *shrugs his shoulders and leans his head back on his ever-present hand.*]

FARROW. [*Scoffingly.*] Oh yes—new tars, platinum bearings and a' engine make no more fuss than de wind. Oh yes, sho'. [*Grunting.*] He prophesies.

[HENRY *starts to reply and then fastens his eyes on* SEENY GRAY *who comes tripping in.*]

SEENY. [*With a round, resonant voice.*] How you-all come on? [*To* HENRY *who rises, somewhat mockingly courteous.*] Good-evening, suh.

HENRY. [*Displaying his gold-chained vest as well as his gold front teeth.*] And how do you do?

FARROW. Miss Gray, this is Mr. Henry—John Henry. Maybe the great steel-driving man, maybe not.

SEENY. [*Stretching out a quick impetuous palm.*] Glad to meet you.

HENRY. [*Bowing over it unduly long.*] The pleasure's mine, all mine.

[*The children on the bed lose their bread and set up a kind of doggish whimpering.* OLD QUIVIENE *comes in and tries to pacify them.*]

QUIVIENE. Wish they mamy'd come on here. [*With a hump of her body from the waist up, she returns to the shed.*]

SEENY. Where'd you say you from?

HENRY. [*Winking broadly at* FARROW *who looks back at him with a puzzled face.*] I ain't said. [*Ramming his hands in his pockets.*] Oh well, sho'—I don't mind telling you. [*Poking up his lips in a whistle.*] I'm jest from around and about. [*Pulling out his watch.*] When did you say we eat? Now reading eight-ten and a half, railroad time.

QUIVIENE [*Coming in with a steaming dish which she sets on the table.*] In a minute, in a minute. Bad-Eye, you seen Zeb Vance anywhere?

BAD-EYE. [*Starting, but never taking his anxious eyes from* HENRY's *face.*] Seed him 'bout hour ago, bound foh de post-office.

QUIVIENE. Oh well then, be a long time waiting foh that window to open. [*She goes back to her cooking.*]

[TOM STERLING *comes into the shed, hangs up his bucket and begins washing for supper.*]

FARROW. [*Hee-hawing again.*] 'Fore God he said you and me'd have trouble—trouble between us maybe to-night.

[SEENY *giggles and looks at* HENRY *with luminous, inviting eyes. Silently* HENRY *turns and walks abstractedly up and down the room. In a moment* TOM STERLING *comes in and stands by the stove warming himself. He is a tall, broad-shouldered young fellow, twenty-eight or thirty, with a square jaw and wide-set direct eyes. He reaches out playfully and scuffs* BAD-EYE's *wool around.*]

STERLING. How you come on, old 97?

BAD-EYE. Awright. [*Looking up at him with humble admiration.*] She ain't come yit.

STERLING. Oh yes—working late again.

SEENY. Meet Mr. John Henry the new boarder, Mr. Sterling. [*The two men shake hands, and as if sensing a sort of antagonism between them, each goes immediately back to his former occupation—*HENRY *to pacing the room,* STERLING *to warming himself at the stove.*]

BAD-EYE. Dis makes three nights she been late comin' from Mr. Green's. [*Suddenly jubilant.*] Lord, if I had tahs on my truck I could bring her home at night. [*Softly.*] Maybe I could.

STERLING. [*His face clouded.*] Work too hard? Sho'—eight dollars a week, and seven-fifty for board and room!

SEENY. [*Chirping up as she flirts her hand coquettishly against* FARROW'S *face and goes out to help* OLD QUIVIENE *with the supper.*] Fifty cents more'n I get.

BAD-EYE. Lawd man, you makes big money. Seven dollars a day.

STERLING. Yeh 'n I got a mammy and sister back in Salisbury to take care of. [*Musingly.*] And that ain't all. [*Fretfully.*] Can't seem to save none. [WILLIE *suddenly giggles and squeals, slapping his body and then his thighs.*]

BAD-EYE. [*Protectingly.*] He thinks he's smart. Thinks he knows sump'n. But he don't.

STERLING. [*Pleasantly.*] That's all right. [*Raising his voice a bit.*] Sho', we're going to get married. Thought you all knew that.

FARROW. We knowed it but we didn't know when.

STERLING. Not so long now.

UZZELL. Got her divorce?

STERLING. Purty soon, next court the lawyer says. [*At the beginning of the conversation about the marriage,* HENRY *has drawn nearer, listening.*]

UZZELL. [*Grunting.*] Unh.

HENRY. How about her man on the road?

STERLING. Never seen him, never want to see him.

HENRY. S'pose he wanter see you?

FARROW. Yeh, s'pose he do?

STERLING. Then he can see me.

FARROW. Mighty mean man, Tom—how come he where he is?

STERLING. [*With a low laugh.*] Well they got him where they can keep him quiet awhile.

HENRY. [*Speaking into the air.*] But they won't keep him long. He'll be here now purty soon.

STERLING. He's got another year to go and by that time, [*Gesturing.*]—well—

HENRY. He'll be here purty soon.

STERLING. How soon?

HENRY. It may be today and it may be tomorrow. . . .

STERLING. [*Angrily.*] Say it out plain.

FARROW. He's a prophesier, Tom.

[STERLING *walks over to the bed and bends over the children pettingly.*]

HENRY. [*Brutally.*] Soon be yourn, won't they?

STERLING. And I don't mind telling the world.

HENRY. What're you gonna do with that club-footed 'un? They say his feet points back the way he come. [*He laughs loudly and* WILLIE *joins him, the tears running down his cheeks.*]

STERLING. [*Standing up—calmly.*] Gonna send him to Gastonia and have his feet straightened. Doctors there can do it. [*Bending again over the bed.*] Don't worry, sonny, them feet 'll be so's you can run like a fox, some these days.

[*The door is kicked open at the right and* ZEB VANCE *comes stepping in, carrying a large package in his hand. He throws his cap in the corner and sits down on the bench opening the package. He is a young mulatto of twenty or more, with bright ferrety eyes and a wizened neck and face. His voice is high like a girl's.*]

ZEB VANCE. [*Calling.*] Come all you rounders if you wanta see What de U. S. Mail done brung to me.

QUIVIENE. [*Coming in from the back.*] Did you git it, honey?

ZEB VANCE. [*Pulling out a suit of clothes.*] Sho' as shooting. [*Taking off his old coat and trying on the new.*] How do she fit, folkses?

BAD-EYE. [*Enviously.*] Look lak it growed on you.

QUIVIENE. [*Picking up his old coat.*] Hyuh, hyuh's a letter.

ZEB VANCE. Yeh, he sent me that too. [*Feeling in the envelope and pulling out a bill.*] A nice strip o' green-back.

WILLIE. Lawd, ten dollars!

ZEB VANCE. [*Springing out on the floor and cutting a caper.*] This here's mah birfday. Shake hands everybody. I'm free and twenty-one.

HENRY. Who he mean by he?

FARROW. You know all things.

HENRY. [*As* ZEB VANCE *skips around shaking hands with everybody.*] Bet I can guess. [*After a moment.*] Sho', I know.

FARROW. Sho', you know.

ZEB VANCE. [*Addressing the crowd, tears of joy in his eyes.*] He's the damndest best man ever was. Ten dollars and a suit of clothes. Going heah in Milly's room and put 'em on.

[*He goes into the room at the left.*]

SEENEY. [*As it were leaning towards* HENRY.] Some celebration—Money, clothes, a gre't big supper.

HENRY. [*Growling to himself.*] White man.

ZEB VANCE. [*Calling from off the left.*] Come hyuh, Levin.

[FARROW *gives a quick look around him and hurries into the room at the left.*]

QUIVIENE. S'pose he was a white man?

UZZELL. His business.

QUIVIENE. All right then.

HENRY. Once mo' and sho' it is.

SEENY. Them two's planning devilment.

WILLIE. [*Quavering.*] Done burning his pocket.

HENRY. Tonight?

SEENY. Oh meebe. Going with me.

HENRY. Maybe not so fast. Le's us, you and me— [*He gestures into the darkness and on.*]

SEENY. [*With a coquettish toss of her head, yet smiling directly.*] I don't mind.

HENRY. All right then, and after supper. When I make the move—shake. [*They shake hands, suggesting a closer embrace.*]

FARROW. [*Coming in as he calls over his shoulder.*] You done said and I give the answer.

QUIVIENE. Everybody set to it; here she is.

[*They all move toward the table and sit down.* HENRY *goes quickly by* BAD-EYE *and hands* SEENY *gallantly into her seat.* WILLIE, *astonished at* HENRY'S *graciousness, giggles with delight and digs* BAD-EYE *frantically in the ribs.*]

QUIVIENE. Come on, Zeb Vance, you're holding up the birthday.

[ZEB VANCE *comes in wearing his new clothes.*]

FARROW. Look out, red-hot mammas, cold weather's coming. Git him momma-mad, make his soul glad!

ZEB VANCE. You said it, old north wind. [*Cake-walking and chanting, he sticks out his chest.*]

> Well, she axed me into her parlor,
> And she cooled me wid her fan,

And she whispered to her mother
"Mamma I love that gambling man."

[STERLING *suddenly gets up and goes out at the right.* ZEB
VANCE *sits down at the table.*]

HENRY. [*Laying his hand on* SEENY'S *convenient one.*]
Where he going?

SEENY. All worried up 'bout her.

QUIVIENE. Help yourself, folkses— Yeh and he needs to be.
Po' thing work herself to death.

UZZELL [*Monotonously.*] Work, work, work.

FARROW. From sun to sun. Two dollars a day, work, work,
work.

UZZELL. Two for you and none for me—half for her.
[OLD QUIVIENE *passes the food around and they help themselves.* STERLING *returns, sits down and falls to his food.*]

STERLING. Mighty cold outside.

QUIVIENE. She'll be on in a minute.

STERLING. Babies been fed? (*Shivering.*) Yeh, mighty cold.

QUIVIENE. Some bread. Milly gonna bring the canned milk
for 'em. Willie, when you get done, you build a fire in her
room.

WILLIE. All right, 'm.

FARROW. [*Half to himself.*] All right'm, mammy.

STERLING. Had enough o' that.

HENRY. Might we have a speech from Governor Vance on
this occasion?

FARROW. Yeh, make 'em a speech, Waw-hoss.

ZEB VANCE. [*His mouth full of fish.*] Can't make no speech,
got to 'tend de vittles.

HENRY. [*Again with a touch of malignancy.*] Make a speech about him what sent the dry-goods and the piece of kale.

ZEB VANCE. Damn fine man, that's all to be said.

HENRY. What color his face?

SEENY. [*Pinching him.*] Sh!

QUIVIENE. Give Bad-Eye some more coffee. Well, his face ain't blue nohow, like the folks from Guiny. [*They rear back from the table laughing, and even* UZZELL *loosens a dry, writhing smile.*]

HENRY. [*Catching* SEENY's *arm sharply.*] Ain't it funny?

FARROW. Sho'.

HENRY. Oh yes, funny when a woman laugh at her bastard.

ZEB VANCE. [*Springing out of his chair with a whine.*] I'll tear his eyes out.

QUIVIENE. [*Quietly.*] He's a stranger, treat him polite.

ZEB VANCE. I'll mash his face in for him!

HENRY. Uhp! Don't let me hurt him, folkses. [*He leans back, his mouth stuffed with food, and smiles calmly at* ZEB VANCE.]

STERLING. Set down there, Zeb. [*Turning towards* HENRY.] Ask Aunt Quiviene's pardon.

QUIVIENE. [*Passing the food again.*] Never mind it, Tom.

STERLING. We'd like to have you ask Aune Quiviene's pardon.

HENRY. The people in hell would like water.

STERLING. [*Standing up.*] What you going to do?

UZZELL. [*Whispering to* HENRY.] Fool, that man'll break you like straw.

HENRY. [*Coolly.*] Well then, sho'. I beg your pardon, Miss Lockley.

[STERLING *sits down and resumes his eating. Presently* MILLY WILSON *comes in from the right wrapped in a thick coat and carrying a package of groceries.* STERLING *gets up from the table and helps her take off her coat.*]

HENRY. [*To* SEENY.] Seem to be mighty loving with another man's wife.

SEENY. Other man's dead, good as dead.

HENRY. Scripture say the dead do come to life. [*He whistles at her and puckers up his eyes.*]

SEENY. Oh—another year and all'll be fixed.

HENRY. Sho'. But many slip twixt the check and the bank. [MILLY *takes off her hat, goes into the kitchen and soon returns with the canned milk mixed in a pitcher. She begins feeding the babies, holding one in her lap and feeding it while* STERLING *feeds the other. They guzzle and squeal and grunt like famished pigs.*]

ZEB VANCE. Had to work extry, Milly?

SEENY. Better come on and finish your supper, Tom.

MILLY. Mis' Green had company and I had to stay and wait on 'em. [*She is a dark, plump mulatto of twenty-five with a wistful face and heavy-lidded eyes.*]

FARROW. Seem like they have comp'ny up there all the time lately.

MILLY. Maybe so. Put him back, Tom, he's finished.

[TOM *lays the baby back in the bed and returns to his supper.* MILLY *takes the crippled child to the stove and warms his feet.*]

QUIVIENE. Come on and get yourn.

MILLY. I et up there, but the fish do smell good.

QUIVIENE. And we got oysters.

[HENRY *sits looking at* MILLY, *half turned from his food.*]

SEENY. [*Stepping her fingers along his arm.*] Better come on. [*Smiling.*] You make the first move.

QUIVIENE. This here's Mr. John Henry, the new boarder, Milly.

MILLY. Yes.

HENRY. [*Without rising or bowing.*] Glad to see you. Knowed about you a long time.

MILLY. [*Smiling frankly.*] You did?

[HENRY *shrugs his shoulders.*]

FARROW. He knows everything past and future.

STERLING. And more, except some things.

[*For a while no one says anything—as they go on eating.* MILLY *sits at the stove, crooning to her child.* FARROW *and* ZEB VANCE *begin to exchange gestures and winks.*]

ZEB VANCE. Right, buddy, right lak de rain.

FARROW. You said, you speak gospel.

STERLING. [*Pleasantly.*] What's up tonight, Zeb?

WILLIE. [*Quavering again.*] Ten dollars got to be spent.

BAD-EYE. [*Mournfully.*] 'Twould near buy a whole new tah.

ZEB VANCE. Nearest that ten'll come to tahs 'll be to ride on 'em.

FARROW. [*Pushing himself back from the table.*]

> The women in their slippers,
> The ladies with their fans,
> Walking up and walking down,—

Eigh, Gov'nor?

ZEB VANCE. And de Gov'nor's wid you.

HENRY. [*With heavy jocularity.*] You see, Mrs. Wilson, the Gov'nor of the sovereign state of North Carolina, the Honorable Zeb Vance, has this day received—this day being his birthday, has this day received, to wit, a suit of clothes and a ten-dollar bill from his pappy. Did you say father or pappy?

ZER VANCE. Be goddamned if I said anything.

QUIVIENE. No cussing at the table.

ZEB VANCE. Why dat stranger fellow come her talking big?

STERLING. Set down again, he ain't going to say much more.

SEENY. Now don't you get to talking big, Tom Sterling.

MILLY. Seeny!

FARROW. That stranger can't help talking big. He a prophet from the land of Canaan. He's like a sow, see anything, see the wind.

[HENRY. *suddenly seizes his coffee cup and starts backward. The group watch him in astonishment.*]

WILLIE. [*Terrified.*] What ail dat man?

HENRY. [*Rising mechanically from the table and carrying his cup before him.*] What do I see? [*Peering into the cup.*] I see trouble.

UZZELL. [*With his twisting smile.*] Wrong, wrong up above his shoulders.

HENRY. Believers, onbelievers! I see, I see.

FARROW. Now 'fore God, what *do* he see?

SEENY. Look out, Levin, that man maybe got power. [*Softly.*] Yeh, he got power, strange power.

HENRY. [*Passing his hand back and forth before his eyes.*] I see sorrow and I see pleasure. Both pleasure and sorrow I see.

STERLING. Where do you see 'em, brother?

QUIVIENE. In the coffee-grounds.

MILLY. What trouble you see?

FARROW. [*Guffawing.*] Tell us the pleasure part.

HENRY. I sees the face of Levin Farrow.

[SEENY *cackles out loud and* FARROW *moves his chair around in discomfiture.* WILLIE *backs away from the table, goes over to the corner at the right rear near the shed and stands looking on in fear.* BAD-EYE *now full of food, and nodding in spite of himself, has laid his head on the table.*]

FARROW. Since you see so much, what you see in my face? Pleasure?

HENRY. Not for you.

FARROW. Oh trouble comes to all, anyhow.

HENRY. [*Stirring the cup with his finger.*] It comes sooner to some than others.

FARROW. How soon?

HENRY. Tonight.

FARROW. Me?

HENRY. Tonight for you.

FARROW. Here man, you cut out that prosticating.

HENRY. In the first place, I see you done lost your gal.

FARROW. [*Turning quickly to* SEENY.] What's he say so big?

SEENY. [*Tossing her head again.*] Let him say on.

HENRY. [*Impressively.*] In the second place, I see pleasure.

FARROW. [*Grinning now.*] Me. Yes suh, that makes it equal. [*He beams unsteadily around at the others who, with the exception of* BAD-EYE, *watch* HENRY *with growing interest. Even* UZZELL *turns his chair around and stares at him.*]

HENRY. Not for you.

STERLING. [*Suddenly slapping the table with open hand.*] John Henry, great steel-driver from the Clinchfield Mountains, you need a git-up for your conjure business. [*Laughing with sudden boyishness.*] Somebody git him a pair o' horns and a bag of fox-fire.

HENRY. [*Holding up his hand.*] Don't believe? I'll make you believe. I see pleasure. [*Bending low over the cup.*] What do I see? [*Suddenly shouting.*] Bad-Eye, Bad-Eye!

BAD-EYE. [*Starting up with a clatter.*] Who dat call me so loud?

WILLIE. [*Running up to* BAD-EYE *and bending over him.*] He see sump'n in dat cup 'bout you?

BAD-EYE. Dat bizness! [*Looking around for his hat.*] Great Lawd—spell bizness!

FARROW. He say it's sump'n good.

HENRY. I see a new truck with brand new tahs.

BAD-EYE. [*Stopping.*] See it all in dat li'l cup?—Pshaw.

HENRY. Bad-Eye, tomorrow morning go out and buy you a set of good cords, first class clinchers, yep.

BAD-EYE. [*Mournfully.*] Dey cost a heap of money. Sixty-four dollars and thirty-two cents.

HENRY. I see money. Sixty-five dollars. [*He waits, looking at* BAD-EYE *genially.*]

UZZELL. [*Chuckling.*] Where you see it?

HENRY. Looking through the cup, I see a stranger done leff it with the garage man. Go get it!

BAD-EYE. [*Pleading.*] Don't joke me? Sho' nuff?

HENRY. Sho' nuff. [*With dead earnestness, raising his hand in an oath.*] That money's there, go git it!

FARROW. [*Leaning vehemently towards* ZEB VANCE.] That

man got the evil spirit or sump'n. Mebbe crazy. [BAD-EYE *eyes him stupidly.*]

BAD-EYE. [*Softly.*] Hunh, ain't nuffin to it!

HENRY. If you don't go at once you lose your money. Any more of you want to know what's coming?

UZZELL. All tricks.

HENRY. Does the Gov'nor want me to tell him something about his pa?

QUIVIENE. [*Shrilly.*] Ain't going to tell him nothing. He done been told.

HENRY. Tell him 'bout the time them white students come out here and you raised hell with 'em?

QUIVIENE. [*Loosing her dignity.*] Shet it up, shet up that fly-trap!

HENRY. Tell him 'bout his pa, big man now, standing up high in the state. Going about with the gov'nor.

QUIVIENE. All done past.

HENRY. I see in the cup he the same man sent po' Bantam Wilson to the roads. A judge! A judge! Oh yus, oh yus, come into co't, come into co't! Goddam! Goddam, I faced him onct.

QUIVIENE. You stop that talking, and git right out'n my house. [*Shrilly again.*] Yeh, and I do mean it!

STERLING. [*Catching* OLD QUIVIENE *by the arm.*] I wanta ask him something.

HENRY. I'm coming to you.

FARROW. Where'd he learn 'bout Bantam Wilson?

STERLING. [*With a touch of triumph.*] Been on the roads with him, that's where.

HENRY. I see in the cup . . .

STERLING To hell with your cup and coffee grounds. You

been doing time, ain't you? And what's all this mess about trouble? I see through you. You learn all this stuff about folks round here from Bantam. [*Moving towards him.*] And I want you to clear out. Making fun of us, unh?

HENRY. Make no difference. Make no difference. When I speak, I speaks truth.

STERLING. You speak no more truth in this house.

MILLY. [*Coming from the stove and stepping between them.*] Let him say it, Tom. [*He puts his arm around her and holds her and the baby to him.*]

HENRY. Sho' and I'll speak. Fixing up for a wedding, heh? Well, there won't be none. [*Looking in the cup again.*] I see Bantam Wilson coming home. [*Throwing the cup against the floor and breaking it to pieces.*] And that's the end of my say. [*He pulls a coin out of his pocket and goes over to* OLD QUIVIENE.] Bad luck not to break the cup, and here's a quarter for it.

QUIVIENE. Lord-a'-mercy, keep it back from me! [*He puts the coin on the table and sits down silent by the stove.*]

BAD-EYE. I'm gwine to dat garage! [*He grabs his hat and dashes out of the house at the right.*]

QUIVIENE. Willie, go build a fire in Milly's room.

[WILLIE *looks fearfully at the darkness in the shed, hesitates a moment and goes out. Presently he is heard cutting wood on the wood-pile.*]

FARROW. Well, Seeny—I was about to forget, Zeb. I'll be back and ready to start about ten— Well, Seeny? Time we's going if we gits to that first pitchter. [*Rubbing his hands and slapping his thighs in anticipation.*] Lord, the funniest man I ever did see, that Charlie Chaplin. Funnier 'n you, John Henry, I say, funnier 'n you, John Henry. [HENRY *makes no reply but sits bent over the stove.*] And a white momma what scorches the screen.

[UZZELL, *now gloomy once more, goes to the wood-box, replenishes the fire and sits down again with his head in his hands.* FARROW *calls with sly softness.*]

FARROW.

> When I get about sixty-five dollars,
> Take my hammer to de captain,
>   Tell him I'm gone, boys,
>   Tell him I'm gone.

[*He takes* SEENY *by the hand and starts towards the rear.*]
I say, John Henry, I mean John Henry. [*But* JOHN HENRY *is silent as before.* SEENY *jerks her hand from* FARROW, *goes to the stove and warms herself.*]

SEENY. [*Blandly.*] Too cold outside to be going anywhere. [HENRY *chuckles softly to himself.*]

FARROW. Here's your coat. We gotta hurry; show starts at eight thirty.

HENRY. I said trouble, I mean trouble—

FARROW. Fire in the hole, le's go.

SEENY. [*Smoothly.*] Ain't going.

FARROW. [*Licking his lips.*] Crying out loud!

SEENY. Mr. John Henry and me have a little date. [HENRY *turns towards him with a snarl.*]

HENRY. Get out, you yellow-faced runt!

FARROW. [*Thunderstruck.*] He'p me get at him, Zeb. Tom, don't let him come here and break up things like that.

MILLY. Don't you bother him!

HENRY. [*Putting his arm around* SEENY *and drawing a knife out of his pocket, his face brutal and malevolent.*] Eigh, by God don't you bother him.

MILLY. Take Sonny in there and be putting him to bed. [*She pushes him towards the door and he goes in. Then she takes the other child in after him.*]

HENRY. Oh yus, oh yus, why don't you and the Gov'nor, the lamb of God, de judge's son come on 'n take dis 'oman from me?

FARROW. [*Bursting into whining sobs.*] Come on Zeb, le's go from here. Goddamn if we don't split de Durham women wide open tonight! [*He throws the new coat at* ZEB, *grabs him by the hand and bursts out of the house.* HENRY *drops his knife back in his pocket, clutches* SEENY *to him and turns up and down the room with her in his arms. She giggles in a sort of terrified joy.*]

SEENY. [*Whispering.*] Ain't never no man been like you before.

[UZZELL *sits up and looks at them with sceptical condescension, and* OLD QUIVIENE, *throwing out her hands in despair, begins clearing away the table.*]

HENRY. [*His face buried on* SEENY'S *shoulder.*] Can you do the hot-box from Georgia?

SEENY. Anything, anything. [*Trying to disengage herself.*] But later, later. [*Whispering.*] I can't breathe.

[WILLIE *comes timidly in with an armful of wood, looks at them in amazement, then tip-toes into the room at the left.* SEENY *breaks loose from* HENRY *and flies to help* OLD QUIVIENE. HENRY *emits a sort of joyous halloo between his cupped hands, strikes a caper or two and then sits down again at the stove, looking heavily at his watch.*]

UZZELL. [*Hoarsely.*] What time by your squash?

HENRY. Bed-time for working men that needs sleep. I don't need it.

UZZELL. Don't work?

HENRY.

>Engineer at night, a brakeman in the day,
>Tell the women in the towns
>>I'm on-a my way.

[WILLIE *comes in and sits down.*]

QUIVIENE. Come dry the dishes, Willie! [*He sighs forlornly and goes out.*]

[STERLING *and* MILLY *are heard talking in low tones as they put the children to bed.* SEENY *comes in from the rear for the last pile of dishes.* UZZELL *goes quickly over to her, his sombre face filled with a hungry look.*]

UZZELL. Hand me a drink of water. [*With one hand he takes the dipper, with the other catches* SEENY'S *outstretched palm.*]

SEENY. [*Softly as she looks at* HENRY'S *bowed back.*] Ed, Bad Ed you used to be.

UZZELL. [*With a wretched sigh.*] Seeny girl.

SEENY. [*Gathering up the dishes.*] I'm sorry, sorry, Ed.

UZZELL. [*Glancing carefully behind him and looking at her hungrily.*] Don't do it. I've travelled the road. I know.

SEENY. [*With quiet hardness.*] Old crows and young birds, Ed. You've said so, you know.

UZZELL. *His writhing smile playing about his lips.*] All right. . . [*Whispering sadly.*] I like you.

SEENY *goes out with the dishes.* UZZELL *returns the dipper to the bucket and stands thinking, his hands shoved deep into his pockets. He speaks softly to himself and then to* HENRY.] Dig a new foundation for the old. Eigh, brother? [*But* HENRY *bakes himself by the stove and says nothing.* UZZELL *gathers up the fragments of the broken cup and lays them on the table.* SEENY *comes to the door with a dish-cloth in her hand.*]

SEENY. Aunt Quivie's all upset, Ed.

UZZELL. Let Zeb go on. [*With a glance out of his shaggy eyes.*] The old crow, the young bird. [*Jocularly.*] Eigh, sister? [*Going to the door.*] Goodnight everybody, and the Gov'nor'll be back in the morning. [*Shrugging his shoulders and pulling his coat-collar around his neck.*] See you at breakfast. If I don't, don't worry 'bout me. [*He whistles softly and goes out through the shed. In a moment he pokes his head back through the shed door.*] ·Oh Seeny . . .

SEENY. Yeh.

UZZELL. Tra-la-la, girlie! [*He closes the door and is heard whistling again as he goes away.*]

QUIVIENE. [*In a sharp, rasping voice.*] Quit slubbering them dishes. [*Muttering.*] Been drying 'em night and mo'ning for three year and won't never learn.

WILLIE. [*Humbly.*] Doing the best I kin.

SEENY. [*With loud teasingness.*] Oughta trained him some 'fore you married him.

QUIVIENE. Looks like plenty others need training around here, sho' God do if my eyes got any sight in 'em.

[*The door at the right opens and* BANTAM WILSON *comes cautiously in. On seeing him,* HENRY *closes the door to the shed.*]

BANTAM. [*Grinning.*] Heah I is, and you too.

HENRY. [*Shaking hands with him and hugging him around the shoulders.*] Early. Didn't expect you till tomorrow night. Crow, little rooster.

BANTAM. Come on a th'ough train. [*Glancing around the room.*] Whah's everybody? Sho' a hell of a dump.

[*He is an ebony black little negro, squat, agile and ape-like, with slender legs and powerful shoulders. His massive hands hang down below his knees.*]

HENRY. All the better though. We can shove off towards Washington on the midnight from Durham.

BANTAM. Mebbe so and mebbe not. [*Winking at* HENRY.] Mought wanta spend a little sleeping wid my 'oman. [*Soberly.*] And dem chillen, I'd lak to see 'em.

HENRY. Suits me. I got a little jimmying for tonight too.

BANTAM. [*Archly.*] Indeed, suh? Uhp, wimmen.

HENRY. [*Chuckling.*] Oh yus, indeed.

BANTAM. Find everything fixed and ready foh the king? [*Sweeping his long arms around him.*]

HENRY. Oh, so-so.

BANTAM. [*Gesturing.*] Who talking in there, and who in there?

HENRY. [*Mimicking him.*] A woman in dere, and in dere.

BANTAM. [*Pulling a tiny revolver from his pocket.*] Look at dis, honey. She spit blood when she speaks.

HENRY. Done told you to go easy. [*Tapping his head.*] Carry your pistol up there.

BANTAM. Hunh, and you wid your knives. [*Looking sharply at* HENRY.] What do you mean by so-so?

HENRY. [*Humming.*] Somebody been there since I'm gone. . .

BANTAM. [*Hiding his pistol and rubbing his hands.*] Anh-hanh, and that's where I come in. [*Abruptly.*] How you come on foh cash?

HENRY. Freshet still rising.

BANTAM. Lord, you cleaned out that gang in Salisbury. They talking about it still.

HENRY. How much you need?

BANTAM. Dunno. Awright den, if you get de cold. [*With*

bland impersonality.] De goddammed white folks turned me loose in these heah old clothes with twelve dollars and a half. Hell of a price foh a yeah's work.

HENRY. [*Somewhat testily.*] Better be glad they let you out out ahead of your time.

BANTAM. [*Musingly.*] 'Fo' Christ, took all dat money to buy my baby. [*He pats his pocket.*]

[*The door at the left opens and* TOM STERLING *comes in.*]

HENRY [*Punctiliously.*] I want you gentlemen to meet one another and be friends. Mr. Sterling, this is Mr. Wilson.

BANTAM. [*Shooting out a huge paw.*] Glad to meet you, suh.

STERLING. Wilson?

HENRY. Bantam Wilson. Jest turned loose from the road. [STERLING *looks at him blankly, then goes and sits down at the stove.*]

BANTAM. Well, if you don't wanta shake hands.

HENRY. Your interest lie mighty close and you oughta be friends. [*Humming.*] Somebody been there while I'm gone. . . .

BANTAM. [*With a low bark.*] Goddamn, he de man?

HENRY. Ain't shooting off my mouth.

SEENY. [*Coming in from the rear.*] My land-a-morning! Who's this in possession?

BANTAM. If it ain't de old gal.

SEENY. [*Calling.*] Aunt Quivvie, come heah and see what the cat's brung in.

QUIVIENE. [*Appearing in the door.*] Lord, Bantam Wilson.

BANTAM. [*Shaking hands with them.*] And how's everybody? And you too, Willie, come on out'n your hiding-place. I ain't gonna hurt you.

[WILLIE *comes in and shrinks away as* BANTAM *fiercely shakes his limp hand.*]

QUIVIENE. Well, everybody set down and keep warm. Willie, punch up the fire. Oh, had your supper?

BANTAM. Et on de way.

[*A long silence comes over the group.* BANTAM *looks inquiringly around the room.*]

QUIVIENE. [*With a start.*] Run away from the roads?

BANTAM. [*Pulling a paper from his pocket.*] Pardoned slam and in the full.

QUIVIENE. Thank Jesus for that. Now you'll rest easy? Plenty of good work up at the college.

BANTAM. [*Lighting a cigarette.*] What? Sweating like a ball o' tallow in de ditch—nuh-uh, not me.

QUIVIENE. Gonna ride on easy street?

BANTAM. Gonna ride Norf. [*Glancing up sharply at* OLD QUIVIENE.] They tell me Milly live heah. Whah she?

QUIVIENE. Well now—oh—she's about.

BANTAM. [*Again archly.*] Outdoors?

QUIVIENE. Oh, mebbe not—

BANTAM. [*Smiling.*] Built to your house de last yeah?

QUIVIENE. No, built nothing

BANTAM. [*Laughing.*] Den she can't be in de house. [*He glances at* TOM STERLING.] You got only three rooms. De shed, dis room and de room there. She ain't in de shed, she ain't in this room, and she cain't be in there.

HENRY. [*Chuckling.*] How come, brother?

BANTAM. [*Rasping.*] 'Cause dat's Mr. Sterling's room.

QUIVIENE. Ain't Mr. Sterling's room.

BANTAM. Oh-ho, then goddam it what're you doing in dat room wid her and the door closed? [*Listening.*] Seem like I hear somebody a-crying in there. [*Chuckling.*] How de babies come on?

QUIVIENE. 'Bout like when you left.

BANTAM. Sonny's feet turn round yit?

SEENY. And they won't till the doctor turns 'em.

BANTAM. Damn de doctors. Keep him away from 'em, if you don't want him ruined. And dey ruin your pocketbook foh you too.

SEENY. Tom there is gonna take him and have him fixed.

BANTAM. [*Easily again.*] Not is, honey, but was. [*Listening.*] They sleeping awright. Who dat crying? [*Calling.*] Don't cry, momma, your papa done come home!

STERLING. Hush!

BANTAM. [*Bounding around.*] Who you talking to?

STERLING. I mean you, and I give you five minutes to get out.

BANTAM. Five minutes, and what's eating you?

HENRY. He don't like you talking that way to his woman.

BANTAM. 'Y God, I'll tell 'bout de 'oman.

[MILLY *is heard sobbing more loudly in the room at the left.*]

STERLING. I tell you to leave. See there, she knows you're back.

BANTAM. Listen, bo, about her in there. Dis minute I gives you your orders.

QUIVIENE. [*Quavering.*] Set down, Tom, that Bantam'll kill you.

STERLING. Just so he lets her alone.

BANTAM. Goddamn it, why you come stepping in twixt me and my 'oman? [*Half piteously.*] Twelve months breaking dem rocks. Let her rain, let her shine. De old hammer swinging all de time. [*Spreading out his huge calloused palms.*] Look-a dere, dem horny hands. I broke enough rocks and drove enough steel down—

HENRY. [*Softly.*] Steel-driving.

BANTAM. And drove enough steel down—amm—from de end of Kayntucky to Alabam. [*Vehemently.*] Twelve months and all de time no word from my 'oman. [*In a worker's singsong.*]

> Let her up—hunh—let her down,
> Muscle dat make—hunh—de world go roun'.

That sun and that rain and in the winter, freeze. No wimmen and no wimmen. Dey all scared. [*Weaving his head from side side.*] And de white folks pass in deir cars and de colored folks pass in deirn and dey look at you lak sump'n quare. [*Savagely to all around him.*] What you know 'bout it? [*To* STERLING.] Wait till you stand by and see 'em beat your buddy till de blood run all over the barrel, yea, de barrel, same like it was made to ketch it in. Talk 'bout de blood of Jesus. [*Shaking his head, he reaches over and gives* SEENY'S *cheek a playful pinch.*]—And den, honey, de yaller gals come out in July wid deir sun-bonnets on, picking blackberries by de way. And dey laugh, and deir laugh sound cool, but dey stand way off. Ax Henry, he know.—[*Fiercely.*] And all de time, my 'oman heah mommicking up wid him. [*Even in his fierceness there is the suggestion of pleasantry.*]

HENRY. [*Coolly.*] A little something, not much.

[*In* MILLY'S *room a child whines and there is a noise of a window being raised.* BANTAM *darts across the room.*]

BANTAM. Ho, little birdie, don't fly away. [*He opens the door and catches* MILLY *as she is trying to jump out of the window.*]

MILLY. Tom, Tom!

STERLING. I kill that Wilson.

HENRY. [*Stepping before him.*] For God's sake, stay out'n that room. He's got a gun on him.

BANTAM. [*As a struggle is heard.*] Dere, dere, honey. Gi' us a kiss. [*With a loud smack.*] Dat's it, several of 'em. A whole armful.

STERLING. Git out o' my way.

HENRY. [*As the women whimper and plead with* TOM.] For God's sake—[*But he gets no further, for* STERLING *hits him a blow in the face, laying him flat on the floor.*]

SEENY. [*Flying at him.*] Stop it, Tom. Don't do that. Something terrible—

HENRY. [*Standing up, a knife in his hand.*] No man hits me like that and live. [*He moves towards* STERLING. MILLY *is heard moaning, as* BANTAM *coos over her.*]

BANTAM. Momma, momma, pritty baby!

SEENY. [*Turning from* STERLING *and throwing her arms around* HENRY'S *neck.*] Come on, le's go, le's go.

HENRY. [*Trying to pull her arms from around him.*] I'll kill de goddamn snake, I'll kill him.

SEENY. [*Kissing him and drawing him towards the rear.*] Come on, come, I'll go with you. [*Whispering, her face against him.*] You know, you know, anything, anything. [HENRY *waits a moment and then, pulling her to him goes quickly out through the shed.* OLD QUIVIENE *sits down with a gasp and lays her head on the table.* WILLIE *turns foolishly about, sees* SEENY'S *coat hanging on the wall, gets it and goes into the shed.*]

WILLIE. [*Whimpering.*] You done forgot your coat.

[STERLING *starts cautiously across the room to the left, when the door opens and* BANTAM *stands forth, hugging* MILLY *to him with one hand and carrying his pistol in the other.*]

BANTAM. Put 'em up. [WILLIE *comes in at the rear, carrying the coat. He stops, terrified.*]

MILLY. [*Gasping.*] Go on away, Tom, he'll kill you, he'll kill you.

BANTAM. I tell you to stick dem hands up in de air.

QUIVIENE. [*Flinging herself before* TOM *and beating on his breast.*] Git out'n the house. For God's sake, git away, and don't bring trouble on us.

BANTAM. I gi' you one minute, den trot. [*He waits.* STERLING *stares at him blankly.*]

MILLY. Oh Lord.

BANTAM. Here goes den. [*He fires twice in close succession.* MILLY *screams and* OLD QUIVIENE *falls in a chair, rocking and moaning in grief.* WILLIE *looks on with eyes astart and then with a shriek flees through the door at the right.* MILLY *tries to claw at* BANTAM'S *face, but with one arm he holds her suffocatingly against him.*] Don't git wild, honey, I ain't killed him. Des' brushing his britches to let him know I means business. [STERLING *looks dully at* MILLY *for a long while and then, turning without a word goes slowly out at the rear.* BANTAM *lowers his pistol and kisses his hand towards him.*] Good-bye, good-bye fohever. [*Turning and drawing* MILLY *into the room, his huge hands spread fanlike on her breast.*] Honey babe, you's a soft bunch o' flowers. Nunh, sweet! [*He closes the door behind him.*]

QUIVIENE. [*Crawling up and making her way to the door at the right.*] Willie, come back honey! Ain't nothing to hurt you now! [*She turns around and goes heavily to the bed. Sitting down, she rocks her head back and forth in her hands.*

Presently she pulls off her shoes, drops her skirt, turns down the cover and wraps herself up.]

[WILLIE *comes cautiously in.*]

WILLIE. Whah is he?

QUIVIENE. [*Her shoulders jerking with suppressed sobs.*] Blow out the light and get to bed, son.

[*He blows out the light, takes off his shoes and trousers and lies down on the cot at the right. The room is dark save for the dim light that comes from the grate of the stove. The shadows on the wall grow more and more faint.* BANTAM'S *caressing voice, broken by* MILLY'S *low sobs, comes into the room. The bed is heard creaking as the ex-convict goes to his long-awaited rest.* MILLY'S *sobs gradually die away to low moans, and presently* BANTAM *is heard snickering, even giggling.* MILLY'S *moans now take on a different tone.*]

QUIVIENE. [*Sitting up in bed and snickering also.*] Hear that, Willie?

WILLIE. [*Whimpering.*] I skeered over heah. Sees dat man wid de pistol.

QUIVIENE. Come and git into bed with me, honey. [*With alacrity he runs and jumps into the bed. She hugs him up close to her and he pulls the covers down tight over his head. The faint outlines on the walls disappear. The peace of darkness, night within and without, enfolds the house and its troubled souls. The door at the rear springs open and* BAD-EYE *comes trampling in.*]

BAD-EYE. Whah is you, folkses? [*Half sobbing.*] Dat man fooled me!

QUIEVENE. Who's you?

BAD-EYE. [*Mournfully.*] De old 97.

QUIVIENE. We want to git our sleep now.

BAD-EYE. [*Plucking his jew's harp in the darkness.*] Whah dat man?

QUIVIENE. He gone out. Go find him.

BAD-EYE. [*Whimpering.*] Yeh, I tell you he done fool me! [*Moving gropingly about the room and then going out the way he came.*] I go show him.

WILLIE. [*Throwing the cover from his head.*] Gonna say my prayers.

QUIVIENE. Yeh, honey, do. [*In the dim light he is seen crouching by the bed.*]

WILLIE. [*Mumbling.*] Our Favver who art . . .

QUIVIENE. [*Joining in fervently.*] Thy Kingdom come, thy will be done on earth as it is in heaven.

BANTAM. [*Inside.*] Somebody at dat window. [*He is heard getting out of the bed.*]

QUIVIENE and WILLIE. Fohgive us our trespasses as we fohgive those who trespass against us.

MILLIE. [*Within.*] Ain't nobody, Bantam. Come back to bed.

BANTAM. Uhp, dere he is! I kill de goddam snake. [*The report of his pistol is heard, followed by the crash of glass.* QUIVIENE *springs out of the bed and crouches down with* WILLIE.]

QUIVIENE. [*Moaning aloud.*] Lord have mercy on us, Lord have mercy.

BANTAM. [*Cracking the door and peering out.*] Shet up your screeching. Jest teachin' him to stay from my window.

QUIVIENE. [*Standing up and wringing her hands.*] Go 'way from here! Go 'way from here!

BANTAM. Ain't gonna be no trouble. De p'lice come, you ain't heerd nothing, ain't been no shooting. Somebody in de hollow killing cats. [*Angrily.*] Git in yo' bed. [*He closes the door and is heard returning to his bed again cooing to* MILLY.] Sweety babe, sugar lump.

WILLIE. [*Springing into bed and wrapping himself up.*] Come hyuh stay wid me.

QUIVIENE. Yeah yeah, honey. [*She goes to him and they both lie wrapped in each other's embrace under the quilts. She croons over him and quiets him like a child.*]

WILLIE. De p'lice, will dey bodder me?

QUIVIENE. They won't bother you, baby.

WILLIE. Don't let 'em git at me.

QUIVIENE. I won't, honey. Rest yourself.

WILLIE. Dat man wid de pistol!

QUIVIENE. HE done gone. Sleep, sleep. [*Willie whimpers and jerks beneath the covers.*] We ain't heard nothing, ain't seen a thing, been asleep, all the time been asleep. [*And soon quiet comes over them and they are asleep. The light goes out of the stove, the shadows are gone from the wall, and all is darkness within and around. Somewhere under the stars* TOM STERLING *is abroad eating his heart out with grief. He will return at dawn. Ah,* BANTAM, *pillow your head well!*]

.   .   .   .

[*In the bright glare of day some months later six striped convicts are digging on a blazing road, swinging their picks aloft and bringing them down. Four others come behind piling out the dirt with shovels. The white dust hides the blackberries in the hedge, and the willow clumps are bent under its weight. The heat of July shimmers across the land as far as the eye can see. Lazy Lawrence dances his fiendish dance. The sweat pours down, the only dampness in the world for the ten mourners on the road. On a stump to the left a guard squats, drowsy, vapid, like a toad. The rifle in the crook of his arm keeps alert, as watchful as* LEVIN FARROW, *its muz-*

zle warns like an eye, it threatens. Fall, picks, and heave arms! On the bankside to the right another guard sits. He also is sleepy, drowsy. His rifle also keeps alert and watches, its muzzle threatens. The convicts dig with their backs to the guards, their faces set down the infinite stretch of road that disappears in a point on the horizon. Like so many soulless puppets, they lift their hands towards the sky and bring them down, never any slower, never any faster. And as the picks come down against the earth with a thud, a husky desperate groan bursts from their baked lips. As rhythmic as the beating of their hearts the "hanh" accompanies the falling of the picks, carrying over long maddening hours of pain until the sun sinks cooling in the west and the guard stirs and says, "Call it a day." At times their voices are raised in a chant, level, patient, as eternal and tough as the earth in which they dig. Sometimes they talk as they work, but not so often, for the staccato of conversation breaks up the rhythmic routine of labor and that's what they're there for—labor, labor, working on the roads. Ninety days on the roads TOM STERLING *and sixty days for you,* BANTAM WILSON. *The judge dropped his tobacco by his foot, rose and gave sentence. Disturbance of the peace. Assault with intent to kill. These niggers, these everlasting niggers, always fighting, always shooting. They've got no sense, they'll never have no sense. Give 'em the law, let 'em feel it. Obedience, peace, peace. This is the republic, these are the institooshuns. Let this be a lesson. Sixty days. Ninety days. Dig, dig. Side by side they dig—*BANTAM WILSON *and* TOM STERLING. *Misery has made them friends, sorrow companions.* BANTAM'S *spirit still walks unbroken,* STERLING'S *has gone under. The feel of iron and abuse of tongues have broken him. His great shoulders are bent, his legs hardly sustain his weight, and his arms fling up the pick and let it fall hour after hour, day after day, with slowly decreasing power. And all the while his lightless face stares at the earth beneath. These are the children—hanh. These are the brethren. The guard on the* *right stirs in his sleepiness and beats at the flies with his hat.*

FIRST GUARD. Rain or shine the old dog-flies stay with you.

SECOND GUARD. [*Lighting a cigarette and passing the package on to the first.*] And the damn musketeers allus drilling for water.

FIRST GUARD. Heigh you, Sterling, raise up that pick and let 'er come down. [*The convicts dig on, accompanying every blow with their everlasting "hanh," saying never a word.*] You hear me? I say put some pep in that digging.

BANTAM. [*After a moment—without looking round.*] He's sick, ain't able to work.

SECOND GUARD. You bastard monkey runt, who's talking?

FIRST GUARD. Hell'll be frozen 'fore you git this little digging done. [*They lapse into silence again. The second* GUARD *stretches his arms in a yawn.*]

SECOND GUARD. Lord, I'm sleepy—sleepy.

FIRST GUARD. Better leave her off a few nights. [*The convicts with the shovels burst into a snicker.*]

SECOND GUARD. [*Brutally, his voice sharp with hate.*] Somebody begging for the little rawhide. [*The four convicts, terrified, push their shovels deeper into the loose earth and pile it out.*]

FIRST GUARD. I want some water.

SECOND GUARD. The goddamed water boy's fell in and drownded. [*Standing up and calling.*] Water boy! Waterjack! Could a-been there and half way back!

[*The diggers begin a low working chant, pitiful and pleading.* "Mercy, mercy," *it calls.* "Water, water, give us some water. Where is it? Where is he? Where is the Great I Am, the Almighty God. Listen now, while us gi' you de call. Eigh Lawd, come wid de 'sponse!"*

CONVICTS.

> I called my people—hanh,
> I said my people—hanh,
> I mean my people—hanh,
>   Eigh, Lawd!

FIRST GUARD. That's right, sing him out'n the bushes.

SECOND GUARD. If it ain't water it's grub, ain't that it's something else. Bear down on them picks! Jesus Christ! (STERLING *suddenly tumbles over and falls with his face flat in the dirt. A convulsive shudder seems to run through the other convicts, but they carry on their digging, never any slower, never any faster.*]
CONVICTS.

> I called my friends—hanh,
> I said my friends—hanh,
> I mean my friends—hanh,
>   Eigh, Lawd!

FIRST GUARD. [*Springing up.*] Heigh now, none o' that, none o' that!

BANTAM. [*His voice rising in a whine.*] He sick, bad sick!

FIRST GUARD. Better got cured 'fore he come here. [*Marching up to the prostrate body.*] Get that mouth out'n the dirt. [*Whirling towards* BANTAM.] Nobody asked for your jowing. [*Eyeing him.*] Want the little cat-tails?

BANTAM. [*Slinging his pick.*] Jesus, Jesus!

FIRST GUARD. Snap out'n it, Sterling.

SECOND GUARD. [*Getting a leather thong from his coat.*] Put a firecoal on his tail and rise him.

FIRST GUARD. Gonna step to it, Sterling? [*But* STERLING *makes no answer.*] He's a stall boy. Hell, he's stalling!

SECOND GUARD. Damn right he's stalling.

FIRST GUARD. This ain't no party.

SECOND GUARD. Hell it ain't no party! [*He smoothes the thong with his hand and looks at the first guard.*]

FIRST GUARD. Make 'em work, make 'em work—that's right.

SECOND GUARD. Work, work—that's what they're here for—work!

FIRST GUARD. Work—work—let him taste it.

SECOND GUARD. [*Raising the strap above his head.*] Thirty-nine, thirty-nine. [*His voice coming out stronger now, more sharply.*] The law, the law! [*But still he holds the leather poised without bringing it down. A low murmur of horror rises among the convicts, growing into their chant, full of hate now, full of begging, but hopeless withal.*]

CONVICTS.

> I called my sister—hanh,
> I said my sister—hanh,
> I mean my sister—hanh,
> Eigh, Lawd!

FIRST GUARD. Hold her a minute, we'll see, we'll see. [*He goes up to* STERLING *and pokes him gently in the ribs with the muzzle of his rifle, but only the twitching back makes answer.*]

SECOND GUARD. Try him in the collar. [*He cuffs him gently in the collar, then with more insistence, at last with vehement roughness. A low whine is heard.*] He's saying something.

FIRST GUARD. [*Bending down.*] Goddamn it, we'll see!

SECOND GUARD. And what song is he singing now?

FIRST GUARD. Don't say nothing. Moans and whines. He don't say nothing.

SECOND GUARD. By God, we'll see. Oh yes, he'll talk. He'll tell us a mouthful! [*The convict working chant grows fuller, the rhythm begins to shape the picks, to hold the rising and falling arms to their labor. The cry for help, for peace, grows stronger—and with it the baffled will, the confused soul sends forth its cry.*]

CONVICTS.

> I called my brother—hanh,
> I said my brother—hanh,
> I mean my brother—hanh,
>> Eigh, Lawd!

FIRST GUARD. Let him have it. [*The Second Guard hands his rifle to the first and then looking around the world as if for a witness of justification, begins to beat the prostrate figure. Again a shudder and the gust of a groan sweep the convicts. They drive their picks deeper in the ground, but never any faster, never any slower.*]

CONVICTS.

> I called my mother—hanh,
> I said my mother,—hanh—

SECOND GUARD. Six—seven—eight—nine—ten.

FIRST GUARD. And now you'll work—and I reckon you'll work.

SECOND GUARD. Eleven—twelve—thirteen—fourteen. [*And the watchers in the skies cry blood, blood—earth, earth, sweet earth receive it. Keep it, save it till the next harvest.*]

FIRST GUARD. Oh yes, he'll work, and I reckon he'll work. [*The* WATER BOY *bursts through the hedge at the left, stands terror-stricken a moment, and then dropping his bucket with a clatter tears down the road. The precious water sinks into the dried earth. Now they chant in hopelessness, and the four with shovels wag their heads, their parching tongues protrude through baked lips. Ah, hope is no more—life is no more—death—death all around us. Grave, grave, swallow us up, hide us away, keep us.*]

SECOND GUARD. Fifteen—sixteen—seventeen—eighteen.

[*Now* TOM STERLING *has reached the end. In a last burst of life he staggers to his feet, his eyes glazed with madness.*]

FIRST GUARD. Go to work. Look out— [*The* SECOND GUARD *turns to grab his rifle but* STERLING *is upon him. He strikes him in the face and beats him to the earth, crushing the stems of the early goldenrod by the ditch and tearing the clumps of knotted lady-thumb.*]

STERLING. [*His voice coming out in a great animal scream.*] Hah—hah—hah. [*He beats the* GUARD'S *upturned face with his fists.*]

SECOND GUARD. Kill him! Kill him! [*The convicts sing on, now their chant rises louder, fresher. Revenge! Revenge! Hope is not perished from us. Our arms are still strong.*]

CONVICTS.

> I called my father—hanh,
> I said my father—hanh,
> I mean my father—hanh,
>   Eigh, Lawd!

SECOND GUARD. Kill him! Kill him! [*The* FIRST GUARD *stands stupefied. Then as if suddenly awakening he steps back, raises his rifle and shoots* STERLING *through the back. He rolls over and lies with face upturned in the burning sun. The* SECOND GUARD *crawls over to the bank and lies stretched out in the grass, his body heaving and jerking with angry, strident sobs. The* FIRST GUARD *stands looking foolishly down at the dead Negro. The four convicts drop their shovels and hover together in a shuddering group, the six sing on, beaten —darkness, night—God sits high in heaven, his face from the Negro, his hand towards the white man. The poor and needy cry in vain, the iron palings hold them.*]

FIRST GUARD. The goddamned fool, he's dead, dead!

SECOND GUARD. [*Sitting up with a high laugh as he wipes the blood from his face.*] Had to kill him, we had to kill! [*Peer-*

ing forward.] Dead as a fly. [*Moaning.*] They's something wrong, something wrong here!

FIRST GUARD. Sing, you bastards. Dig, you sons of bitches! [*And the body lies still. Once it knew swiftness, legs that ran by the cabin, played in the cornfield. Eyes that knew starlight, knew moonlight, tongue that knew singing. As they say in the song, and I lay this body down. In the cool hedge the fly says "zoom." And a buzzard wheels by the flat disc of the sun. And they dig and they sing. O earth, give us answer! Jesus hear us!*]

CONVICTS.

> I called my Jesus—hanh,
> I said my Jesus—hanh,
> I mean my Jesus—hanh,
>   Eigh, Lawd!

QUARE MEDICINE

CHARACTERS

OLD MAN JERNIGAN.
HENRY JERNIGAN, *his son.*
MATTIE JERNIGAN, *Henry's wife.*
DOCTOR IMMANUEL, *a patent-medicine vendor.*

TIME—*Several years ago at the close of a winter day.*
PLACE—*A farmhouse in eastern North Carolina.*

QUARE MEDICINE

THE *scene is the combined sitting-room and bedroom of the* JERNIGAN *house, with a fireplace to the left, a sewing-machine to the right and a table in the center of the room. The floor is carpeted with bright straw matting, and everything bristles with tidy primness. A door is at the center back and one at the left rear. The window at the right center, neatly curtained, shows a streak of sombre autumn fields filling up with the blue dusk of a fading winter day. From another part of the house the voice of a woman can be heard shrilly singing "Rescue the Perishing, care for the dying." The elder* JERNIGAN, *walking with a stick, comes carefully in at the rear door shivering with cold and carrying a mug-cup in his hand. Below a mass of white hair his face shines out like a ruddy autumn apple, and his whole person suggests the toughness and durability of a dried hickory root.*
Half-way across the room he stops and listens to the singing.

JERNIGAN. [*Sharply imitating.*] "Rescue the perishing, care for the dying!" [*He moves over to the fire and sets his mug to warm; after which he takes a bottle from the mantel, pours out some medicine in a spoon and swallows it. He sits down and stretches his hands to the blaze with a grunt of satisfaction. In a moment he feels the cup and takes a long drink. The woman's voice calls from off the right.*]

VOICE. Father!

JERNIGAN. [*Starting.*] Ah-hanh! What is it?

VOICE. [*Nearer.*] Father—fath—er!

JERNIGAN. [*Moving towards the door at the left.*] What is it, Mattie?

VOICE. Supper's 'bout ready. Where's Henry? [*The singing begins again, fading towards the kitchen.*]

JERNIGAN. [*Calling futilely after her.*] He's feeding up and'll be here in a minnit. [*He listens awhile and then reseats himself thoughtfully before the fire. Presently there is a heavy scraping of feet on the steps outside and* HENRY JERNIGAN *comes timidly in at the rear. He is a big awkward farmer of thirty or more, hesitating and shy. He takes his seat silently and wearily in a rocking chair, being careful not to touch the whitewashed hearth with his feet. The old man looks at him closely.*]

JERNIGAN. Tired out, ain't you? Hyuh, try some o' this 'simmon beer, I jest dreaned the barrel.

HENRY. [*In a slow, fumbling voice.*] I don't want none o' that, I believe.

JERNIGAN. Unh-hunh. [*They both lapse into silence, staring before them. Soon the elder* JERNIGAN *peers through the window at the winter sunset.*] Gonna be cold, Henry, cold. Robins been flying towards the south all day. [HENRY *says nothing.*] You're tireder'n common, ain't you, Henry?

HENRY. Yeh. [*Lifelessly.*] Wore out, wore out.

JERNIGAN. [*Taking his bottle from the mantel.*] Hyuh, take this last dost of Doctor 'Manuel's tonic. [HENRY *shakes his head.*] Well, I will then. [*He pours out the last drop and swallows it.*] Doctor said he'd be by today. 'Bout night and he ain't hyuh yit. You better git him to give you something, ye better, Henry, you're looking thin, thin.

HENRY. He ain't no doctor, he's a humbug.

JERNIGAN. Lard help my life!

HENRY. Wonder that mess don't kill you—old branch water and chemicals he's mixed up, I betcha. [*He sighs heavily, listening to the song in the kitchen.*] That old man's crazy with his poetry and talking and medicine!

JERNIGAN. Hunh, not hardly. [*Solemnly.*] 'Tain't body tired what ails ye, Henry, is it? [*After a moment he jerks his thumb in the direction of the song.*] Still singing, Henry. There it is.

HENRY. Yeh, I know.

JERNIGAN. Ah-hah, but folks will marry jest the same. She's worse'n ever, Henry. Good she is, religious good. Cooking and sewing and scrubbing and all fixed up fer tonight. Look over there on the machine at what she's got finished fer them there Hindoos or whatever they are. There's my coat I bought in Dunn five years back at Old Man Ransome Taylor's sale!

HENRY. [*His eyes travelling heavily about the room.*] What's she got on fer tonight?

JERNIGAN. Another one o' them there meetings. Old Mis' Pate and her gang's coming hyuh to sew fer the heathen and them that's starving over in the old world. [*Staring at him intently.*] This religious mess is gonna kill Mattie off ef you don't git up manhood enough to stop it. Sing and talk, sing and talk, Lard, I caint stand it no more.

HENRY. I—I cain't—I ain't gonna put my authority on nobody. She's her own boss.

JERNIGAN. Own boss! She's her own boss and our'n too. Well, ef you're scared of her, all right. They ain't no help fer it. [*He turns towards the fire, patting his foot forlornly on the floor.*] But, Henry, ye ain't gitting no fun out'n living, and right now's the time ye ort.—And as fer me—I been wanting to talk—[*Hitching up his chair.*]—to you 'bout this. Why the name o' Old Scratch you don't up and putt down yer foot I cain't see. [HENRY *says nothing.*] But ye won't. [*Half to himself.*] He ain't got no backbone, lets everybody run over him. [*He reaches for his cup and drains*

down the last of his beer in an angry gulp.] Ye didn't git
that from yer mammy ner from me, Henry. [*He mocks the
singing in the kitchen.*] "Rescue the perishing—"

HENRY. [*Suddenly standing up.*] I cain't have no row with
nobody, not with her nohow, I tell you. [*At the door.*] I got
to go part the cow and calf. [*He slams the door behind him
and the old man jumps in astonishment.*]

JERNIGAN. Dinged ef he didn't slam the door—hee, hee, hee.
Good fer you, Henry, good fer you! [MATTIE, *a fair faced
young woman, comes in from the left, singing and carrying
a stone churn in her arms. Despite her housewifely certainty
of action, there is an indefinite feminine frailty about her.*]

MATTIE. What's good for Henry?

JERNIGAN. [*Hurrying in confusion to his chair.*] Nothing,
Mattie, nothing at all. [*She looks sharply at him a moment
and then sets the churn by the hearth.*]

MATTIE. I'm putting the milk here to turn. I wisht you'd
look at it every now and then and stir it with the dasher.

JERNIGAN. All right, Mattie, all right.

MATTIE. And mind, don't you spill none o' that old beer on
the hearth.

JERNIGAN. I won't, Mattie, I won't.

MATTIE. What'd Henry go out for?

JERNIGAN. To git the calf away from the cow.

MATTIE. [*The words piling out.*] I bet he didn't wipe his feet
when he come in. And did you? [*Staring on the floor and
following* HENRY's *trail.*] No, he didn't—just look at the
dirt, just look at it. [*She hurries into the room at the left
and returns with a broomsedge broom.*] Here, sweep it up,
Father. [*She pushes the broom into his hand.*] I've got to go
back to my batter. [*She sticks her head out the door at the
rear and calls.*] Henry—Hen—ry! Supper! [*She turns back

into the room and old JERNIGAN *falls to sweeping.*] Sweep it towards the hearth, towards the hearth, Father, and mind the milk, don't git it full of dust. [*She goes out singing, beginning where she left off.*]—"from sin and the grave—"

JERNIGAN. [*Sweeping.*] Lard, Lard A'mighty, was ever martel man so persecuted! [*Leaning on his broom and musing.*] There he is— [*Nodding his head to the right.*]—pore soul, not at peace in his own household, going about like a man with the mulligrubs, cain't sleep, cain't eat, worried, worried down to the ground. And there she is—[*Nodding to the left.*]—reading the *Christian Herald* and hearing about dirt and disease and famine over in Azhy till she ain't fit to live with. Listen to her, listen to her, will you? What's to become of me, Old Moster only knows. What, to come to this, to this in my old age and me—[*Thumping on his chest.*]—yeh, me, old and with a crippled leg from marching in Furginny! [*He wipes his sleeve across his eyes and goes back to sweeping. Presently he stops and begins to muse again.*] Putts me to sweeping, she does, and churning and gitting up the eggs, and following old setting hens around. And she's had me at the wash-tub like an old woman, she has. Damn it! [*His voice sags over the oath.*] I ain't no woman. If Henry ain't got the grit to say something, I have. It's "Father do this, Father do that, Father—Father—Father!" But ding it all, she's a good girl. It's that drot'n old bell-cow of a Bella Pate and her gang what's got her worse'n she ever has been. I wisht a starm would come up and blow the whole shooting-match of 'em clean to Roosia or wherever it is. Then they'd git enough o' them there heathen, I reckon. But they ain't got no right to interfere with me, not a bit. [*He puts a hand into his pocket and holds up a small tin box in his left hand and a plug of tobacco in his right.*] Here they come and set 'pon me about my tobacco. Chew chewing-gum, chewing-gum, they say, to save fer the heathen and to pertect my health. [*He rattles the tin box.*] And I've chewed that wad o' stuff till I cain't git rid of it in my sleep. Cain't wear it out, cain't by no means. I'm done of it, I am. Have to slip off and hide to chew my tobacco, and all in a land o' freedom. [*He stands thinking, then goes to the door at the left and calls.*] Mattie, air ye busy?

MATTIE. Yes, I've got my hands in the dough!

JERNIGAN. All right. [*He stealthily bites off a chew from his plug, drops his tin box back in his pocket and spits in the fire with grim happiness. Just as he is leaning to spit a second time, the door opens suddenly at the left rear, and* MATTIE *comes in with a cloth. Old* JERNIGAN *draws back, and begins sweeping in a flurry of embarrassment. He calls out testily.*] Thought you was busy. Ain't I doing all right?

MATTIE. Sweep it clean, Father. I forgot this cloth for the churn. [*She raises the lid from the churn and stirs the contents around with the dasher.*] It's all right and ready, lacking just a bit, for churning. Don't you let it slosh on anything while you're a-churning it. [*She wraps the cloth around the handle of the dasher. The old man is sweeping and watching her out of the corner of his eye. While she is bent over she sees something on the hearth that attracts her attention. She rises up to her height and with a sharp note in her voice turns upon him.*] Mr. Jernigan—

JERNIGAN. Nah, nah, Mattie.

MATTIE. Signs don't lie, and there's signs of it there on my hearth. [*Working around the room and watching him furtively.*] Right here in my front room! Ain't you got your mouth full of tobacco right this minute? [*He shakes his head.*] Yes, you have, yes, you have. [*She stands looking at him as he sweeps.*] Father, why don't you say something, cain't you talk? [*He makes little movements of agony and finally chokes.*] Yes, yes, you are chewing right now. Spit it out, spit it out! Don't stand there and swallow that juice, it'll kill you. [*In desperation he runs to the fireplace and explodes into the fire, and stands coughing with a nauseated look on his face.*] I'll get you some water! [*She hurries out

*and reappears immediately with a glass of water and a bat-
tered wash-basin full of claying material.*] Here drink it,
and take this pan and rag and clay the hearth over. [*After
drinking the water, he ruefully gets down on his knees and
begins work. She goes to the machine.*] Hurry and get it
done, I got supper nearly cooked. [*She sits down and begins
sewing and singing* "How firm a foundation—"]

JERNIGAN. [*Indicating the garments.*] Air they fer the
heathen?

MATTIE. They are that.

JERNIGAN. [*Timidly.*] 'Course you know best, I reckon. But
how you know they wear britches over there?

MATTIE. [*Staring at him in amazement.*] Who ever heard of
folks not wearing britches! You know they'd put 'em in
jail for such, if they didn't.

JERNIGAN. [*Venturing.*] I hearn they don't wear nothing
over there but a string around their waist to tell where the
middle is.

MATTIE. [*Pedalling furiously.*] You men don't care, of
course, care 'bout nothing but your farming and your crops.
Why, it's in the *Christian Herald* where the little children
just go through the woods in big droves gnawing the bark
off of the trees they're so hungry. We've decided to give up
our breakfast and send the cost of it to them.

JERNIGAN. That's why you didn't eat breakfast this morning.
Well—you et a whole lot more fer dinner to make up fer
it, didn't ye?

MATTIE. [*Sharply and with a nervous note in her voice as
she gets suddenly up from the machine.*] Father, take all this
mess out when you get done—that old 'simmon beer cup,
and that old 'Manuel patent medicine bottle, and don't forget
to carry the clay pan out—[*She goes out at the left. Her
song is heard rising in the distance. Old* JERNIGAN *continues*

claying the hearth, muttering to himself. HENRY *comes in at the rear.*]

HENRY. [*Stretching his legs out carefully towards the fire.*] What's the matter with the hearth *now?*

JERNIGAN. [*Setting the pan in the corner by the wood-box.*] Nothing, nothing, Henry. She thought she saw a speck on it somewhere.

HENRY. You must a-been chewing tobacco ag'in.

JERNIGAN. Well, why shouldn't I chew it?

HENRY. Yeh, yeh, I wisht you could in peace.

JERNIGAN. You'd be better off ef you'd go back to chewing.

HENRY. I know. But I promised her I'd quit and I have.

JERNIGAN. I used to chew it 'fore it quit raining in Africky or wherever it is and 'fore old Bella Pate brung her sanctified self around here, I did, and they was some joy in having a far then, and some reason for having a farplace too. [*Tapping on the andiron with his stick.*] That's what it's made fer—to spet in.

HENRY. [*Timidly and somewhat hopefully.*] Why don't you talk it out with Mattie. [*Earnestly.*] I wisht you would.

JERNIGAN. Durned ef I didn't come purty nigh telling her something a while ago. [*He catches* HENRY *by the arm.*] Now look-a here, Henry, you'n me's got to do something. The thing for you to do is to walk down the road tonight and meet Mis' Pate and them folks and tell 'em they cain't come up here to carry on no prayer-meeting and sewing business. Tell 'em to go som'r's else. Tell 'em to go to—hell!

HENRY [*Shrinking away.*] I cain't do that, I cain't. Lord, you're near 'bout gone to cussing.

JERNIGAN. And tell 'em yer wife ain't gonna have nothing else to do with sich.

HENRY. [*Quickly.*] I tell you what, you do it.

JERNIGAN. I would in a minnit, Henry, but you're the head o' the house and you better, it's yer place to. [HENRY *turns himself about before the fire.*]

HENRY. Mebbe they won't come tonight, and before they meet another time mebbe we can figger on something to do.

JERNIGAN. Hunh, they'll be hyuh, all right.

HENRY. [*Staring off.*] I hear they's mad dogs about. One bit at Dick Ryall's child this evening.

JERNIGAN. [*Studying.*] Well, that may break up the meeting, but I won't believe it till I see it, not me. Take more'n mad dogs to stop religion. You stand up to Mattie, I tell you, putt the britches on and wear 'em yourself. Lard, I cain't understand you. Why you let her impose on me in my old age the way you do I cain't see. [*He turns away and sits down in his arm-chair.* MATTIE *comes in with a tin bucket in her hand.*]

MATTIE. I've got to go across the fields to Mis' Ragland's a bit— [*Suddenly stopping.*] Henry, go right back out that door and wipe off your feet.

HENRY. [*Mumbling.*] I thought I cleaned my feet. [*He goes outside and is heard scraping his shoes on the edge of the porch.*]

MATTIE. Sweep it up, Father. [*He gets the broom and sweeps.*] I got to borrow some soda from Mis' Ragland and she wanted me to bring her a jar o' jam.

HENRY. [*Coming back into the room.*] I'll go over there for you, Mattie.

MATTIE. No, I'll go, and you-all go on and git your supper. I've put the biscuits in the stove, and they'll be ready by the time you wash and get to the table. Now Henry, don't let them biscuits burn. [*She goes out.*]

JERNIGAN. [*Scornfully.*] Jest look at her—didn't have a bit o' business over there, jest wants to go over see what old

Nonie Ragland's got made up for the heathen. Henry, you got to lay the law down, I tell you.

HENRY. Yeh, yeh.

JERNIGAN. Now, I'm gonna talk straight to you. Women is like mules and all dumb brutes, Henry, you got to break 'em 'fore they'll work.

HENRY. Nah, nah, I cain't do that. [*There is a knock on the porch.*]

JERNIGAN. Who kin that be? [*Happily.*] That's my doctor, I betcha. [*The knock is repeated at the door.*]

HENRY. [*Raising his voice in sudden irritability.*] Go on away! Go 'way!

JERNIGAN. [*Staring at him.*] What— Come in, come in! [DOCTOR IMMANUEL *comes in.*] I knowed it was you, Doctor, I knowed it was you. [*The* DOCTOR *is a man of medium height, about fifty years old, dressed in a cheap threadbare dark suit, celluloid collar and dark tie. His coat hangs low and nearly to the knees, clerical-like. Despite his cheap dress there is an indefinable air of distinction about him; something scholarly, something forlorn in his pale clean-cut face and dark piercing eyes. He carries a well-worn medicine case in his hand. As he enters the door, he pulls off his derby hat, disclosing a huge mop of long black hair streaked with gray and resting like a bolster on his neck and shoulders.*]

DOCTOR. [*In a deep level voice.*] Masters of this house, friends—

JERNIGAN. [*Pushing up a chair.*] Come right in, come right in and make yourself at home. [*The* DOCTOR *lays his hat on the bed at the right and puts his case in a chair. He moves in a sort of dream-like, mask-like manner, intent upon his business and paying little attention to the two men.*]

DOCTOR. [*His voice moving in a level chant, half-singing as he opens his case.*] What can I do for you tonight? What can

I do for you tonight? [*He takes out bottle after bottle, shakes it, squints at it towards the light, and replaces it, chanting as he does so.*]

> As you all know, wherever I go,
> My name is Immanuel,
> I treat you well, I make you well,
> Sound as the sweet church bell.

[*He turns suddenly on old* JERNIGAN *who starts back in surprise.*] Now what is it, brother? What can I do for you?

JERNIGAN. [*Fetching his bottle.*] Another bottle. I just drunk the last.

HENRY. [*Growling.*] Another bottle of stump water, dishwater, rainwater.

DOCTOR. [*Holding up the bottle.*] Doctor Immanuel's Universal Remedy! Right it is and very fit. Distilled from secret weeds and herbs by mystic processes. Cures internal ailments, cuts, burns, bruises, is an antidote for poisons, can be taken internally or externally. For swelling in the joints, leg sores, sore throat, convulsions, dizziness, fits, and general disorders. [*The words roll from him in a flood. He turns towards old* JERNIGAN, *fixes him with his eyes, and suddenly sings out.*] What is your trouble, brother? Are you healed, better or— It's cold tonight, cold tonight, and ice on the pools in the lane.

JERNIGAN. In my knee, you remember, in my knee. [*He slaps his hand to it.*] I'm getting better, doctor, slowly, slowly.

DOCTOR. [*Holding his hand up in assurance.*] Slowly but surely, certainly, absolutely. Another bottle and you walk straight as any man.

> As you all know, wherever I go,
> My name is Immanuel.

I always make you well,
As any man will tell. . . .

[*His voice drops to a whisper and he hums under his breath, the while he is putting away the empty bottle and getting out another. He hands the bottle to old* JERNIGAN.] The price is one and a quarter now, brother. Prices have gone up, prices are going up. The demand exceeds the supply. [*Again he chants.*]

I travel from morning till night
Curing and fixing things right.
From night until day
I'm on a-my way—

[*He begins placing his bottles back in his case.*]

Seeking the saddened sight—

[*Again he whirls upon the old man.*] Is the knee all that troubles you? Have you other troubles, diseases of the body or the soul?

JERNIGAN. [*Shaking his head quickly.*] Nanh, nanh, I'm all right saving my knee.

DOCTOR. [*Picking up a small bottle and holding it lovingly before him.*] Now here is a remedy, *the* remedy, the heart and soul of the matter, the help for the world's evils. Down in Egypt, the country of darkness, it was discovered. Dug out of the tombs of the powers of evil. Hid away they had it, but my agent discovered it, sent it to me, here it is. [*Reading.*] Dr. Immanuel's Egyptian Tonic. [*Suddenly barking like an auctioneer, as* HENRY *jumps in his chair.*]

Two dollars a bottle, two dollars,
Going at two dollars.
Are you weak and heavy laden,
Sore distressed, sad distressed?

It will cleanse of evil passion,
Restore you bowels of compassion,
Accidents, diseases chronic—

[*Shouting.*]

The marvelous Egyptian Tonic.

[*He sticks it out at old* JERNIGAN.]

Two dollars once, two dollars twice—
Going at two—

JERNIGAN. [*Backing away from him as he fumbles in his pocketbook for his money.*] Nanh, nanh, this bottle's enough. Here's yer dollar and a quarter. [*The* DOCTOR *takes the money impersonally.*] Come up to the fire and warm yourself.

HENRY. [*Looking at old man* JERNIGAN *significantly.*] Anh-hanh, what'd I tell you? [*The* DOCTOR *closes his case and goes to the bed for his hat.* HENRY *calls to him bitterly.*] You better look out down in that creek for mad dogs.

DOCTOR. [*Turning back quickly but with dignity.*] Mad dogs?

HENRY. Yeh, dogs that are mad. Mad dogs. One of 'em bite you and you'll be madder'n you are now.

JERNIGAN. Yeh, you git bit and you'll foam at the mouth and gnaw bedposts and cut up terrible like Sarah Williams done 'fore she died. She run out in the yard and screamed, and they tried to ketch her but she run off and lay down by the hedgerow and died biting her legs and arms and barking like a dog.

DOCTOR. [*Quickly taking a tiny package from his case.*] Doctor Immanuel's Mad Stone, good for all bites and poisons. Bring it near the afflicted spot and it seizes upon it—[*Clapping it to the top of his hand.*]—and sucks out the poison. Five dollars apiece, five dollars. [*Gazing at it fondly.*] This mysterious stone was taken from the belly of a bewitched deer, killed by the old prophet of the Cape Fear. [*Barking again.*] Five dollars apiece, five dollars, going at five dollars. [*He pushes the stone quickly out at old* JERNIGAN.]

JERNIGAN. Nanh, nanh, I ain't run mad.

DOCTOR. Five dollars— Five dollars once, five dollars twice— five dollars— [*Suddenly he stops and stares at* HENRY *as if perceiving something remarkable and strange about him. He mechanically wraps up the stone and drops it back in the case, never taking his eyes from the young man. He moves toward him and walks obliquely around him. Old* JERNIGAN *watches him with open mouth. As the doctor approached him,* HENRY *turns and follows him suspiciously with his eyes.*]

HENRY. Hyuh, hyuh, what you up to? [*The* DOCTOR *continues to stalk him. He draws back dramatically and points a sharp finger at* HENRY.]

DOCTOR. [*Grotesquely.*] Trouble.

JERNIGAN. [*Jumping and giggling nervously.*] Trouble, hee-hee!

HENRY. [*Staring at him.*] Trouble?

DOCTOR. [*His words beginning to pour out in a roll.*] I see upon that brow suffering. My name is Immanuel. I am needed, needed here and now. [*Looking at him in anguish.*] You are weak and heavy laden. Tell me. Speak forth your heart. I am come that ye might have rest from your suffering. Speak forth, thou unbeliever.

HENRY. Hyuh, hyuh, I ain't gonna have no monkey shines. [*With a touch of entreaty in his voice.*] Stop it now.

DOCTOR. [*Shaking his head mournfully.*] I must help you. I feel the call of pain. Speak forth your heart.

HENRY. [*Turning towards old* JERNIGAN.] What's he up to nohow?

JERNIGAN. Now, now, you needn't ax me. [*There is a*

long silence while the DOCTOR *stares fixedly at* HENRY.]

HENRY. [*Looking anxiously about the room and presently bursting out.*] I tell you to stop looking at me thataway!

DOCTOR. Trouble, trouble, suffering in the countenance of that face! [*Imploringly.*] Speak, speak, I have remedy for suffering. I can help and aid thee. [*He clasps his hands and waits.* HENRY *stirs uneasily in his chair and old* JERNIGAN *teeters nervously on his feet, beating his thighs with the back of his hands. At last old* JERNIGAN *explodes.*]

JERNIGAN. Well, you air in trouble, Henry!—In a way ye're in the deepest sort of trouble. [*Muttering.*] Me too, and me too.

DOCTOR. [*Triumphantly.*] Ah—hah! Speak, speak!

HENRY. [*Half in wrath and half in perplexed fear.*] Well, what'n the name of Old Scratch you want?

DOCTOR. Speak forth the evil that is possessing thee.

HENRY. [*Twisting about.*] You tell him, Pa, if they's any evil to be told.

JERNIGAN. Him and me's been seeing a right smart o' worry lately. We was talking about it before you come.

DOCTOR. I know, I perceive it.

JERNIGAN. [*Going on haltingly.*] As the scripture putts it, he's married to a wife. [*He stops.*]

DOCTOR. One had his land, one had his yoke of oxen, another had his wife and could not come. As set forth in the gospel according to Luke.

JERNIGAN. [*Eagerly.*] That's it, doctor, his wife's tuk possession of everything hyuh.

HENRY. Now, now.

JERNIGAN. Well, she has. And that there doctor kin help you, I done told you he could. [*He steps nimbly out into the room and sweeps it with his arms.*] Look a' there, will you?

Look at that there h'a'th. Clean as a sheet. And the floor and everything. A speck o' dirt got no home hyuh and we ain't nuther. [*Pointing to the sewing-machine.*] And look over there at that there sewing. My good coat and britches gone fer good, all fer the heathen over the water.

HENRY. You mought stop trying to tell everything.

JERNIGAN. Well, you tell it then.

HENRY. Go on then and say what you wush.

JERNIGAN. All right and I will as shore as you're born. That's just it, doctor, she's plumb tuk with religion and sweeping and talking.

DOCTOR. Where is the lady of the house?

JERNIGAN. Off, off.

DOCTOR. A common case, a common case. The man must stand up and be the master. The scripture tells as much.

JERNIGAN. [*Jubilantly.*] There you air, Henry, there you air. [*Jerking his thumb at* HENRY.] But he won't, he won't, not him. He sets lak a wedge in the rain and takes it every bit. Big as a house he is and ain't got no backbone in him more'n a sack.

DOCTOR. Timid? Afraid? Lacking in manly courage?

HENRY. [*Wrathfully.*] Go on and have it your way!

DOCTOR. Doctor Immanuel will provide. He can cure.

JERNIGAN. You cure 'em both and I'll pay you. Fix it so's I kin chew my tobacco in peace and here's a five dollar bill fer ye. [*He pulls out his pocketbook.*]

DOCTOR. I shall cure them, I must cure them, I *will* cure them. Amen!

JERNIGAN. Do that and this here's your'n. [*He flaps a bill in his hands. The* DOCTOR *begins to pace up and down the room, pushing back his hair and mumbling to himself.*]

DOCTOR. [*Snapping.*] When will the lady of this house return?

HENRY. She just stepped acrost the field. But you needn't be planning none of your mess, I ain't gonna take no part in it.

DOCTOR. Mess! Mess! [*He resumes his walk.*]

JERNIGAN. [*Becoming excited.*] I dunno what you gonna do, Doctor, but I jest beccha you do it. [*Gleefully.*] I bet he does, Henry. Yeh, she'll be right back.

DOCTOR. No sooner said than done. [*Whirling upon* HENRY.] I can cure you both. I can bring peace and order into this distracted home. I can make a man of might out of you. I can make you a mighty man in Israel, both in deed and in word. I can bring back humility and love to the erring woman's heart. Yea, [*Lifting up his voice.*] I can prepare a proper helpmeet for you in your distress. [*Thundering and glaring.*] But—but—have you faith in my powers?

HENRY. I dunno— I dunno— Hah, crazy!

JERNIGAN. [*Ecstatically.*] Try to raise up yer faith, Henry. [*Grinding his hands in excitement.*] Hurry up, Henry, hurry up, she's gonna be back in a minute.

HENRY. [*Shaking his head weakly.*] I'm scared of all this business. How I know he won't kill me or something or hurt her.

DOCTOR. Kill! Hurt! [*His jaw falling open in amazement.*] Alas, young man, your words are wild, wild and full of poison to my kindly heart. [*His tone suddenly changes to anger.*] Take your own benighted way then. I offer you peace, you choose strife. So be it. [JERNIGAN *grasps* HENRY'S *arm in supplication.*]

JERNIGAN. Henry, Henry, try it, try it, boy!

DOCTOR. [*Raising a warning hand.*] But listen, before I depart over the creek.—[*To himself*] A mule there swelled

with the colic— Behold salvation is at hand and you re-
fuse it.

JERNIGAN. Air ye crazy, Henry? There he is now going
off.

HENRY. [*Beginning to show an unwilling interest under the*
DOCTOR'S *spell.*] Well,—

DOCTOR. [*Picking up his hat.*] I shall say no more.

JERNIGAN. Henry, Henry, don't let him go off like that there!
[*The* DOCTOR *picks up his case and moves towards the*
door.]

HENRY. Well, if you're shore you won't hurt me ner her, I
mought—

DOCTOR. [*Apparently no longer interested in him.*] Well, goodnight and may you endure your punishment as befits a suf-
ferer so blind. [*He grasps the door knob.*]

JERNIGAN. Henry, Henry!

HENRY. Are you shore you won't hurt me?

DOCTOR. Faith! Have you faith?

HENRY. [*Standing up with sudden decision.*] Well, I'll try it
then, by God! Where's your medicine? Bring it on. [*With an*
amazingly agile bound the doctor springs back into the
room.]

DOCTOR. Saved! Saved! [*He opens his case and searches in*
its depths. Extracting two tiny bottles, he holds them up in
his hands. HENRY *sits down again watching him with open*
mouth.] Ah, here they are, Doctor Immanuel's Cure for the
Unhappy Soul. The one is red, the other gray. The red is
for the rich blood of manhood. Drink it and you become
masterful, fearless, a tamer of the weaker sex. They will bow
down to you, worship you, feed upon your words of wisdom
as upon honey-dew. Let the woman drink the gray and the
man the red. He becomes the lord of his house and his goods.

She becomes the meek and lowly helpmeet. There she sits by the fire silent, gentle and sweet. There he sits her master, her lord.

JERNIGAN. [*His eyes shining.*] Listen at him, Henry, listen at him talk.

DOCTOR. [*Lifting up the red vial.*] I remember, I remember. I see in the past. It is a night of storm. The moon is sick and pale and wasting in the west.

> The pale moon doth rain,
> The red moon doth blow,
> It bringeth water in its beak.
> The white moon doth neither rain nor snow.

I rise up in my dreams. Doctor Immanuel comes forth from his couch at the midnight hour, for now it is the time to seek for the cure of unhappy souls. Silently I go through the forest towards the appointed place. The rain and the wind they comfort me on my journey. I go forth alone in the forest, under the watchful heavens. The signs are right in the sky, it is the time of the bull, and the bull means life and more abundant life. [*He waves his hands before his face and treads up and down the room acting out his journey.* HENRY *and old* JERNIGAN *stare at him as if mesmerized.*] I go by the elder bush in the pathless swamp, I touch the sorrel tree, and place my hand upon the bark of the smooth bay tree. I mount the hill and taste of the sweet sassafras and a bit of the bitter pine, and I, Doctor Immanuel, as the cocks begin to crow, come to the place of the silent old man and he waits for me. He has had his dream. Together we go far to the east, he with six dried sticks of the bloody mulberry and I with six of the nameless bush under our arms. We come where the young strong man died for love and his rich red blood ran into the ground. There we set the pot and build the fire. [*His voice takes on a hypnotic monotone and he moves back and forth in the room with the queer unreal steps of a jumping-jack.*] And into the pot Doctor Immanuel casts his one and two and three. And likewise the silent one casts his one and two and three which shall not be named till time is done. The bottles are brought forth and filled. The silent old one to his home again which none but two can find. And Doctor Immanuel forth into the world to heal the distressed. [*His voice dies away and he hums to himself.*]

HENRY. [*Breaking from the spell.*] Ain't he crazy right?

DOCTOR. [*Picking up the gray vial and throwing up his hand.*] And hark! [*He stands with his hand uplifted, and they wait.*] It is night, a night of peace. The farmer sleeps his toil away, and the stock rest in the stall. The seeds wait in the earth, in the warm ground. The poor birds sit in the hedgerow and the snake goes not forth to prey. And now the old moon sleeps in the new moon's arms, hanging in the heavens above the three dark pines. [*Again he falls to striding up and down the floor.*] Doctor Immanuel is forth from his couch. The signs are right. The virgin walks in the sky. He comes to the three dark pines and waits in prayer. And the three maids of the deep swamp minister unto him, they minister unto him. Out of the darkness they come with song and with dancing, their heads hanging low and their rings shining and their garments flashing silver with the flames of gold. [*He turns and stares at* HENRY *who watches him groggily.*] From the mud of the turtle and the scaly snake they come, rising out of the deep night time, out of the mire and swampy slime, where the owl and the bat and the fever are. They rise, bringing the cure, the gray cure, the draught of humility, of peace. [*He stares at the gray vial and stands lost in thought. Presently he turns, his voice humming.*] Drink the red and be filled with life and power; drink the gray, become the meek and gentle of the earth. Doctor Immanuel has said his say! [*He begins walking back and forth across the room.* HENRY *and old* JERNIGAN *stare at him as if fascinated. Far off a woman's voice is heard singing. It draws nearer, and* MATTIE *passes around the house, singing "Rescue the Perishing," and goes into the kitchen.*]

HENRY. [*Swallowing hard.*] Hyuh, they's something quare!

JERNIGAN. He's gonna cure you, Henry. He is! Sink yer trust in him, Henry!

DOCTOR. Come, drink the drink! [*He closes his case and sets the two bottles on top of it.*] Call the lady of the house. She shall have the gray.

HENRY. [*Starting from his dream, sidling up to the bottles, and staring at them suspiciously.*] Mought be something in it, mought not. [*A queer unreal smile breaks over his face and he comes up to the doctor and stares at him intently.*] All right, dinged if I don't do it. Dinged if I don't! [MATTIE'S *sharp insistent voice is heard in the kitchen.*]

MATTIE. Father! Fathe-er-r! Henry! Henr-y!

JERNIGAN. Drink it, swallow it down, Henry! Can't be no worse'n [*He turns and mocks* MATTIE.] Father! Henry! and [*singing.*] "Rescue the perishing—" Go on, Henry.

[HENRY *picks up the red vial, uncorks it and smells it and sets it down, then takes up the gray one and does likewise.*]

HENRY. Why it don't smell like nothing a-tall.

DOCTOR. [*Stopping in his walk and looking at him piercingly.*] Bid the lady of the house come in.

HENRY. [*Throwing his head about and beating himself as if trying to fight off the* DOCTOR's *influence.*] You call her, Pa. [*The door flies open at the left and* MATTIE *springs in with a pan of burnt biscuits in her hands.*]

MATTIE. [*In a shrill nervous voice.*] Look what you've done, both of you. I told you not to let the biscuits burn. [JERNIGAN *looks at* HENRY *and* HENRY *looks at him.*]

JERNIGAN. [*Finally.*] I thought Henry was looking after them biscuits.

HENRY. [*Fumbling.*] I didn't even think of 'em, Mattie.

MATTIE. I know, I know. That's just the way it is. That's just the way it is. That's always the way it is.

DOCTOR. Madam, lady of this house!

MATTIE. [*Starting back.*] Oh, I didn't see you, Doctor 'Manuel. Put some wood on the fire, Father. When'd you come, Doctor 'Manuel?

DOCTOR. Madam, when you appeared in the door we were in the midst of a most momentous question.

MATTIE. What'n the world is all this to-do about? You'll have to tell it quick, I've got to hurry and get supper. We are sewing here tonight—[*With a weary, defiant look towards* HENRY *and old* JERNIGAN.]—sewing for the heathen.

DOCTOR. Madam, after tonight you will not bother about the heathen. You have enough trouble in your own household. We are solving that momentous question.

MATTIE. What in the world is all this to-do about, I ask you?

DOCTOR. [*With high dignity.*] Madam, behold the two bottles there. The one is red, the other gray. The red is for your husband, the gray for you.

MATTIE. Needn't think I'll drink any of your crazy mess.

DOCTOR. The husband will drink the red and take charge of his household. You will drink the gray and obey him in what he says hereafter.

MATTIE. The Lord help my life! [*Turning to* HENRY] Have you gone out'n your head same as him, to be taking on to such stuff?

HENRY. [*Timidly.*] Try and drink a little bit, Mattie. It won't hurt you! He says it's good for you.

MATTIE. The dog's foot!

HENRY. [*With a hint of determination in his voice.*] He's done said if I drink that stuff you won't know me for another man. [*Decisively.*] And I've said I'll drink it.

DOCTOR. He's going to drink his and you're going to drink yours.

MATTIE. That I'm not. I've never heard of such. Henry Jernigan, you must be crazy to fool with him.

HENRY. Yes, I'm gonna do it. I'm plumb tired of sich a mess of things. I'm gonna change it or die a-trying. [*With a lunge he grabs one of the bottles and throws the contents down his throat.*]

MATTIE. [*Screaming.*] Henry, it'll poison you! [*Henry stands tasting with his lips. A foolish smile breaks over his face.*]

HENRY. Why, it ain't no more'n—

[*The* DOCTOR *brings his hand down on* HENRY'S *shoulder with a whack and stares significantly at him.* HENRY'S *eyes gradually narrow in comprehension and he turns and walks back and forth across the room thinking. The* DOCTOR *moves around as if unconcerned. Suddenly* HENRY *springs into the air with a yell. Old* JERNIGAN *starts back and falls over a chair.*]

JERNIGAN. Lard, Lard a-mercy!

MATTIE. [*Running up to* HENRY.] Henry, Henry, honey, what is it?

HENRY. [*Tearing wildly around the room and shrieking.*] I'm pizened, pizened! Help, water, I'm afar inside. [*He doubles over in pain.* MATTIE *pursues him wringing her hands. All the while the* DOCTOR *walks ecstatically and yet unconcerned around the room, carrying on his automaton-like actions and his monologue.*]
DOCTOR. [*Chanting.*]

As you all know, wherever I go,
My name is Immanuel.

I treat you well, I make you well,
As sound as the sweet church bell.
Down the road I travel,
Going in rain or shine,
Healing the sick and afflicted,
No medicine like unto mine.
This I tell who comes like Immanuel.

HENRY. [*Falling into a chair and slobbering heavily at the mouth as he gasps.*] Pizened! Pizened! Help, water! [MATTIE *throws her arms around his neck.*]

MATTIE. Run, Father, run and bring the bucket of water. [*The old man shoots into the kitchen and back like a streak. All the while* MATTIE *is crooning over* HENRY *and rubbing his face and forehead feverishly.*] Oh, darling, honey. What can I do? [*She breaks into wild sobs.*]

JERNIGAN. Hyuh, hyuh, drink some water, Henry. [HENRY *springs out of his chair, knocking* MATTIE *from him. He souses his head in the bucket and drinks, spits out great mouthfuls of water on the floor and empties the bucket over his head. Then he stamps the bucket to pieces, shrieking and yelling.*]

MATTIE. Run for the doctor, run for the doctor!

DOCTOR. I am Doctor Immanuel at your service, madam. [MATTIE *turns and glares at him a moment and slaps him in the face.* HENRY *snatches up the broom and begins chasing the doctor around the room and beating him. The doctor makes an effort to get his case and hat as he is pursued, calling out.*] This is wrong, wrong! Ye do not understand. [*He opens the door and flees into the night.* HENRY *falls into a chair and rocks back and forth, groaning and moaning.* MATTIE *comes sobbing up to him.*]

HENRY. [*Whirling and seizing* MATTIE *by the throat.*] Who are you? I know: Mattie. You sew for the heathen and worry your husband's life out about dirt. Now in the grave they'll be plenty of dirt. And you sing, and you sing; and you talk and you talk. [*He grabs the remaining bottle and uncorks it.*] Drink this here bottle o' stuff.

MATTIE. [*Clenching her teeth and fighting back.*] I won't, I won't! It'll poison me, it'll kill me!

HENRY. [*Pulling open her mouth and pouring the contents in.*] Nunh—unh, I reckin it won't! [*She swallows and coughs and strangles, then drops to the floor crying.* HENRY *strides about the room kicking the furniture to pieces and throwing out his shoulders and shouting.*] I'm a new man, a man o' might, a he-man in Israel! [*Turning upon* MATTIE.] And you have drunk the drink. You gonna be humble down, a help-mate. [*He drops back in his chair in a dying posture.*]

MATTIE. Oh, Henry, Henry, baby!

HENRY. When I'm gone, take care of Pa. Let him live in peace. Let him have his tobacco and spet in the far. [MATTIE *crawls on her knees before him and lays her head in his lap, weeping.*]

MATTIE. Get the doctor, Father. Hitch up and go for the doctor. [*Old* JERNIGAN *starts for the door.* HENRY *jumps up and snatches him back.*]

HENRY. You ain't, you ain't. Let me die in peace. [*There is the sound of a medley of voices outside. Women gabbling in excitement.* MATTIE *climbs up to her feet and runs to the door.*]

MATTIE. Is that you, Mis' Bella? Come here, come here quick. Henry's poisoned and he's a-dying. [*The gabble and excitement outside increases. A voice replies from the yard.*]

VOICE. I'm coming, Mattie, I'm coming. [*She is heard coming up on the steps.* HENRY *gets up from his chair and begins to bark like a dog, blubbering and growling.*]

HENRY. [*Shrieking again.*] I' been bit by a mad dog. [*He barks.*]

VOICE. Lord a-mercy, he's run mad! [*A low murmur of horror rises from the women outside, followed by shrieks and then the sound of running feet.* HENRY *rushes out of the door barking and pursuing them.*]

MATTIE. [*Looking at old* JERNIGAN *through her tears!*] He ain't been bit by no mad dog!

JERNIGAN. [*Stuttering with excitement.*] Mebbe that's the way the pizen works. That doctor said he got it a quare way in the middle of the night and a storm on and a' old man helping him.

MATTIE. He's crazy. [*Wringing her hands.*] Why'd you let him give Henry that stuff? The mess I took won't nothing, weak as water! [*She goes to the door calling piteously.*] Henry! Henry! [*Old* JERNIGAN *comes up to the bottle she has dropped and looks at it.*]

JERNIGAN. [*With a shout.*] He's tuk the wrong medicine, Mattie! He tuk that there gray stuff and you tuk the red!

MATTIE. [*At the door.*] Henry! Henry! [HENRY *comes back on the porch and gives a farewell bark.* MATTIE *runs out and throws her arms around him. He flings her from him and strides into the room. His shoes are covered with mud. He goes to the fireplace and stamps it off on the hearth.*]

JERNIGAN. [*Running up to him excitedly.*] Hyuh, hyuh, you tuk that gray stuff. Look, look!

HENRY. [*Waving him off.*] It don't make no difference. 'Twon't nothing but water. [MATTIE *comes in and stares at him as he casually cleans his boot on the hearth.*]

MATTIE. [*Whimpering.*] What's happened, Henry? You seem—

HENRY. I been cured, that's what. The medicine done it. [*He gets up, looks around the room, goes over to the machine, gathers up the clothes for the heathen, picks out a coat and trousers and throws them at the old man.*] Here, there's your

Ransome Taylor coat and your britches. The heathen ain't gonna git 'em. [*He wipes his shoes with the other garments and then calmly goes to his chair and sits down.* MATTIE *has been looking on a moment and then with a glad cry of comprehension falls on her knees by him and lays her head sobbing in his lap.*]

JERNIGAN. [*Dropping in his chair thunderstruck.*] Well, I be durned if I ever seed the beat! [*He thinks a moment, and then bursts out in a low musical chuckle. His face spreads into a grin that breaks over his face in a thousand wrinkles. He cuts a caper on the floor, stopping now and then trying to comprehend what has happened.* HENRY *sits solemnly stroking* MATTIE'S *head. The door is cracked open at the rear and* DOCTOR IMMANUEL *pokes his head in.*]

DOCTOR. Masters of this house—

HENRY. [*Turning and snarling.*] Hanh—Scat! [*He barks and the* DOCTOR *slams the door. After a moment* HENRY *calls old* JERNIGAN.] Pa, go and tell him to come in and get his hat and case. [MATTIE'S *sobs gradually die away.*] Yeh, I know, poor child. I did scare you, didn't I? [*Only a whimper from* MATTIE *and hugging of* HENRY'S *knees answered him.*]

JERNIGAN. [*At the door.*] Come on in, doctor, and get yer stuff. He ain't gonna hurt you. [*The* DOCTOR *comes gravely in and gets his case and hat.*]

HENRY. Pa, give him that five dollars.

JERNIGAN. [*His sides shaking with enjoyment.*] Hyuh, hyuh, it is. You done it, Doc, same as you said you would.

HENRY. And you needn't come back. I don't need you! [*He lifts his head with decision written on his face.*] Lemme have a look at the plug of tobacco, Pa.

DOCTOR. [*At the door.*] Remember that I am always at your service. Peace abide with you and this house always. I am on my way now to another patient.

HENRY. That's all right, doctor. You needn't bother about us. We ain't gonna need you no more. Are we, Mattie?

[MATTIE *shakes her head.*]

DOCTOR. [*Going out.*]

> As you all know, wherever I go,
> My name is Immanuel.

[*He closes the door and his chant dies away in the night.*]

HENRY. I said, Pa, I'd like a look at that tobacco.

MATTIE. [*Raising her head.*] Don't you spit on—

HENRY. [*Crushing her back on the floor.*] Nanh, nanh, I tell you I been cured. I'm boss. [*Breaking into a loud roaring laugh.*] Horray! Horray! I'm another man. I'm cured, I'm boss. Gimme that 'backer. [*The old man hands it to him eagerly.* HENRY *bites off an enormous chew and hands the plug back. Old* JERNIGAN *hesitates a moment and then also bites off a mouthful. A look of deep content comes over him. He snuggles into a chair and chews.* HENRY *chews. They look across at each other.* HENRY *signifies to the old man with a motion of his hand that he spit first. Old* JERNIGAN *with signs refuses.* HENRY *spits profusely and loud in the direction of the fire. Old* JERNIGAN *does likewise.*]

JERNIGAN. [*Eyeing* HENRY *slyly, as he rolls his tobacco sweetly in his mouth.*] Hee—hee! [MATTIE *sits hugging* HENRY'S *knees.*]

HENRY. [*Nodding happily and wisely.*] Unh-hunh-yeh. [*They sit saying nothing. Presently* HENRY *looks over at the old man and laughs suddenly and deeply.*]

JERNIGAN. What?

HENRY. I run them there women right into the mudhole out there.

JERNIGAN. [*Beating his thigh gleefully.*] Hee-hee! Hee-hee!

HENRY. I shore did. [*They lapse into silence. By this time*

MATTIE *has somewhat raised her head and is staring contemplatively by* HENRY'S *chin into the fire.*]

JERNIGAN. [*Shivering a bit and stirring the fire.*] Gonna be cold Henry, cold.

HENRY. Yeh.

JERNIGAN. Robins been flying towards the South all day. [*They both lean towards the fire and spit.*]

SUPPER FOR THE DEAD

CHARACTERS

FESS OXENDINE, *a Croatan Negro.*
VONIE OXENDINE, *his wife.*
OLD QUEENIE, *a Negro conjure-woman.*
LIL ⎱
FURY ⎰ *her two daughters.*

TIME—*The latter part of the nineteenth century.*
PLACE—*In a Cape Fear River swamp in eastern North Carolina.*

SUPPER FOR THE DEAD

THE *sun has gone down over the Oxendine clearing and a sort of steaming night-sweat creeps up and around the cabin from the feverish surrounding swamps.* FESS OXENDINE, *a powerful Croatan Negro of middle age with a swarthy copperish face, stands by the pig-pen holding a bucket in his hand and watching his pig eat slops. The pig finally finishes his guzzlings and squeals and gnaws at the rails for more, but* FESS *pays no attention to him now, watching on with unseeing eyes. The dusk gradually thickens in the little field, swamp owls begin their mournful calling, and presently a mocking-bird bursts into a lonely chatter in the one pear tree near the garden.* FESS *with a mutter shakes his shoulders and looks morosely around at the sky. The spectacle of the west burning in a flame and the clouds marching in glory seems to irritate and awe him. With a low oath, he lurches across his few potato rows and into the house. Sitting down by the fire-place, he begins to dip snuff, now and then running his hand through his mop of heavy hair.*

In the back of the room is a bed and to the left of that a broken-down cot. A rough eating-table is in the center. Three or four pots and pans hang to the right of the fire-place and in the corner a cupboard contains some provisions and a few cracked dishes. There are two or three chairs with untanned cowhide bottoms. A door at the right opens to the outside, and in the left wall is a wooden window with a double-barreled shot gun above it. Old clothes are hanging on nails about the room.

FESS. [*Slapping himself and muttering.*] Mon, dem domn

muskeeters seem lak try to eat you up. [*He beats about him with his ragged felt hat and sits listening.*] Why 'on't she come on hyuh? And dem owls, dem owls, seem lak worse dan useter. [*He lights a sputtering lamp, sets it on the table and resumes his seat before the hearth. Presently he lifts the lid from the spider sitting near the coals.*] Hunh, left me nary a bite t'eat. Knowed it. Min' take my cowhide when she come and beat the clothes off'n her. Whah she gone nohow? [*Pondering.*] Sump'n in her mind, dat's a fac'. [*He wanders to the door, looks out, and gives a sharp whistle. As he waits with no reply, his face grows distorted with anger, and he yells.*] Heigh, you, Vonie! 'Come out'n dat 'ere swamp ef you's down dere.' [*His hound shakes himself in the yard and coming up into the door leans against his leg. The brute's gesture of kindliness infuriates him and with a savage kick, he hurls him from him. In a burst of anger he springs across the room, jerks down the gun and hurries to the door.*] Gwine shoot dat God-domn dog. Git f'om hyuh, you dirty suck-aig devil! Allus in de way. [*He raises his gun and fires, and the dog runs screaming across the field. He fires a second time and stands listening to the screams of pain dying towards the swamp. Then, heaving a great sigh, he sets the stock of the gun on his foot.*] Unh-hunh, I been telling dat Nick to keep out'n my way. Anh, dat purty sudden dough, shooting him lak dat. [*Chuckling.*] Sho' tore up his tail wid dem shot, I betcha. [*He stands thinking.*] Seem lak eve'y-thing gitting wrong wid me. My haid des' flies all to pieces. [*Shaking himself.*] Wish't I could fohgit dat 'ere dream I had—oh—Lawd! Next thing I'll be putting a load o' shot in dat Vonie. [*He gets two shells from the cupboard, reloads the gun, and replaces it above the window; after which he sets about stirring up the fire and preparing supper. He places a frying-pan on the coals and begins hacking off huge slices of white side meat at the cupboard. While he is thus occupied,* VONIE *shuffles quietly in. She is a middle-aged Negro, dressed in dirty rags, all hips and feet and with a pole-like chest. One eye is missing from her head, leaving a red membraneous slit between her lids. Her face is dead and sagging and unrelieved by any vitality even in her one good eye. As she enters,* FESS *whirls upon her with a shout, raising the knife in his hand.*] Yeah, and where you been to, 'oman?

VONIE. [*Dragging off her bonnet and sitting quietly in a chair.*] Off.

FESS. [*With a guttural snarl.*] Reckon I knows it, and you gone de whole evenin'. [*Seizing her and putting the knife against her throat.*] Gooder min'er rip yo' gullet open. Whah you been to, I axes you?

VONIE. [*Choking out the words.*] Off, off a little piece.

FESS. [*Crushing her down in her seat.*] Spet out, spet out! What you up to. [VONIE *closes her eye and drops her head limply against his hand. He gives her throat a little sharp prick and steps back from her with a threatening chuckle.*] All right, I'll find out. Better not be up to no tricks, you know me—

VONIE. [*Wiping a trickle of blood from her throat with her apron and speaking in a thin stifled voice.*] Gouge t'other eye out, anh?

FESS. [*Throwing his knife down and slumping in a chair.*] Mon's 'oman tell de shuriff on him orter have 'em both bored out wid a chunk o' far.

VONIE. Ain't no shuriff dis time.

FESS. Better not be. But you act so quare all day long! Sump'n in yo' mind?

VONIE. [*Quietly.*] Dey is.

FESS. [*Softly as he punches up the fire.*] Still worrying 'bout it—'bout sump'n?

VONIE. Mought.

FESS. Quit it, quit it, cain't be ho'p.

VONIE. Mought could a mont' ago. [*Bowing her head in her hands.*] Po' little thing!

FESS. [*Eyeing her.*] Hanh?

VONIE. Po' little thing.

FESS. [*Sharply.*] Hyuh now, thought you done say all mebbe foh de best.

VONIE. Mebbe . . . [*Levelly.*] But den I been turning it in my haid. [*She darts a quick look at him and stares at the floor.*]

FESS. Dat what you been doing off in dem woods?

VONIE. Ne' mind.

FESS. Don't talk too sharp wid me, nigger. [VONIE *suddenly breaks into a low sardonic and toothless laugh.* FESS *turns and gazes at her in astonishment, then shrugs his shoulders carelessly.*] Yo' misery mak' you laugh lak dat?

VONIE. Mebbe.

FESS. [*Bounding out of his chair.*] 'Y God you stop dat and git a move on you 'bout my supper. [*He moves toward her.*] Hyuh I been waiting, and I got to hurry to de swamps.

VONIE. Better not go to dat still tonight.

FESS. Hunh?

VONIE. I hearn de depities is on to it. Dey watch tonight?

FESS. Dat de truf?

VONIE. [*In the same impersonal voice.*] Mebbe.

FESS. [*Stopping uncertainly.*] Hyuh . . . Quare you telling me dat. Seem lak you'd want 'em to git me, way dey done t'other time.

VONIE. Don't want 'em to git you dis time.

FESS. Not if you wants to keep dat haid where it belongs.

[*With a touch of kindness.*] Whah'd you heah 'bout dem officers, Vonie?

VONIE. Over de creek.

FESS. What you doing over dere?

VONIE. A little business.

FESS. [*Raging.*] A little business! Cut out dat making fun of me. [*With a sudden thought.*] You ain't tell dem officers dey find me hyuh, has you?

VONIE. I ain't told 'em nothing.

FESS. Cain't see what you planning.

VONIE. [*Giving him another quick glance.*] Lonesome hyuh by myself now. Be bad wid you in de pen.

FESS. [*Somewhat softened.*] Sho' den I set wid you.

VONIE. [*Going on in cold impassiveness.*] Too lonesome and her not wid me hyuh.

FESS. [*Gruffly.*] Yeh, but I be hyuh wid you now.

VONIE. Mebbe.

FESS. [*Staring at her in angry amazement.*] What'n de name o' God you mean, 'oman, wid all dat mebbe talk?

VONIE. [*Smiling queerly.*] How long since it happened?

FESS. Don't put no membrance 'pon it. Fohgit it, let it go by.

VONIE. 'Bout a mont', ain't it, since us found her in de water?

FESS. Well den, 'bout a mont'!

VONIE. New-moon night?

FESS. [*Hurriedly.*] Don't know, cain't 'member all dat. Quit fetching it up, I tell you. [*In a decisive voice.*] She up above now, at rest. Preacher say she good girl.

VONIE. [*With sudden vehemence.*] Her wuh good too, but den somebody wuh mean.

FESS. [*Softly.*] How come?

VONIE. Who put her in dat creek and drowned her?

FESS. Done told you she must had slipped in when she fishing.

VONIE. Why ain't you tried to find out who 'twas, you her daddy?

FESS. She got drownded, dat's all.

VONIE. [*Crying out.*] Fess Oxendine, who done it, who wuh de man?

FESS. [*Snapping.*] How de hell I know? [*He quickly goes over to the bed and lies down.*] I gwine lie and rest a minute. Git on now and fry me dat meat.

VONIE. [*Beginning to beat on her knees.*] Some ob 'em say she drownded herself and gone down to hell. Dey say it dat day at de graveyard.

FESS. She fell in I tell you and got dat fish-line all wropped 'round her neck. Dat choked her down.

VONIE. [*Standing up.*] And what you doing las' night talking 'bout fishlines in yo' dreams? And one time you hollered out and call her purty flower.

FESS. [*Starting and then speaking cunningly.*] Et too much o' dat grease and dat meat, mak' me have bad dreams. Quit dat worrying. She gone on up to heaben. Sho' she sorry foh you and me way down hyuh.

VONIE [*Mournfully.*] I gwine find out whah she gone.

FESS. Hunh?

VONIE. Find out.

FESS. [*Snorting.*] You must be crazy or sump'n. How you gwine do dat?

VONIE. Find out who done it too.

FESS. [*Sitting up on the edge of the bed.*] How you mean?

VONIE. Help coming hyuh. Us gwine find out.

FESS. [*In a low voice.*] Who coming?

VONIE. I been over to Aunt Queenie's.

FESS. [*Springing out of bed.*] Dat 'oman ain't coming in my house.

VONIE. Her and de twins is coming hyuh in a few minutes.

FESS. [*Getting his gun.*] Dem snake folks come in hyuh, I fill 'em full o' lead.

VONIE. She don't keer nothing foh dat.

FESS. Whah dey now?

VONIE. Dey come by de graveyard to git some de dirt off'n her grave.

FESS. I'll kill 'em, I tell you.

VONIE. [*Sitting down again and watching him intently.*] Nunh-unh, you won't. Lead won't bodder 'em, and 'sides, dey'd han't you and destroy you wid deir power.

FESS. Hunh, dat hain't business! What dey gwine do hyuh?

VONIE. Dey show you.

FESS. [*Setting his gun down against the wall.*] Pshaw, dey cain't hurt me. Keep strong in de haid, dat's all. Mess wid me and I git me a stick and frail 'em out'n hyuh.

VONIE. [*Laughing toothlessly again.*] You de only man'd say dat.

FESS. [*Throwing up his head.*] And I's de man kin do it too. You low-down niggers all got no mo' sense dan a gang o' sheep. Fess Oxendine ain't dat sort. He got de white folks' blood in him, and dat old Indian chief wuh my grandpap. [*Boldly.*] Yeh, let 'em try all deir mess t'won't skeer me.

VONIE. [*Cryptically.*] Sho' you too much man foh de nigger trash.

FESS. All dat business 'bout Jack-muh-lantern and dat Plateye—hunh, I seed 'em and never 'twon't nothing but old fox-far or lightning bugs. [*Laughing.*] And you niggers all freezing wid fear of' em.

VONIE. Sho', dat's all. [*She goes to the chimney and taking a little brown packet from a nail, throws it into the fire.*]

FESS. [*With a shout.*] Heigh, what you doing?

VONIE. [*Returning to her chair.*] Sho' you don't keer 'f I burn up my little trick. Dey ain't no power in it, you said many a time.

FESS. [*Moving towards the fire.*] You don't want to burn it up now wid old Queenie coming hyuh.

VONIE. Queenie ain't gwine hurt me. [FESS *stops, and* VONIE *laughs sarcastically.*] No, he ain't skeered o' nothing. He strong in de haid and all-powerful. [*In a monotone.*] Fess Oxendine de mighty man o' de Cumberland swamps, don't hadder put no 'pendance in no conjuh bag. He strong enough widout it, de wild buck of de river. How many men has he cut to de hollow? And de wimmen, and de wimmen! Bad Fess dey calls him. [*Teasingly.*] Bedder not let dat little bag burn up.

FESS. [*Throwing back his shoulders.*] Domn dat little bag! What I keer? [*Turning and kicking her.*] Git now and fix my supper.

VONIE. [*Laughing again.*] We all eat supper togedder.

FESS. Hunh?

VONIE. Supper foh de daid.

FESS. What's dat?

VONIE. Us gwine feed her, po' little thing.

FESS. [*Mumbling in perplexity.*] Dat studying 'bout it got her wrong in de haid. [*There is a noise outside and old* QUEENIE *stands in the door.* FESS *looks at her a moment and then sits quietly in his chair near the fire. The old woman comes in, followed by her twin daughters. She is an incredibly ancient* GUINEA NEGRO *of a bluish-black color, drawn and skinny, with bright little eyes, and dressed in a single garment of dull red flannel. She walks with a stick and carries a little leather satchel on her arm. The twins, dressed in the same dull stuff, and holding hands, follow her into the room. They are about sixty years old and walk with short quivering palsied steps, their tiny bonneted heads rising above their shoulders with the grace and litheness of two snakes. As they enter they fasten their beady eyes on* FESS, *who moves closer against the wall.*]

QUEENIE. [*Motioning with her stick and speaking in a husky jerky voice.*] Set over dere. [*The twins move over and sit down on the edge of the bed. Old* QUEENIE *looks carefully around the room and smiles triumphantly as her eyes rest on the packet burning in the fire.*]

VONIE. [*Rising and placing her a chair.*] Set down and rest yo' se'f.

QUEENIE. [*Huskily.*] Who dat man?

VONIE. Dat Fess, de daddy o' her. [FESS *watches her narrowly, abstractedly pulling out his snuff-box.*]

QUEENIE. Sho' dat Fess. [*Pleasantly.*] Bad man, ain't you, Fess?

FESS. [*Growling.*] What you doing hyuh in my house? [*He turns his head away and begins dipping.*] Old 'oman what de snakes useter suck. [*A sudden gleam comes into* QUEENIE'S *eye, quickly passing away.*]

QUEENIE. How you all gitting on?

FESS. Gitting on all right and you might take dem two bastards off my bed and hit de grit from hyuh.

QUEENIE. Don't mind us, Fess. D'ain't no harm in us. [*Looking at him pleasantly.*] Gimme a bit o' yo' snuff, Fess. [*She smiles kindly at him. The twins lean forward expectantly.*]

FESS. Sho' I don't mind dat. Hyuh. Help yo'se'f. [*She takes the snuff and puts some in her lip and nose.*] You don't seem so quare adder all. [*Old* QUEENIE *suddenly sneezes and then inhales with a deep breath of delight.*] But dem two 'omans on dat bed—

QUEENIE. [*Sneezing again and smiling at him.*] Dey po' harmless chillun. But ain't dey purty, Fess? I calls 'em my two snakes. Talk to him, chillun. [*They lick their tongues out at him.*]

FESS. [*Starting back.*] Great God, dem things ain't human! [VONIE *sits down and says nothing.*]

QUEENIE. Oh, dey kin talk bedder'n dat. Dey kin says words at times. Po' things, got marked by a big rattlesnake pilot bit me in de swamp 'fo' dey was bawn. [*She sneezes again, gazing indulgently at* FESS.] Look at deir little haids and deir little black eyes, des lak a snake foh de world. [*She sneezes again and the twins grow more and more excited, their heads appearing to rise higher and higher on the stems of their scrawny necks.*]

FESS. Mak 'em quit looking at me dat-a-way. [*She hands the snuff-box back to him.*]

QUEENIE. Dat mighty good snuff, Fess. [*She sneezes twice in rapid succession and turns and looks at the twins. Their tongues begin to flutter between their lips as they look hungrily at their mother.*]

FESS. [*Suspiciously.*] Why you sneeze so? [VONIE *looks up intently.*]

QUEENIE [*Speaking gently over her shoulder.*] Good snuff, Fess, good Lord o' God. [*She opens her mouth, wrinkles her nose, and then sneezes sharply. The two women sit up stiff and straight on the bed.* QUEENIE *shouts out.*] Seben times, chillun, seben times! [*She totters to the door and looks out over her left shoulder.*] Dere it is, dere's de new moon behime dat poplar. All ready, fixed and ready, fixed and ready.

FESS. [*Standing up.*] Don't you start dat 'ere business, I tell you.

QUEENIE. [*With a sharp gesture.*] Set down in dat cheer, nigger man, set down. [FESS *gradually sinks back in his chair, waiting.*]

FESS. [*Muttering.*] But min' what I told you.

QUEENIE. [*Raising her head and speaking in the air.*]

> God befo' me,
> God behime me,
> God be wid me.

LIL and FURY. [*Whispering.*] God be wid me.

QUEENIE. Dat right, talk out, speak fo'th chillun. Dere was po' li'l Miny drownded in de creek. Whah she now?

LIL and FURY. Whah?

QUEENIE. Mebbe in heben, mebbe in hell, mebbe walking in de swamps. [VONIE *bows her head on her knees.*] Us gwine find out, gwine raise huh ghos' f'om de daid and feed huh, gwine see who kill huh.

LIL and FURY. Who kill huh.

FESS. [*With a brutal laugh.*] Reckon you won't be gitting de daid back hyuh. [*He reaches for his gun and lays it across his lap.*]

QUUEENIE. [*Touching* VONIE'S *bent back with her stick.*] Fetch me huh dress and bonnet. [VONIE *rises and gets a dress and bonnet from a nail in the wall.* QUEENIE *places a chair to the table, spreads the dress over it, and puts the bonnet on top, forming a crude dummy.* FESS *watches every movement with skeptical braggadocio. Old* QUEENIE *calls.*] Chillun!

LIL and FURY. [*Softly.*] Yeh, mam.

QUEENIE. Kin you heah me?

LIL and FURY. Us heah you.

QUEENIE. Kin huh heah me?

LIL and FURY. Huh heah you too.

QUEENIE. [*Chuckling.*] Us gut de power?

LIL and FURY. De power.

QUEENIE. Fetch me de free plates and de bowl. [VONIE *goes to the cupboard and brings the dishes to the table. Old* QUEENIE *sets them out, a plate before the dummy, one at each end of the table and the bowl in the middle.*

FESS. Sech a pack o' fools!

QUEENIE. Come to de table, chillun. [*With jerky steps they move over and seat themselves, one at each end of the table.* QUEENIE *opens her satchel and takes out a dirty little paper bag and empties it in the bowl.*] Po' in, po' in dirt f'om huh grave.

LIL and FURY. De graveya'd dirt.

QUEENIE. [*Pulling out a handful of herbs and placing them in the bowl.*] Bring me de far-coal, 'oman. [VONIE *brings a fire-coal on a piece of wood.* QUEENIE *takes it in her hand and blows on it.*]

FESS. Great God, it don't burn her!

QUEENIE. [*Dropping it into the bowl.*] Blow on it, chillun. [*They bend their heads toward the center of the table and blow in the bowl. Presently a curl of smoke rises upward.*] Breave dat smoke down in you. [*They inhale the fumes and sit stiffly back in their chairs looking unblinkingly at old* QUEENIE. *The old woman draws several pieces of white meat from her satchel and places one in each of the three plates.*] Eat dat, chillun. [*They begin eating.* VONIE *comes up near the table and stands watching.*]

FESS. What dat dey eating? [*Horrified.*] I bet to Christ dat rashers of dead folks!

QUEENIE. See anything yit?

LIL and FURY. [*Dreamily.*] Not yit, Mammy.

QUEENIE. [*Pulling out three dark objects resembling frogs and placing them on the plates.*] Eat dat, chillun. [QUEENIE *peers into their eyes as they eat.*] See yit?

LIL and FURY. See little bit.

QUEENIE. [*Huskily.*] What dat, chillun?

LIL and FURY. Sump'n 'way, 'way in a big snow field.

FESS. [*Jumping out of his chair.*] God A'mighty, dey eating frawgs. [QUEENIE *waves her hand behind her and* FESS *gradually sinks back in his chair, staring at them with open mouth.*]

QUEENIE. Look clost, look clost. Is dey people dere?

LIL and FURY. People dere.

QUEENIE. Huh dere?

LIL and FURY. Cain't see um. [OLD QUEENIE *pulls out more dried herbs and puts them in the bowl. Thick clouds of smoke pour upward and settle about the room.*] Breave it, chillun, breave it. [*She takes a little red flannel pouch out of the satchel and pours some white powder in each of the three plates. The twins wet their fingers and dip the powder into their mouths.* QUEENIE *coaxes them on.*] Look down, 'way down yander in dat t'other place. Look down.

LIL and FURY. [*In a far-away voice.*] Us looking.

QUEENIE. Kin see dere? [*They suddenly draw back horrified.*] Look, look dere, I tell you.

LIL and FURY. [*Shuddering.*] Ah! [*They close their eyes and sway from side to side.*]

QUEENIE. [*Sternly.*] Look down dere, I tell you. [*She pulls out a handful of hair and casts it into the bowl. There is a quick puff of flame upward, and* LIL *and* FURY *rear back with a low moan.*]

VONIE. [*Dropping in her chair with a cry.*] Don't make 'em look, don't make 'em. Dey done see sump'n bad. [*She hides her face in her arms.*]

QUEENIE. Look down dere!

LIL *and* FURY. Kin see now.

QUEENIE. See huh?

VONIE. [*Shrieking.*] Po' little Miny down dere in hell! [*She covers her head with her apron.*]

QUEENIE. Keep yo' eye on huh, don't lose huh. [*She begins to chant as she draws fetishes from the satchel and arranges them on the table.*]

> Feathers, cakes and beans and cawn,
> Thumb of de bastard son jist bawn.
> Spider, wasp and field-mice tongue.

FESS. [*Shooting out of his chair with a yell.*] I done see dat-ere bonnet move on de cheer! [*He jerks up his gun.*]

QUEENIE. [*Chanting.*] Eye of a man de gallus hung.

FESS. [*Snarling, as he cocks his gun.*] You quit dat conjure business, don't I shoot you. [*He suddenly starts for the door, but old* QUEENIE *steps before him holding up her stick.*]

QUEENIE. You ain't gwine out'n hyuh, black man, till we's done. [*With a quick movement of her stick she bends down and draws a line on the floor from the door to the fireplace, enclosing* FESS.] You step over dat line and you fall daid. Stay back dere, man, and don't move. Do, I ruin you fohever. [FESS *puts out his foot as if to step over.* QUEENIE *watches him with uplifted hand and the twins moan loudly. Finally he slinks back to his chair and sits down shivering.*]

FESS. All right, God domn you! I wait and see what you up to.

QUEENIE. [*Laying out more fetishes.*]

>Devil's snuff and de dried dog brains,
>'Oman's scabs dat died in chains.
>Ground calf-tongue and de black cat's bone—

[*Raising her voice in a high pleading.*]

>Come up, Miny, git yo' own!

FESS. [*Beating himself with his hat.*] Dat domn smoke mak' me feel quare. [*Huskily.*] Hunh, I keep strong in de haid, dat's what. Dey cain't hurt me. Dat old bonnet dere limp as a rag yit.

VONIE. [*Whining under her apron.*] Miny, Miny!

QUEENIE. Whah she now, chillun?

LIL and FURY. Kin hardly see, 'bout gone.

QUEENIE. Keep looking, keep looking. [*She takes out a small egg and breaks it in the bowl. Then she pours a small bottle of fluid in.*]

>Black snake ile and rain-crow aig,
>Puts de stren'th in the ghostes laig.
>Make um power of muscle and bone—
>Come up, Miny, hyuh's yo' own.

LIL and FURY. [*Softly.*] Hyuh's yo' own.

FESS. [*Yelling.*] I see what you adder now. You wants to ha'nt me. [*Cocking his gun.*] But you ain't gwine do it. I'll blow yo' brains out wid dis here. [*He levels the gun at them.*] I gi' you jest one minnit to git out. [*Old* QUEENIE *pays no attention to him, her head lifted up as if straining toward a vision.*]

LIL and FURY. [*Joyously.*] Us see um now. Huh coming.

QUEENIE. [*In loud exultation.*] Coming!

FESS. Hyuh goes den, and dat's de las' o' you. I shoot de old black 'un fust.

LIL and FURY. Huh in de field out dere now.

QUEENIE. [*Throwing her hands up and down in the air.*] Yis, yis, I feel it.

FESS. [*His face distorted with rage.*] I shoot both o' dem eyes out. [*He pulls the trigger, but the hammer refuses to fall. He tries the other one.*] Dem domn hammers stuck. [*He raises the gun again. Old* QUEENIE *turns and looks at him with a low devilish laugh.*]

QUEENIE. Come on, Miny, hyuh's yo' own.

LIL and FURY. Hyuh's yo' own.

FESS. [*With a shriek.*] She done got dat gun—a spell on it! [*He throws the gun from him and whirls to his chair. Sitting down with his back to the women, he clasps his head between his knees, rocking and moaning.*] My haid done all gone slam to pieces. O, Lawd, have muhcy on me! [*He cowers in his seat.*]

LIL and FURY. Huh in de yard out dere now.

QUEENIE. [*Ecstatically.*] Yis, yis, fetch her in. [*Calling loudly.*] Supper, Miny! Come to yo' supper!

VONIE. [*Throwing her apron from her head and sitting up calm and straight.*] Call her, call her, lemme see her onct mo'.

QUEENIE. [*Turning and looking through the door.*] Look dere, look dere. Huh out dere at de well drawing water. [*The low rumble of a whirring windlass is heard.*]

FESS. [*Raising his head.*] Listen at dat, listen at dat! [*Crouching down on the hearth.*] Dat's a ha'nt at my well. [*He sits shivering with terror.*]

LIL and FURY. De ha'nts draw water at his well.

QUEENIE. [*Staring out in the deepening dusk.*] De ya'd's full of 'em, all come back wid huh. Fess, you is a lost membuh.

[*Reaching out her arms towards the night and pleading.*] Come in hyuh, Miny, come on. Call to huh, chillun. [*Breathlessly.*] Call to huh.

LIL and FURY. [*Beating their heads against the table.*] Heah us Miny, heah us. Come in. De supper is waiting, de supper is fixed.

QUEENIE. Look! Look! She 'bout to tuhn back. Feel foh huh, Vonie. Huh gwine back in de field wid all dem others, de little 'uns and de big 'uns. Dey gwine back to de swamps.

VONIE. [*Lifting up her voice in a wail.*] Miny, Miny, come to yo' po' muh dis night!

QUEENIE. Huh coming, huh coming in. [*Addressing the spectre.*] Dat's it, honey, dat's it, come on in. [*Her voice trembles and slobbers with eagerness, and she begins patting her hands softly together, keeping time with her foot on the floor.*]

VONIE. [*Screaming.*] Dere she now. [*She sits petrified in her chair. A little ragged Negro girl with downcast eyes comes quietly in at the door and seats herself at the table. She is about sixteen years old, with swelling breasts and a plump oval face. She begins eating food from the plate.*]

VONIE. [*Murmuring over and over.*] Miny, Miny, is dat you, chile? Den you ain't daid, thank God. [*She stares at her with fascinated eyes.*] Fess, Fess, dere's Miny, come back to us!

FESS. Tain't nothing, tain't nothing. Don't you look at dat. [*Suddenly old* QUEENIE *begins to caper back and forth across the floor, breaking out into senseless ecstatic words.*]

QUEENIE. [*As she capers.*] Tibbity-bibbity, tchee-tchee-tchee— Tchee-tchee-tchee. Purty little flower.

LIL and FURY. [*Falling on the floor before the little girl.*] Purty little flower!

QUEENIE. [*Waving her arms aloft.*] Lily o' de valley.

LIL and FURY. [*Making obeisance.*] Little scrushed Lily.

QUEENIE. [*Singing.*] De rose o' Sharon.

LIL and FURY. Rose o' Sharon.

QUEENIE. Mean man pulled de little flower f'om its bed.

LIL and FURY. Mean man pulled.

QUEENIE. He hadder die.

LIL and FURY. Gut to die.

QUEENIE. Who wuh it, honey?

LIL and FURY. Who wuh it? [*The little girl continues eating her food, saying nothing.*]

QUEENIE. [*Crying out.*] You, Fess Oxendine, look up hyuh and see yo' dawtuh!

FESS. [*Beginning to sob.*] I cain't see huh, have muhcy on me!

QUEENIE. Look up, I tell you. [*She stretches out her hand and FESS slowly lifts his head from the floor.*]

FESS. [*Gasping.*] Who dat? [*Joy breaking in his voice.*] Why dat— Glory to God, dat little Miny come back! [*He staggers to his feet and goes towards the table.*] Den you ain't daid, thank de Lawd. Dat all a dream I had. Look at you and you so purty. Honey, come hyuh to me. [*He suddenly breaks into loud sobs.*] Thank de Lawd, thank de Lawd. [*As he approaches the table, the little girl backs away in terror and moves towards the door.*]

VONIE. Miny, Miny!

QUEENIE. Tell us who de man? [*Without lifting her head, the little girl nods at FESS.*] I knowed it, he de man whut ruint you and make you drownd yo'se'f. [*She reaches into the bowl, and a galvanic shock seems to run through her. She throws bits of the bowl's contents towards the door and the little girl disappears into the darkness.*]

VONIE. [*Starting up and wailing.*] Whah she gone? Gi' huh back to me, gi' huh back!

QUEENIE. [*Throwing part of the mixture on* FESS.] Hyuh de man!

FESS. [*Screaming and clawing at the back of his neck.*] Let me loose! Who dat got me! [*He falls writhing and howling on the floor.*]

QUEENIE. Dere he, Vonie, he de man mix wid he own flesh.

VONIE. [*Breaking into a loud laugh.*] Look at da' bad man lying dere cutting up on de flo'. Dat you Fess, de old swamp buck?

FESS. Couldn't git huh out'n my mind. She so purty. [*Clawing his clothes from him.*] Ooh—let me loose! [VONIE *picks up the gun and suddenly fires both barrels into* FESS's *back. Then she flies out through the door calling pitifully after the little girl.*]

QUEENIE. [*Her face illumined.*] De power come down to us. [*She sprinkles* LIL *and* FURY *with the contents of the bowl and they rise from the floor with transfigured faces.*]

LIL and FURY. De power.

QUEENIE. [*Skipping and chanting.*] Us re'ch and call and de daid do answer.

LIL and FURY. [*Beginning to skip with her.*] Do answer.

QUEENIE. [*Weaving a pattern around* FESS' *dead body.*] Hallelujah!

LIL and FURY. [*Beginning to pat their hands.*] Hallelujah!

[*The dance quickens as they sway and bow and chant.*]

QUEENIE. Us call and git answer.

LIL and FURY. Git answer.

QUEENIE. De supper fotch um.

LIL and FURY. [*In ecstasy.*] Fotch um down.

QUEENIE. Supper foh he daid.

LIL and FURY. Foh de daid.

[*The twins continue dancing around the body, as Old* QUEENIE *goes hopping around the table, raking her charms and fetishes into her bag. Their breath comes through their teeth in a hissing sound.*]

QUEENIE. [*Dancing towards the door.*] Tibbity-bibbity-tchee-tchee-tchee.

LIL and FURY. Tchee-thcee-tchee. [*They disappear through the door, their gibbering dying across the fields.*]

SATURDAY NIGHT

CHARACTERS

JOHN DAY
MRS. DAY
POLLY, *their daughter.*
JOSHUA, *their son.*
JOE HARWELL, *a neighboring boy in love with* POLLY.
ALLEN JONES, *a neighbor.*
MACK LUCUS, *a fiddler.*

TIME—*The present.*
PLACE—*A farm in eastern North Carolina.*

SATURDAY NIGHT

IF *the crops are not too pushing, the farmers usually end their week's work at Saturday noon. After dinner you will find them congregated in the neighboring village, buying rations, swapping news, politics, and sometimes religion until evening comes. The boys have gathered over at the old-field baseball diamond where with run and shout and a little cussing they play their hearts out till darkness drives them home, perished for water and with the seat of their trousers dragging the ground. And if times are not too hard the old man will return with ice and vanilla flavoring to make cream for the children. And everybody will have some fun between the heat of the fields behind and the loneliness of Sunday coming on. Thus it is on a particular Saturday night in summer at the home of* JOHN DAY, *a hardworking tenant farmer. Two or three men are sitting in the bare moonlit yard before the house, talking about their crops, and hopes for the future. And since the earth in its kindness provides them with a metaphysic as well as daily bread, they now and then vouchsafe a word concerning God and the nature of the universe. It is about nine o'clock at evening and the moon is high in the sky. Stretching around the house and away, the fields of cotton and corn cast up a silvery radiance in the air. Behind the old barn over there a whippoorwill is cutting a rust. A young woman opens a door and comes out on the low vine-clad porch. The glow from a lamp inside pours out after her, revealing morning-glories climbing the posts and varicolored flowers set in tin cans along a shelf to the left. Through the door and across the room beyond a little porch is seen at the back of the house where a water-shelf is built and where a tall, motherly woman is dishing up ice-cream for a swarm of children. The young woman returns into the*

*house—evidently the expected one has not come—and closes
the door behind her to keep the bugs and gnats from streaming in. The men in the yard eye the night and go on with their
talk, with gaps of silence between their speeches.*

MACK LUCAS. [*Turning a gleaming fiddle in his hand.*] Nice
and cool out here.

JOHN DAY. Purty cool and nice.

LUCAS. The cream was good.

DAY. It was that.

LUCAS. Corn out there—growing fast—hear its j'ints pop.

DAY. Purty good. That whippoorwill's a mess, ain't he?
White bowl o' milk! White bowl o' milk. Why do they say
that, you reckon? [LUCAS *sighs and looks out before him,
his long thin fingers tapping on the violin.*]

LUCAS. Dunno. They don't say it. Just sounds like it.

DAY. Funny.

LUCAS. You're a strong man, John Day, and I'm a weak
one. I'm thinking of it.

DAY. [*Teasing.*] What is it, judge?

LUCAS. You got crops and children. [*Whistling.*] And I got
a fiddle. [*Suddenly animated.*] Like that bird, maybe, with
no home but his song, and the rain pouring.

DAY. Here's some tobacco—try it, Mack.

LUCAS. Yes.

DAY. What ails that boy? [*Calling.*] You Joshua—hurry up
with your cream and bring your banjo out!

ALLEN JONES. [*Looming up in the darkness.*] Booh! [*He is a
jolly man and given to tricks.*]

DAY. For goodness sakes! Light and cool your saddle.

JONES. Started the music yit, Mack? Couldn't miss that.

DAY. Waiting for Joshua to git his bait o' that cream. [*The door opens again and the young woman comes out on the porch.*]

JONES. Heigho, Polly.

POLLY. [*Disappointed.*] Good evening.

DAY. Go in and git you some cream, Allen.

JONES. [*Spitting loudly over his shoulder.*] Lord, I et a supper would kill a bull. Eddie brought some croakers back from Duke. [LUCAS *draws his bow across his fiddle in a few plaintive notes.*]

DAY. Well, have some tobacco.

JONES. Just put in a chew. [*Sitting down quickly and heavily.*] How's the world with you all?

DAY. All right.

LUCAS. Still the world.

DAY. And you?

JONES. Moonlight and sunshine, boys.

DAY. Rain?

JONES. When needed. [*Laughing.*] Not moonshine. He ain't come, has he? [*Nodding towards* POLLY.]

DAY. At home trying to find his collar-button maybe. Slow—but stiddy.

LUCAS. [*Playing almost inaudibly and murmuring.*]

> I been a-courting, mother.
> Make my bed soon for I must lie down.

JONES. Reckon he and Polly'll ever come to a' understanding?

DAY. I dunno. Ef they don't somebody'll die single.

JONES. If he ain't been hyuh every Sa'd'y and Sunday night for the last three years, I'm a bull calf.

DAY. [*Shouting.*] Joshua! Call him, Polly.

[*The young woman goes into the house.*]

LUCAS. Sixty year is a long time to live!

JONES. Uh-uh now, always thinking of something.

DAY. Long, and not so long.

JONES. Long one way, not so long another.

LUCAS. [*Flirting out the bar of a jig.*] Long, measured by experience.

JONES. Well, I'm just forty-one and ain't never been sick.

DAY. Young. And Mack and me is old. [*Reaching over and touching* LUCAS *on the shoulder.*] We've been through a lot.

LUCAS. More'n we'll have to again.

DAY. That's right. [*Jocularly.*] Well, there's some pleasure in knowing that, even. How many miles you reckon you've ploughed in your life, Allen?

JONES. Maybe a thousand or two, I don't know.

DAY. Polly and Joshua got to figgering the other day—they're always at some mess—to see how far I'd walked behind the plough in my life. Lemme see. I had walked a' average of twenty miles on a ploughing day, and I averaged about sixty-five ploughing days to the year, and this summer I've been at it fifty years. [*Addressing the young woman who has returned.*] How many miles did you say I'd walked behind the plough?

POLLY. Over sixty-five thousand.

JONES. My Lord! That many miles in the ploughed dirt!

DAY. [*Almost excitedly.*] That's just behind the plough, folkses. More than twice around the world, ain't it; Polly?

POLLY. Yes.

DAY. [*Poking* LUCAS *in the ribs.*] She believes the earth's round.

LUCAS. It's square, and flat, like a table, anh?

JONES. The Bible speaks of the four corners.

POLLY. What about them that's been around it?

JONES. [*Almost whispering.*] Edgycation.

DAY. Powerful.

LUCAS. [*Looking up at the moon.*] I was putting up fence-posts for the Squair yistiddy, and I dug up a rock. [*Musing.*] I thought to myself it had been there forever and ever.

DAY. God put it there.

JONES. [*Taking off his hat and spitting reverently.*] He shore did. God made it and put it there.

LUCAS. I dunno so much about that.

JONES. [*Even more reverently, with a touch of eagerness and awe.*] We've hearn it said you're 'bout a plumb inhf-idel.

LUCAS. I've wondered about things—some.

DAY. God was always, Mack.

LUCAS. From the beginning?

JONES. Forever and ever.

LUCAS. [*Again drawing the bow across the strings.*] How long is that?

JONES. All of time—can't be 'magined, except God does it.

DAY. [*Reverently.*] He holds time in the hollow of His hands.

LUCAS. [*Softly.*] He's got hands?

JONES. [*As if quoting.*] Lifted up with His hands. [*Suddenly confused.*] I hearn the preacher say Sunday—

DAY. Say sixty-five days for ploughing—that leaves three hundred days. [*Beginning to chuckle.*] Say I walked five miles a day on them days—and I do, shore I do—any day.

JONES. Every bit'n grain of it.

DAY. How many miles that .nake a year, Polly?

POLLY. Fifteen hundred miles a year.

DAY. And fifty years, not counting boyhood.

POLLY. Seventy-five thousand miles.

JONES. Smart, Lord! Same as them doo-jiggers in the bank.

DAY. [*Soberly.*] Ain't that a spell of a piece!

LUCAS. About as fur as to them stars. Wisht I'd done all my walking on a path going there.

[*There is a sound of footsteps at the right and a big, hulking young farmer, all dressed up, comes into the yard, hesitates a moment and then sits down in an empty chair near* LUCAS.]

DAY. Hy, Joe.

JOE. Hy, Mr. Day.

DAY. Some 'freshments on the back porch and Polly's there on the front. [JONES *snickers and* LUCAS *turns his face more intently towards the stars.*]

JOE. Yessuh.

DAY. How's your daddy?

JOE. Doctor says he's got to go to Richmond now.

DAY. Is?

JOE. To try to burn it out'n him.

JONES. I bet it'll hurt! They took out head and all that time from Aunt Minty's jaw. She said it hurt like a red-hot arn being shoved through. Pore soul, didn't do her no good.

LUCAS. Man was born to suffer. It was said so.

DAY. [*With gentle reverence.*] Like a shadow it said, and his race is soon run.

JOE. [*spasmodically.*] Muh says he'll never stand it, cause it's right at the base of his skull.

[*On the porch* POLLY *begins whistling to herself.*]

JONES. Gitting lonesome?

POLLY. There's some good vanilla ice-cream, Joe.

JOE. [*Feeling his high collar.*] Believe I'll go help Josh clean out the can. [*He starts into the house but gets no further than the porch.*]

JONES. [*In a sudden, loud voice, as if reciting.*] And after all them millions of miles walking, what have you got? Have you got a house? No. It belongs to the Squair. Have you got a horse? No. A mule? A buggy? No. All belongs to the Squair. [*Quietly.*] I'm just talking like business, you know. Got little enough myself.

DAY. I ain't made much—so.

JONES. And you got your children. But we all got them.

DAY. And you got your experience.

LUCAS. And we all got that.

DAY. [*Gesturing towards the shadowed porch where* POLLY *and* JOE *are ensconced.*] A hardworking man for you, Mack. [LUCAS *says nothing.*] Strong as a bull. Work, work, work. That year of the railroad and he fifteen, he saved a hundred dollars. But pop the question? No sir, skeard.

JONES. Can pull a stack of fodder in a day. Knowed him to do it. What! music! Same as old Broadhuss squeezing juice from a flint rock. Blest if he couldn't do it, my daddy said.

DAY. Put eleven hundred dollars in the bank last year. [*Chuckling.*] But scared to death of Polly.

LUCAS. [*Fingering his fiddle more often, and now and then sticking it to his chin.*] I used to play for his daddy many a time—and made something out'n it too. And Joe likes it. Too many people is ag'in' the fiddle these days, John.

DAY. I don't see no harm in it.

JONES. Still the preachers rair about it.

LUCAS. They think it's a' evil-spirited instrument. [*Whiffing out a faint tune.*] But it ain't.

DAY. I believe religion's right. Breakdowns is bad.

LUCAS. [*Forlornly.*] Religion's bad as break-downs—sometimes. Plenty o' people cut up in their religion.

JONES. [*Now spitting loudly again.*] Yes they do.

DAY. Aye, but we got to have it.

JONES. 'Member that preacher at Angiers? Tried to walk on water. He had planks hid under it to walk on. [*Slapping his thigh with his hat in glee.*] And then one day the boys found it out and moved the plank. [*He rears back and roars with laughter.*]

LUCAS. [*Bouncing across the strings.*]
And old Joel Tart announced to the world he'd been give the gift of reading from above. And a great crowd come a-Sunday to hear him do it. Later on they found he'd got it by heart from a preacher. Now John, that was a come-off.

DAY. And Joel's sister Nannie was said to've spoke real Chinaman's talk in the church onct and she did from what they said. [*Humbly.*] It was the spirit in her tongue.

[JOSHUA *comes out on the porch with a lamp in one hand and a banjo in the other. He is a stout, husky lad of eighteen or twenty. He sets the lamp down on the porch, and in the light the faces of the others are visible.*]

JOSHUA. Lord, what a supper I've et. [*He comes out into the yard and sits down, tuning his banjo. The rather sheepish* JOE, *now that he and his vivacious sweetheart are visible in the light, slides his chair away from her.*]

JOSHUA. What is it, Mr. Mack? [*Smothering a grin in his blouse.*] Hee-hee!

LUCAS. [*His mournful, haggard face lighted with a smile.*] Something short 'n easy. Anything—The Drunken Soldier. [*Rosining up and shooting his bow across the strings in a preparatory whorl of sound.*] They like that piece up in Wake County.

JOSHUA. [*Begging on bended knee.*] Lead her out'n the stall. [*He whangs out a flood of chords, and they begin to play. JONES rolls his tobacco back in his jaw and clasps his hands in rhythm.*]

DAY. [*Nodding at JOSHUA.*] Cain't he play it?

JONES. [*Looking up at the moon and braying.*]

> Oh the night's a little dark,
> And the roads a little muddy,
> And I cain't ride straight,
> And I cain't ride study—

DAY. [*Calling.*] How's that, Joe?

JOE. [*Stealing a look at POLLY.*] Right fine.

[*LUCAS and JOSHUA wind up with a flourish. Several little children, dressed in their night-drawers and gowns, come to the door of the porch and peep out.*]

CHILDREN. Pa, we want to hear it.

MRS. DAY. [*Coming out and leading them in.*] Well, hear it in bed then.

JONES. I'll declare!

CHILDREN. [*In the house.*] We want to hear 'em play! [*LUCAS and JOSHUA impatiently amble up and down the necks of their instruments.*]

LUCAS. I always liked the Mountain Dew piece.

JOSHUA. [*Crowding close to him in intimate fellowship.*] No better made.

[POLLY, *as if piqued at the interruption of her lovemaking, leaves her chair and sits down on the edge of the porch.* JOE *looks pleadingly at her and then stares heavily at the floor. Without more ado, the two musicians are off with The Mountain Dew. As they play,* JONES *falls in with his patting and old* DAY *leans back in his chair, a smile softening his rugged, weather-stained face. At first* JOE *pays little attention to the music, then presently he is seen beating the floor softly in time with his feet.* POLLY *ever and anon steals a glance at him.*]

JONES. Lord, it brings a heap o' things back to me. [*The music stops and* LUCAS *leans over to his partner.*]

JOSHUA. [*Casting up his eyes joyously.*] That's it too. [*Announcing to those around him, running a medley of chords the while.*] The Arkansaw Traveller, folkses.

[MRS. DAY *comes out and sits down on the steps, dipping snuff and placidly spitting in the yard.*]

LUCAS. [*With a high tweedle-de-dee.*] There was a traveller in Arkansaw. . . . [*As the monologue goes on,* JOSHUA'S *whang-whang serves as a background for the presentation of a traveller and farmer in conversation.*]

"Hullo, stranger."
"Hullo, yourself. If you want to go to hell, then go there yourself."
"Play the other part of that tune."
"There ain't no other part."
"Why don't you cover your house?"
"Can't cover it when it's raining. In dry weather, it don't leak a drap."
"What makes yore corn look so yaller?"
"Fool, I planted the yaller kind."
"How did your taters turn out?"

JONES. [*Cracking his palms.*] Won't never sich fools.

LUCAS. "Didn't turn out, fool, I dug 'em out."
"How fur to where the road forks?"

"Been living here fifty year. It's never forked yit."

[MRS. DAY *is heard chuckling softly to herself.* JOE *becomes more and more absorbed in the music, now unconscious of* POLLY'S *bright eyes.*]

LUCAS. "Can I ford the river?"

"Reckon so, the geese can."

"Wisht you'd head that steer."

"The devil, looks like he's got a head on him."

"I mean stop him."

"Ain't got no stopper."

[JOSHUA *lets out a loud hee-haw, and abandons himself to his banjo.*]

LUCAS. "I mean turn him."

"Looks like he's got the hairy side out."

JOSHUA. Worse 'n the old gray mare. Hee-hee!

LUCAS. "Lord, Lord, tote's the rag off 'n the bush. I hired to a man—and he sent me to the swamp to split rails—teeta-ta-ta—told me to choose out the tall trees—the straight trees—for they would split better—and I went and hewed—and I sweated and I spewed—that night when I got home—he asked me how many rails I'd split—and I told him when I got done o' the one I was on— Tee-ta-ta-ta—and two more—I'd have three.—Lord God, he fired me—fur I'd been trying to split—them old sweet-gums."

[LUCAS *breaks out in a mournful laugh.*]

JONES. He won a gold piece with that at the court-house onct. I seen him do it.

DAY. The years come and go, Mack, but you ain't lost a bit o' your power.

LUCAS. Allen's pap liked it too.

MRS. DAY. [*With sudden animation.*] The last dance I was at Mack played it.

JONES. [*Springing up with a whoop.*] Already ploughed forty miles today, but I feel frush—frush!

POLLY. Mr. Jones!

JONES. [*Throwing his hat behind him and moving out in an open space.*] Let her go then.

DAY. I don't mind. Cut up.

JONES. Gimme a reel, real Furginia reel. [LUCAS *strikes a few notes.*] Yeh, that's all right. [*He clasps his hands for attention as if he were on the dance-floor.*] Get ready.

DAY. Blamed if he don't mean business.

JONES. [*Moving over towards the porch.*] Le's cake-walk a little.

POLLY. I could do it some, but—

JONES. Aw, John don't care.

DAY. Go to it.

JONES. Gimme the Paul Jones.

LUCAS. [*Who has grown mildly excited.*] Listen folks, everybody. [*He plays the opening bars.*] Formation.

JONES. [*As* LUCAS *begins to fiddle.*] Let the figgers roll. Formation. Longways for six couples, women in one line and men in the other. Hurry up there if you don't want the sun to find you waiting. All right Polly Day, here I go. Come and jine me while the dew do fall. [*He begins to dance, bowing and scraping and turning to imaginary ladies around him. As he dances he calls the figures for his own partial execution.* LUCAS *and* JOSHUA *pound on the ground, and old* DAY *leans back and stares at the sky, his ears cocked as it were and drinking in the music.* JONES *shuffles, bounds, cavorts, all the while squealing out his commands.*] Forward

and back!—Swing with your right hand!—[*He stretches out
his right hand to* POLLY.] How're you tonight, Rosebud?
Purtiest gal from here to the river. Hah!—Swing with the
left hand! Hah!—How's that my honeysuckle queen?—
Swing with both hands!—How's that?—Allemande. [*As he
turns, he fastens his eyes on* POLLY *and dances his way over
to her.* POLLY *looks directly at* JOE *a moment, and then comes
out to meet* JONES' *outstretched hands.*]

JOSHUA. Go to it, Polly, we'll feed you.

[*Old* DAY *makes a motion as if to stop her, and then returns
to his apparent watching of the heavens.* LUCAS' *face seems
to grow more and more haggard as the fury of the music
increases—as if some grief were gnawing within him. It's a
way he has of showing his deepest pleasure.*]

JONES. Right hand to partner, and reel. [*He swings* POLLY
*around and around as if going down the line. Each time she
turns she looks at* JOE's *bowed form.* JONES *pants and blows.*]
Faster! Let's get up some feeling here. [*Shouting.*] Up the
centre. [*With galop steps he drags* POLLY *across the yard.*
JOE *looks up, patting his feet, and* POLLY *looks back as she
dances.* JONES *gasps.*] March! [*He holds* POLLY *closer to him
as the music flies.* JOE *half rises from his seat, and* POLLY's
eyes beckon him on.] Down the centre!

JOE. [*Bounding out of his chair.*] I'll do it too. [*He runs up
and snatches* POLLY *loose from him.*]

JONES. What!—Great guns!

JOE. [*His face almost white with fright.*] I could—almost—

JONES. [*Wiping his streaming brow.*] Le's see you dance with
her then.

POLLY. [*Softly to* JOSHUA.] Play as fast as you can.

JONES. [*Gruffly as he sits down in his chair—almost with a
touch of anger.*] Le's see you dance with her, tessie boy.
Naw, you can't do it. [POLLY *dances up and down the yard*

alone. The music goes on. JOE *hesitates now after his sudden outburst, makes a movement in, draws back, moves again hesitatingly after her.* JONES *fans himself with his hat.*] Look at him! Le's see him do something.

JOE. [*Following* POLLY.] I can't dance—much—none—maybe —[*Shyly.*] but I'll try, I swear I'll try it if I hurt.

JONES. Hah-hah! Come on now, le's see you show your raising.

MRS. DAY. His father was one of the steppingest men there was.

JONES. Shoe-leather couldn't hold him.

MRS. DAY. I danced through to the blood one night with him.

DAY. Pshaw, listen at her.

[*As* POLLY *moves by* JOE, *he reaches out and timidly seizes her hands, then around the waist.*]

JONES. Let the music pour out! [JOSHUA *and* LUCAS *wrap themselves over their instruments.*] Here we go!

[POLLY *and* JOE *run up and down the yard, cross, bend and bow in a crude sort of rhythm. They shuffled a jig, they waltz and fox-trot together. Then, as they proceed, they seem to find a common rhythm. Old* DAY *watches them narrowly and jubilant, significantly nodding now and then to those around him.*]

JOSHUA. Hee-hee, Lord, Lord!

JONES. Hooray! Hooray for you, Joe! Did you ever expect to see it, folkses!

DAY. [*Excitedly.*] I bet him and Polly pulls off something yet. [*To the woman on the steps.*] See that, Mellie?

[JONES *jumps up and stamps his hat in the dirt.* JOE *and* POLLY *now whirl along in their new, crude dance.*]

JOE. [*His flushed face near hers.*] Tell 'em to play faster.

POLLY. You holding me so!

JOE. Play on, Joshua. Tear up your banjo, I'll buy you another. [*Softly to her.*] All right then, and I'll hold you! My God A'mighty.

JOSHUA. [*Finally dropping his banjo.*] I done played the skin clean off o' my fingers.

[LUCAS *gradually lets his music die down to a low moaning in the strings. He sits looking out before him as if lost to the scene of which he is a part.* JOE *suddenly kisses* POLLY *with a loud smack.*]

JONES. He's done it. [*Digging his hat out of the dirt.*] I'll swear if he ain't done it.

JOE. Yeh, and I mean it. [POLLY *stands with downcast eyes.*]

DAY. [*After an embarrassed silence.*] A fiddle's some good adder all.

JONES. They went to church a lot but that didn't bring 'em to.

JOE. [*Softly.*] Le's go out walking in the moonshine.

POLLY. Yes.

JONES. [*Singing.*]

Oh, when will the wedding supper be, unh-hunh.

MRS. DAY. Allen, don't start that right off.

DAY. Tomorrow if you say so. Go up to the Squair's with the license—

JOE. [*Manfully.*] Better in fall when crops are housed.

[POLLY *tugs shyly at his arm and they go out of the yard and down the road.*]

POLLY. [*Timidly.*] We're going for a walk, just a piece.

MRS. DAY. Come back in a little bit. [*She bows her head, and for no reason at all falls to weeping silently in her apron.*]

JONES. You'll have a fine son-in-law, and he'll own land.

LUCAS. [*Still fiddling softly.*]

> I walked through the trees, and I walked through the hills,
> And I ask you to tell me if you can,
> You know what a rock is, you know what a tree is,
> But what is the soul of man?

JOSHUA. [*Repeating in a bass voice.*] And I ask you tell me if you can—[*Quiet comes over them and for a long while there is nothing to be said.*]

DAY. [*Trying to say something.*] The young will go on and the old will go on.

LUCAS. It was made to be so.

JONES. Great guns, right here before us all!

DAY. Aye. [*Clearing his throat.*] Bad weather.

JONES. [*Looking out towards the moon.*] Yeh, rain.

DAY. A star close to its edge and a ring-around.

JOSHUA. Look at them little white clouds. Cold like snow.

JONES. Lonesome looking up there. [*The moonlight bathes their lifted faces with its pale shine.*]

DAY. Like a wide field. I've seen 'em so in March.

JOSHUA. A long ways there and back.

LUCAS.

> You know what the moon and the stars may be,
> And the width of the salt sea land,
> But where is the man can answer me,
> What is the soul of man?

JONES. [*Sighing.*] Uh-uh. [*After a moment.*] On a white

night like this, every stump looks like an old man with a beard. I'm 'bout a-skeared to go home, hah, hah.

JOSHUA. That was a come-off. Right in the open!

DAY. On a night like this I rid a mule once to see Mellie there, and he got skeered of a stump and he th'owed me. Then he run all around me, same as folks, a-laughing at me. I reached me a rail and laid down by a bush and when he come by I whammed him in the burr of the ear and piled him— Toreckly he got up [*He goes on telling the story. We hear him no more, leaving the four moonlit faces and the bowed figure on the step. Somewhere the lovers are abroad, laying their plans for the long, fat winter coming on.*]

THE MAN WHO DIED AT TWELVE O'CLOCK

CHARACTERS

JANUARY EVANS, *a hard drinking, superstitious old Negro.*
SALLY EVANS, *his grand-daughter.*
CHARLIE MCFARLAND, *a farm-hand in love with Sally.*

TIME—*The present.*
PLACE—*A farmhouse in eastern North Carolina.*

THE MAN WHO DIED AT TWELVE O'CLOCK

THE *scene is a room in the Evans home. A door at the center back opens into a narrow hall, and to the left of this is a battered iron cot with a clock above it on a rude shelf. A fireplace is at the right front, and a window near, before which are several splint-bottomed chairs. At the left front is a washstand made of a pine goods-box, unpainted and partly covered with newspapers, on top of which are a pail of water and a drinking-gourd. A pair of dirty overalls, a shirt or two, and a ragged hat hang on nails in the joists at the right. It is near the noon hour.*

SALLY EVANS, *a plump, neatly dressed chocolate-colored girl, is sitting in a chair near the center of the room sewing. She sings as she sews.*

SALLY

> Fall o' de evening I go down de river,
>> Sailing in a boat so fine,
> A-riding on de waters, waters,
>> Talking to dat love of mine.
>
> A-weeping by de river, river,
>> Dere's where my true-love found me.
> Call to me, kiss me, hug me,
>> Bofe of his arms around me.

There is the sound of footsteps in the hall, and CHARLIE MCFARLAND *stands in the doorway. He is a well-built, open-faced Negro of twenty or more.* SALLY *drops her sewing and stands up quickly, smiling at him brightly.*

SALLY. I do declare, heah you is, Charlie boy, quicker'n I thought.

CHARLIE. [*Coming up to her and patting her shoulders affectionately, but with a gloomy abstraction.*] Yeh, yeh, baby chile.

SALLY. Ain't you gwine kiss me?

CHARLIE. 'Scuse me, 'scuse me, sho' I is. [*He bends to kiss her and she throws her arms around him and hugs him tightly to her.*]

SALLY. Oh, me, me! Des' think of it, tomorrow we gwine be married foh good!

CHARLIE. [*Forcing a smile.*] Yeh, yeh.

SALLY. Take a seat and rest yose'f. [*He sits down and hangs his hat on his knee.*] You got through ploughing soon, didn't you?

CHARLIE. Unh-hunh. I told Mr. Byrd 'bout you'n me helping out in de school-breaking tonight, and what wid de wedding and all he said I could quit at de finish of de upper piece.

SALLY. When he want you back?

CHARLIE. A-Tuesday. Dat'll give us Monday foh de picnic on de river. [*Hesitating.*] It would have ef—ef it all had come off de way we's planning.

SALLY. Come off? Sho' its coming off. And of a-Sundays we kin go to other places, way up to Fuquay, Summerville, no telling whah, traveling round too.

CHARLIE. Kin? How we gwine do dat?

SALLY. Dat's my susprise foh you, but I'll tell you dough. Listen, sugar, we gwine take part o' dat five hundred dollars and buy us'ns a little Fo'd. Den we kin burn de wind, round and about.

[*He shows little elation at the prospect.*]

CHARLIE. Ef us gits dat money, you means.

SALLY. Why you so misdoubtful all of a sudden? Ain't no *ifs* and *ands* in it.

CHARLIE. Mebbe so, lak as not adder all dey is.

SALLY. [*Anxiously.*] Why you so jubious dis mawning? Grandpap ain't gwine hinder us. You been saying all de week dat he's a changed man.

CHARLIE. Yeh, yeh, I was a-thinking dat-a-way.

SALLY. And he has changed too. He won't go ag'in' his vision. I'm sho' o' dat now. Bofe of us thought 'twas all bluff at fust and e'en you got me into believing he was new bawn and now seems I got to 'suade you. Whut's de matter? Last night at de practice you was lak a lark, so happy and everything setting to our hand and Grandpap in a good humor wid you. [*With a sudden start.*] Lawd, you ain't gitting out'n de notion is you, and Arth gwine foh de license dis evening?

CHARLIE. [*Vehemently.*] Naw, naw, I tell you t'aint dat.

SALLY. Well, whut is it, den? Is you gitting skeahed o' Grandpap ag'in? You know well's I do dat since de morning he heard de devil talking in de air and saying he's coming foh him some day at twelve o'clock, he's been lak a clean-washed lamb.

CHARLIE. Yeh, he was lak dat.

SALLY. He ain't cussed nary a word nor touched a drap o' liquor. And, Charlie, hon, yistiddy he told me sweet as pie dat he done forgive you dat telling de sheriff 'bout his making liquor.

CHARLIE. [*Miserably.*] Dat was yistiddy dough. He knowed long befo' dat 'twas de sheriff skeahed me into telling on him, fur as dat's concerned.

SALLY. And tomorrow foh de wedding present he's gwine

turn over all dat money Muh and Pap left me. Now you hearten up if dat's whut ails you.

CHARLIE. Hey, he mought. But my mind tells me he'll keep executing on it des de way he has since dey died.

SALLY. [*Going back to her chair and picking up her sewing.*] Cain't see why you worry. We three's gwine live on heah happy as you please. Look at dis devil's costyume you gwine wear tonight in de play. Booh!

[*She whirls towards him, holding up a long red tight-fitting suit, horns, tail, and hoofs attached. Two terrifying eyes and a wide grinning mouth glare out at him.*]

CHARLIE. [*Starting back in alarm.*] Lawd, hyuh, hyuh, don't shake dat thing at me!

SALLY. Ho, ho, ho! I sho' has made a' awful critter, ain't I?

CHARLIE. [*Coming up and touching it gingerly.*] Lawd, Lawd, dat's a turble sight. Reckon 'twon't th'ow de folkses into fits when I comes stepping crost de stage wid dat thing on?

SALLY. [*Sitting down with the garment in her lap and beginning to sew again.*] I got to finish dis left-hand hawn; den you kin take it on wid you. I was gwine have it all done and complete foh you if you hadn't come early. Mought a-put it on and skeahed you wid it.

CHARLIE. Yeh, and I'd a-tore up de road gwine 'way from heah. Wouldn't had no devil in de dialogue tonight, been a-roosting in de swamp. [*He sits down forlornly and watches her sew.*] You's raght handy wid a needle, ain't you?

SALLY. Is dat. And, boy, I'se gwine make you mo' shirts and things dan a few. And knit! I kin knit, too. [*Jokingly.*] You better not think of th'owing me ovah heah at de last. Ain't many gals good at housekeeping lak me.

CHARLIE. [*Uneasily.*] Hyuh, hyuh, don't talk lak dat. It hurts me worse'n it do you to think o' putting it off.

SALLY. Putting it off? We ain't gwine put it off.

CHARLIE. [*Wretchedly.*] Don't seem no way out'n it.

SALLY. Way out'n whut?

CHARLIE. Everything's busted to pieces, dat's how.

SALLY. Is! How come?

CHARLIE. You don't know whah Uncle Jan is, do you?

SALLY. [*With satisfaction.*] Hunh, dat I do. In de bottom chopping his cawn. He's off dis mawning wid his hoe by sunrise. Needn't worry 'bout him.

CHARLIE. [*Bitterly.*] In de bottom! He's in de bottom of a drunk, de old fool!

SALLY. [*Incredulously.*] Hyuh, don't be trying to skeah *me* now.

CHARLIE. Trying! I wisht I had to try.

SALLY. Dat's too serious to be joking 'bout. Tell me de truf.

CHARLIE. I'se telling you de truf. He mought a-gone off dis mawning wid a hoe, but when I come by Luke's sto' up de road few minutes ago dere he sot on a box wid a co'-cola bottle in his hand, beating and a-flamming and a-cussing at de wind.

SALLY. (*With a wail.*) O Lawd!

CHARLIE. When he seed me a-coming, he fell to lambanging and telling 'em all to let him make at me. Dey had to hold him back or I'd a-had to cave in his haid. Dere's yo' new-bawn lamb and follower of Jesus foh you. He's gut fed up on pizen liquor. He was so mad at me dat he 'gun to spit and spew all over de flo'. Said he's coming raght on home and shoot me full of holes if he found me heah. [*Wrath-fully.*] Hurry and git dat last hawn fixed, I gut to be moving. Lawd, I won't feel lak cutting up no shines tonight.

SALLY. [*Her hands lying limp in her lap.*] O Lawd, whut kin we do? [*A sob breaks in her voice.*] And heah we was wid everything fixed foh good.

CHARLIE. He 'bused me black and blue in de face. Said all I wanted was yo' money and dat I'd never git it. He had it hid whah nobody could find it and he's gwine let Luke have it to put in his sto'. [*Standing up from his chair and clenching his fist.*] Wisht to Gohd I had dat Luke Ligon heah in dis room, I'd frail him to deaf.

SALLY. We gut to do something, I tell you. Dat Luke git his claws on my money and dat's de end of it. [*They both sit thinking, wretched.*] When Grandpap comes cain't you'n me shet him up and make him give it up to us or tell us whah it is?

CHARLIE. Yeh, and dat man'll cut you all to pieces wid a knife. He's mean and he full o' liquor. And 'sides you ain't twenty-one. Dey'd have de law on bofe of us. [SALLY *gets up and moves nervously around the room.*] Gimme dat costyume and lemme leave. Wisht to de good Gohd he'd a seed de devil dressed in dis suit in his vision, and I reckon he'd a-not been back in his weekedness so soon!

SALLY. [*Stopping in her walk.*] Kin you see him coming? I gut a idee.

[CHARLIE *goes to the window and looks out.*]

CHARLIE. [*Excitedly.*] Yeh, yeh, yonder he comes down de hill and walking all over de road. Gimme dat and lemme git away.

SALLY. Wait a speck. [*She wrinkles her brow in thought.*]

CHARLIE. Why foh?

SALLY. I believe I got a way to fix him.

CHARLIE. Hurry up. How you mean?

SALLY. [*Picking up the suit.*] Skeah him, dat's how.

CHARLIE. Wid dat?

SALLY. Yeh, I b'lieves we kin do it.

CHARLIE. He mought shoot us.

SALLY. I'll hide his gun.[*She runs to the corner, takes the gun, unloads it, and throws it under the bed.*] Now gimme de shells. [*She gets a box of shells from the wash-stand, opens the window at the right and throws them far out.*]

CHARLIE. Whut you mean to do?

SALLY. [*Growing excited.*] Listen. Look at dat dere clock, neah 'bout twelve. Well, when twelve straks, Grandpap is gwine die.

CHARLIE. Die? We—we ain't gwine kill him, is we? Naw suh, I ain't—Sally you,—

SALLY. I hopes we won't kill him, but he's gwine think his time's come.

CHARLIE. [*Turning quickly back to the window.*] Oh— Hurry up wid yo' plans den, yonder he is now down by de branch place.

SALLY. [*Breathlessly.*] It des flashed on me lak a streak. It's dis. He had de vision dat he's gwine die some day at twelve when de devil comes foh him. Dat's whut de devil told him. Well, when he comes in heah to lie down and sleep off his drunk I's gwine set up a monstrous heap o' wailings and screechings sorter lak I has to do in de dialogue, 'cepting worse. You be shet up in de entry dressed in dis heah suit. I'll skeah him to deaf wid my talk 'bout signs and sich, and den when de clock straks twelve you come in to git him. Lawd, he'll git religion dis day, see'f he don't.

CHARLIE. How you know we kin do all that? He might git something and brain me wid it, I tells you.

SALLY. Dat he won't. He's gwine be skeahed worse'n he's ever been. And he'll cough up dat money, and tell all his sins, and 'fo' he's got straight ag'in, we'll be all fixed. And he ain't never gwine know it wa'nt de devil adder him. Boy, we'll sho' have all de under-holt yit.

CHARLIE. [*Staring at her.*] Lawd, Lawd, you's de sharpest gal I ever did see in dis world.

SALLY. Dis heah's de time to be sharp if we's gwine git married tomorrow. Now, hyuh. When you come in wid yo' devil's suit on, you talk to him, ax him all sorts of question. He'll tell everything. [*Bubbling over with excitement.*] Yeh, yeh, we gut him whah we want him at last. And I'll make out all de time dat I cain't see devil or nothing. [*Coming up to him and hugging him in courageous ecstasy.*] We gwine have some fun out'n him. Adder today I bet my hat he'll be a shouting Christian.

CHARLIE. [*Warming to the game.*] All raght, honey, dis heah's de time. I'll stick to you. And talk 'bout cutting a rust at dat schoolhouse? I's gwine make a to-do wid dat old man whut is one!

SALLY. Now you slip in de entry and shet de do' and doll up. We gwine have a sober man on our hands in a few minutes. Hurry, hurry, dere he is coming by de woodpile.

[*She pushes the costume into his hand and hurries him out at the rear, quickly picks up the loose scraps of her sewing and hides them under the mattress; after which she sits down in her chair and bows her head in her hands. Old* JANUARY *is heard singing outside, and his white head dodders by the window. In a moment he is heard grunting and stumbling in the hall. He creeps in at the rear and stands clinging to the door-facing with long, skinny hands. He is just drunk enough to be quarrelsome and fearful. He is dressed in an old shirt, open at the front, and a pair of overalls too short for him, below which stick out his enormous black, horny feet. His hat is gone, and his hair flares up in a white tangle around his shrunken ebony face. As he comes in, he looks at* SALLY *and carries on his song.*]

UNCLE JANUARY.

> I tells you onct—I—tells you—twice,
> Niggers in hell foh shooting dice—

Pharyoh's army got drowned,
Oh, Mary don't you weep.

[*Waving his hand gaily.*] Heah I is, drunk and r'aring to go!
[SALLY *pays no attention to him. Staggering forward, he
sits down on the cot and moves his head around in a circle,
mouthing and letting out deep groans. He stops and stares at*
SALLY.] Hyuh, you! Is dat you, Sally? Whah's dat dog of a
Charlie? [*Making an effort to get to his feet.*] Unh—hunh,
I knows. [*His head swaying in drowsiness.*] I—know, I's
gwine shoot his lights out. Dat's whut I come foh.

SALLY. [*Looking at him sadly.*] He ain't heah, he's gone.

UNCLE JANUARY. Anh-hah, bedder be. Dat rascal want my
money. Ain't gwine git it, nunh—unh. [*He falls back on the
bed and stretches himself out.*] Tell him if he's heah when I
git over my good time I's coming foh him wid a gun.— I's
a-coming foh— [*His voice trails off. He lays his head back
with a great sigh and closes his eyes.*]

SALLY. Don't you lay down lak dat. Wake up, wake up!

UNCLE JANUARY. [*Mumbling.*] Shet up dat racket, shet up
and let a' old man sleep—sleep—whut needs it. [*He begins
puffing away and snoring.*]

SALLY. [*Coming up to the cot.*] Grandpap, grandpap, git up,
dey's a turble time coming on you!

UNCLE JANUARY. [*Dreamily and slapping at her.*] Git—
to-o-o-ff—o—off. [*He falls to snoring regularly.*]

SALLY. [*Talking to herself.*] Whut I gwine do? Hyuh, hyuh,
I gut to rise him out'n dat liquor. [*She looks apprehensively
at the clock, which lacks twenty-five minutes till twelve.*]
Bedder fix dat clock 'bout right to suit me. [*She goes to the
clock and moves it up ten minutes.*] Reckon dat'll give me
egzactly time enough. [UNCLE JANUARY *is puffing steadily
away, at every third or fourth breath making a sort of whistling sound through his lips. She stands watching him closely,*

thinking.] Now I gits ready to sail on him. [*She goes over to a broom in the corner and gets a long straw, returns to the cot, and begins to tickle his nose.*]

UNCLE JANUARY. [*In a faraway voice, smacking his lips.*] Lemme 'lone. Uh—m—uh—m.

[*She tickles his nose again, and he falls to sneezing, his grizzled head and calloused feet being jerked violently upward with each movement of his diaphragm. Every convulsion is followed by a combined wheeze and shout.*]

SALLY. [*Angrily.*] Ain't he a sight on earf! I'll wake him yit. [*She bends down and begins blowing a heavy blast in his nostrils. He rears and bucks and beats the air as if fighting flies. Then as she blows a heavier blast than ever, he begins champing like a horse and suddenly spits in her face. She starts back with a smothered exclamation of wrath.*] You nasty, stinking rascal, you done spet raght kuh-dab on me! [*She wipes her face and tweaks him by the nose, calling loudly.*] Grandpap, Grandpap!

[*As he groans and crawls up to a crouching position in bed she slumps down in her chair and begins sobbing in seemingly heartbroken grief. Presently he slides his thin legs out on the floor and sits on the edge of the bed, holding his head in his hand.*]

UNCLE JANUARY. Who dat bothering me so? Lawd, I's perished foh water. Cain't sleep, cain't rest. [*He blinks uncomprehendingly around him. Slapping his forehead with his hand, he quavers childishly.*] Oh, my haid hurt! [*He gets to his feet and makes his way across the room to the bucket.* SALLY *carries on her moaning and rocking, watching him out of the corner of her eye as he drinks several gourdfuls of water and gives his head a drenching.*]

SALLY. [*With a sudden shriek.*] O Lawd have mercy on us!

UNCLE JANUARY. [*Turning and staring at her in amazement.*] Who dat! Heigh! Whut de name o' Gohd ails you!

SALLY. Oh, don't go away and leave us, don't you go!

UNCLE JANUARY. Hyuh, hyuh! Whoever dat is cutting up so, you stop it. [*Shouting at her.*] Sally, you git de linimint and rub my haid. Lawd, why you r'aring so? [*He starts towards his cot, smacking his lips and stretching his toothless mouth in great gapes.*]

SALLY. [*In a storm of grief.*] Too late foh linimint, too late. [*Moaning.*] Nothing kin help you now to flee from de wraf to come. Gohd done sent his sign!

UNCLE JANUARY. [*Sitting on the edge of the cot, twisting his head, and spitting on the floor.*] Whut sign? Tell me whut ails you, I says. Is somebody daid? Oh, my po' haid!

SALLY. Not yit, not yit, but when dat dere clock straks twelve somebody's gwine be.

UNCLE JANUARY. Is? You say somebody gwine die? [*Jerking his head up.*] Gohd a'mighty, who it is, chile!

SALLY. Don't you use de Lawd's name dat-a-way, don't you do it! And you des' ten minutes from gwine to the t'other world. O Lawd, have mercy on dis sinful man! [*She buries her face in her apron.*]

UNCLE JANUARY. [*Belching lugubriously.*] Hunh, whut t'other world? What sinful man is dat?

SALLY. It's so, Grandpap, it's so. Yo' vision's gwine happen.

UNCLE JANUARY. [*Blinking at her.*] Whut vision?

SALLY. You know whut vision. And when dat clock straks twelve you'll be daid as a nit. I's seed signs, plenty o' signs.

UNCLE JANUARY. [*Sitting up straight.*] Whut signs? Whut signs? Tell me dat. Hyuh, hyuh, set up and speak fo'th. [*He watches her anxiously, his drunkenness clearing.*]

SALLY. [*Turning in agony on him.*] Pray, pray, 'fo' it's too late. Lawdy, O Master, make him to see his danger! [*She rocks back and forth.*]

UNCLE JANUARY. Shet yo' mouf, dry up, I tells you. I ain't gwine die ner nothing, oo-h—ooh!

SALLY. Oh, yeh you is, yeh you is. Lemme tell you de signs I seed and you'll pray den all raght, but I feah it'll be too late —too late.

UNCLE JANUARY. [*Swaying from side to side and beginning to look uneasily about the room.*] Signs! Tell me whut signs, I axes you.

SALLY. Ev'y since nine o'clock dis mawning till few minutes ago dat old dominicker hen been crowing. And she ain't crowed none since dat day last spring Mis' Penny died.

UNCLE JANUARY. [*Fear creeping into his voice.*] Air you sho' 'twas de old dominicker, Sally?

SALLY. Sho? Dat I is sho'. And dat ain't all, dat ain't de hunderth part. All de whole o' last night de deaf bells been a-ringing in my haid, rung so I couldn't sleep.

UNCLE JANUARY. [*Growing more and more sober, patting his foot nervously against the floor.*] Mebbe dat don't mean me, sho' it don't mean me.

SALLY. [*Shaking her head sadly, and wiping the tears from her eyes.*] Cain't be nobody else, cain't be, and you done had a vision 'bout it. And listen to dis—listen now to de turble warning. Early in de pink o' de mawning I was out in de gyarden and heahd de hell-hounds crossing de sky.

UNCLE JANUARY. [*Horror-stricken.*] Lawd-a-muhcy, did you? [*He locks his arms around one knee and stares at her with wide eyes.*]

SALLY. I did dat. Thought den I wouldn't tell you, but now you come home drunk I gut to do all I kin to save you. [*Twisting her hands together and lifting up her eyes.*] O Lawd up dere in Heaben, help save him 'fo' de devil come foh his soul.

UNCLE JANUARY. [*Stretching his hand towards her in supplication.*] Sally, Sally, don't you squall lak dat.

SALLY. And when dem hounds passed over dis heah house dey des' swooped down and moaned and howled louder'n ever. Den dey passed out'n heahing 'crost de creek.

[UNCLE JANUARY *snaps his head around and looks at the clock which now lacks five till twelve. With a groan he slumps down on the cot.* SALLY *continues her moaning and praying. Presently he raises his head and pipes feebly.*]

UNCLE JANUARY. Was dey—was dey any mo' signs, Sally? Quick, quick, tell me all you seed.

SALLY. [*Shivering and crouching down in her chair.*] Oh, but I cain't tell you de last and most awfullest one of all, I cain't—[*sobbing loudly.*] I cain't tell you!

UNCLE JANUARY. [*Putting his hand weakly to his heart and gasping for breath.*] Whut was it? Lemme know—know de wust.

[*She waits, without replying. He stares at the clock, his tongue lolling in his mouth. When it clicks preparatory to striking, she turns wildly upon him and shouts.*]

SALLY. I was out dere at de pig-pen feeding de pigs raght adder you went to de bottom, and I seed a devil's hole by a pine stump, and I bent down and listened—and whut did I heah, oh, whut did I heah? I heahd wailing and grinding and hosses neighing way down dere in hell. And dey was loud screaming and wild laughing and rattling o' chains, and I could see a great far roaring. Den de fuss stopped, and I heahd two voices talking, and one of 'em—one of 'em . . . [*She suddenly stops and bursts into loud sobs again.*]

UNCLE JANUARY. [*His eyes bright with terror.*] Whut did dey say? Whut did dey say?

SALLY. One of 'em said de devil was a-coming foh you today at twelve o'clock. [*Screaming.*] And it's twelve raght dis minute. Pray! Pray! [*She springs out of her chair and rushes wildly from the room.*]

UNCLE JANUARY. [*Falling on his knees by the cot and crying out in a high, slobbering voice.*] Gohd ha' muhcy, Gohd ha' muhcy! [*The clock begins to strike. He backs across the room from it, watching it as if hypnotized.*] Dere you go—dere you go hurrying off de pass of time! [*He wags his finger and almost chants in the extremity of his fear.*] One—two —th'ee—fo'—five—ha'f gone—ha'f gone—six—seven—and eight—and nine—now it's ten—'leven—de last one—twelve! [*He stands closing and unclosing his hands in stupefaction, shivering as if with an ague. He waits, swaying with weakness, but nothing happens. The clock goes on ticking merrily. He opens his eyes and stares around, slaps his body, listens, then cackles hysterically.*] Glory—glory to Gohd, it's all a mistake! I's safe—safe as a dollar—hooray! [*As he starts towards the door, it opens and the devil, horned, tailed and hoofed, slides in. With a squeak* UNCLE JANUARY *falls like a log on the bed and lies looking at the approaching horror with piteous eyes. A moaning sound comes through his lips and he clutches blindly at his throat. A whine that gradually rises into words bursts from him.*] Ha' muhcy! Ha' muhcy! A speck o' time. Gimme one minnit—one.

[*The* DEVIL *comes nearer and stares down at him.*]

DEVIL. [*In a hollow voice.*] January Evans, two weeks ago you was give warning 'bout yo' weeked life, but you wouldn't heed it, and you went a-tempting Gohd ag'in today. Now it's too late—too late—yo' time's up. Yo' soul belongs to me and tonight I roasts you in hell!

UNCLE JANUARY. Ha' muhcy! Ha' muhcy! [*Great drops of perspiration cling to his brow.*]

DEVIL. [*Thundering.*] Muhcy! Gohd A'mighty's offered you muhcy seventy long yeah and you kept a-spetting in his blessed face.

[SALLY *comes in weeping.*]

UNCLE JANUARY. [*Crying out as he spies her.*] He'p, he'p, Sally! Come heah, come heah and git him off.

DEVIL. And dey shall call foh muhcy and dey'll be no muhcy.

SALLY. [*Looking down at him in great sorrow.*] Ain't you gone yit, Grandpap?

UNCLE JANUARY. [*Pleadingly.*] Git de gun and shoot him, Sally! [*He makes a feeble effort to rise, but falls back, gasping for breath, wailing.*] Shoot him, run him out'n dis room!

SALLY. [*Looking around.*] Who? Run who out?

UNCLE JANUARY. [*His jaw dropping down like a dead man's.*] Cain't you see nobody heah in de room?

[*The* DEVIL *folds his arms and waits.*]

SALLY. Dey ain't nobody but you'n me. [*She bends quickly over him, her breath caught with fear.*] Is you seeing something, grandpap? Is you?

UNCLE JANUARY. [*Pointing weakly.*] Dere, dere! It's de devil! [*Screaming.*] See him dere grinning at me!

SALLY. [*Starting back with a sharp moan.*] Oh, Lawd, he's gwine out, he's gitting to de River Jordan. Don't let his soul be lost! [*She drops in her chair and rocks back and forth.*] Ain't no hope now and de devil done come foh him.

[*The* DEVIL *takes another step toward his victim.*]

UNCLE JANUARY. [*Putting out his hands to ward him off.*] Somebody come he'p a po' old man. Come heah, folkses! He'p! He'p! [*He begins to whimper.*]

DEVIL. Make yo'se'f ready to go. 'Fess yo' sins. Beg fohgiveness.

UNCLE JANUARY. Cain't you heah dat talking now, Sally? [*Pleading.*] Cain't you heah nothing?

SALLY. I don't heah nothing. Whut's he saying to you? Oh, he's gitting neah de gates of de other world!

UNCLE JANUARY. He tells me to—to—'fess my sins. Yeh,

yeh, I 'fesses and axes fohgiveness. Oh, Lawd wipe 'em off'n dat Book.

DEVIL. Own up, own up all yo' meanness and it'll be easier on you in dat pit.

UNCLE JANUARY. [*In a small voice, speaking as if in a dream.*] I been a turble man all de days of my life. I's sorry foh it all.

DEVIL. Dat makes it easier den. Whut you been doing mean lately?

UNCLE JANUARY. Yeh, I'll tell it all. I'll tell. Me'n Luke's gut us a new still at de head of de pond—put it in yistiddy. Fohgive me foh dat. [*His voice grows weaker.*]

DEVIL. What else? Speak, man, yo' time is short.

UNCLE JANUARY. [*In a faraway voice.*] Cain't 'member—no' more—dat's all—all.

DEVIL. Dat ain't all. Don't you try to fool wid de sperits of de other world. How 'bout dat money b'longs to de gal name' Sally?

UNCLE JANUARY. Yeh, yeh, dere—dere behime a brick up inside de farplace—all dere—give it to her. Dat was a sin, I knows now. [*His voice coming back stronger.*] Yeh, yeh, and Charlie—I wants her to marry Charlie, dat was a big sin. I sees it now. [*Panting.*] Lemme live to make it all right— gimme des' a day.

DEVIL. You swear to turn all her money over to her and let her marry Charlie.

UNCLE JANUARY. [*Eagerly.*] Yeh, I swears—I'll git de license—anything. [*He closes his eyes and beats on his breast for breath. He goes on in a weakening voice.*] And I'll never drink anudder drap—nary—un. Growing dark heah—whah is you, Sally? [*He feels around him on the bed.*] Sally, Sally!

DEVIL. Den if you swears—[*He stops and peers at* UNCLE JANUARY *who lies limp and still. In alarm.*] Whut's de matter wid you, Uncle—whut's happened, January Evans?

[UNCLE JANUARY *makes no reply.* CHARLIE'S *voice alarms* SALLY *and she hurries to the bed.*]

SALLY. Whut you done, Charlie? Whut—

CHARLIE. [*Bending over him, fearfully.*] Dey's something bad happened.

SALLY. Oh, me! [*Calling loudly.*] Grandpap! Grandpap! [*He makes no answer and she shakes him vigorously.*] Wake up! [*She falls to rubbing his hands feverishly.*] We got to do something raght quick. Lawd, s'pose'n he dies or something. Rub his feet, quick, his hands is cold! [CHARLIE *begins rubbing his feet.* SALLY'S *voice rises high in fear as she rubs faster and faster.*] Tell me, whut kin we do? Kin we git a doctor or somebody?

CHARLIE. I don't know—rub him, roll him. [*They both roll him back and forth across the bed.*] Feel his heart.

SALLY. Cain't tell wh'ah it's beating or not. Run, git de bucket o' water and le's put some on him. [CHARLIE *brings the bucket in a rush, hesitates a moment, and then dashes the contents full in the old man's face.*]

CHARLIE. Dat'll bring him if anything will.

SALLY. You'll drown nim. Why we ever want to do dat foolishness nohow? [UNCLE JANUARY *begins to sputter and cough.* SALLY *cries out joyously.*] Thank Gohd, he's coming back! Hyuh, you run git dem clothes off'n you. Th'ow him into fits he sees you. Git! [CHARLIE *runs out at the rear.*] Grandpap! Grandpap! [*He opens his eyes and gazes at her. She bends down and kisses him on the forehead, her shoulders shaking with grief. Presently she controls herself.*] You ain't daid, is you Grandpap? Oh, you's alive! Thank de Lawd!

UNCLE JANUARY. [*Raising himself up with difficulty on his elbow.*] Whah is I? [*His voice is humble and sweet. Suddenly he looks around terror-stricken.*] Whah dat devil?

SALLY. [*Impetuously.*] Grandpap, we— [*She catches herself in time and stands waiting, laughing and almost weeping at once.*] Dey ain't no devil, and you's safe in yo' own bed.

UNCLE JANUARY. [*Finally working himself into a sitting position.*] Dey *was* a devil, and I was a praying foh help. [*He turns excitedly to* SALLY.] Think of it, chile, I been *daid;* dat's what I has—

SALLY. Daid? We thought you was and poured water on trying to save you.

UNCLE JANUARY. And I been daid. De devil come and got me—raght dere he stood plain as de pa'm o' yo' hand—in de middle o' de flo'. And when I done promised everything, he took me off in de dark, sailing, sailing, and finally we come back where it was light. Den I woke, and heah I is. [*He puts his feet out on the floor.*] Honey, I done been treating you wrong, dat devil made me own up. Yo' money's in de farplace dere. Every cent but a few dollars I borrowed, and I'se gwine go raght off and git 'nough to pay you back.

SALLY. [*Laughing hysterically and twisting her hands.*] Dat's all raght 'bout a few dollars, and I don't keer foh nothing since you's back wid us. [*Overcome with excitement, she sits down and stares at him.*]

UNCLE JANUARY. [*Beating his thigh with his skinny hand and blinking before him.*] Des' think of it, chile, I was r'ally daid, I b'lieve—in fact I know I was. Dat vision was eve'y bit so. and all dem signs you seed. Couldn't be no mistook 'bout dat devil, he come foh me. [*Shaking his head.*] Dunno dough des' how I gut back heah. [*He sits lost in wonder.*]

SALLY. I believes you was daid too, foh a while—couldn't feel no heart-beat, no nothing.

UNCLE JANUARY. No *b'lieve* 'bout it—sho' I was plumb gone to de udder world. [*His voice falling into humility.*] Ol' Master been good to me, too good, Sally, and I's gwine try to serve him de rest of my days. [*He begins to whimper again.*]

SALLY. Don't cry now.

UNCLE JANUARY. He gi'n me des' dis one chanct to come back —dat devil said he mought gimme anudder trile. Reckon you could git a-holt of Charlie? I wants him to know I's—I's willing foh you and him—willing and happy raght down to de bottom.

SALLY. He come 'bout de time you was tuk wid yo' spell. He's outside now.

UNCLE JANUARY. Is? [*He stands weakly up.*]

SALLY. Yeh, I'll call him. [*She goes to the door.*] Charlie! Charlie! [*He comes in, buttoning up his shirt.*]

UNCLE JANUARY. [*Clinging to him.*] I des' had de greatest 'sperience to martal man a few minnits back. I died stone daid.

CHARLIE. [*Gently getting loose from him.*] Aw, you don't mean daid?

UNCLE JANUARY. [*Almost defensively now.*] Daid eve'y bit and grain. And I'se come back foh anudder chanct. You ain't gwine never be boddered wid me no mo'. I makes frien's wid you now to de judgment day.

CHARLIE. [*Somewhat remorseful.*] Lawd, Uncle Jan, you's too good to us all of a sudden.

UNCLE JANUARY. Naw suh. [*He stops suddenly and a light breaks over his face. He whispers to himself.*] Daid, daid as a do' nail, and now heah I is. [*In loud exultation.*] Dere was dem men in de Bible, and now dey's me. [*He hitches up his suspenders and throws his hands out wide.*] Git behime me, folkses, git behime! [*He scrambles out at the rear, calling joyously.*] Ay, you Luke! I's gut a mess to tell you!

[*Wondering, they watch him go, and then their eyes turn towards the fireplace.*]

UNTO SUCH GLORY

CHARACTERS

BROTHER SIMPKINS, *an itinerant revivalist preacher from 'way off yonder.*
WALT ENNIS, *a young farmer.*
LANIE ENNIS, *his wife.*
JODIE MAYNARD, *her brother.*
SUT MAYNARD, *her father.*

TIME—*The latter part of the nineteenth century.*
PLACE—*Eastern North Carolina*

UNTO SUCH GLORY

In rural North Carolina—and most Southern States for that matter—we begin to think about the Lord when late July and August come. Crops are laid by—corn hilled and cotton ploughed for the last time, even tobacco-curing held in abeyance—and every little church from Bethel to Shiloh is rocked for a week by the fighting paradox of God and the Devil. Then it is that the way of the transgressor grows hard. Little children are herded terrified into the fold, the drunkard denies his dram, the profane man softens his speech, and shy, tough-knotted old fellows with land lawsuits greet each other gently as "Brother." Then too the way of the chicken grows hard. He is slaughtered by the thousands and his plucked feathers blown heavenward by the impersonal winds. The smoke-house suffers its onslaughts, the bin is visited and revisited, the pig is snatched and barbecued, the watermelon and "mushmelon" patches are devastated. The tired housewife sing. "Blessed be the name," sweats and grows sick before a red-hot stove, and the farmer's last dollar is pleaded forth from its hiding-place. For now it is that the preachers are abroad in the land. And now too the city cousins and kin are down like Assyrian kings to eat and talk of the pleasures of farming and the open air—and to attend "big-meeting." Through it all the providing farmer moves quiet and subdued, comforted by the presence of the men of God and vaguely hoping to profit somehow thereby. He listens to the blarney of the city-bred, his impassive face concealing the superiority he knows is his. To the preachers he is all respect and gentleness. And bless God, even when he suspects their thievery and quackery, he comforts himself that the True Message can never be contaminated by scurvy containers—a metaphysic St. Thomas himself could not surpass—and ac-

*cordingly under all pomp and circumstance his faith remains.
There are exceptions, of course—for instance one of the
farmers depicted in this piece. But all glory to the general
type, for I doubt that even in the time of Piers the Plowman
when the land was likewise overrun by heavenly grafters was
the burden borne more dutifully and stoically. But wonderful
cures were wrought then and wonderful cures are wrought
now, and the response now as then remains a general and ir-
rational "hallelujah." And these gentlemen go their rounds
and will go. Let them. They saved me and they may save
others—preachers thin and wan and holy; preachers fat, oily
and unctuous; preachers dashing and handsome crying out
with pleasurable anguish the story of their red-light days—
God wot; preachers Hebraic, awful and thundering. They
will go their way in the service of imagination and the Lord.
Thanks be . . . Where is he who used to leave his photo-
graph to delight the daughters?—it meets me now from many
a country mantelpiece— He is still doing the Lord's work
and passing the plate to pay the photographers. And he who
was wont in the old days to leave more real and distress-
ing images of himself behind? He, too, pursues his labors
to the glory and profit of God. All honor to them and their
brethering. Let us continue to feed and clothe them and leave
the subtlety of an ethic to furnish them forth to action. For
fairies and fierce convictions are salty savor to a land.
So it is as the curtain rises on* LANIE ENNIS *sweating up
supper on a hot August evening for a carnivorous man of
God. She is a rather pretty young country woman, neatly
and plainly dressed, with large babyish blue eyes and a quick
bird-like step. From behind a door on the left come desul-
tory sounds of a booming voice lifted in exclamations,
snatches of song and hallelujahing.* LANIE *stands listening a
moment with a steaming dish of food in her hands. She places
the food on the table and waits, abstractedly fingering the
chain of a locket around her throat.*

VOICE. [*Within.*] Hallelujah, hallelujah.

LANIE.[*Softly.*] Hallelujah! [*The sound of her own voice seems to wake her from her abstraction and she moves swiftly through an open door at the right onto the porch and calls out through the darkness.*] Come on to supper, Walt!

A VOICE.[*Near at hand, outside.*] I'm coming.

[LANIE *turns back into the room and goes into the kitchen at the rear.* WALT *enters at the right, carrying a bucket. He is a hot sunburned young farmer below medium height, slender and wiry and with a steel-like hardness about him.*]

WALT. Got any slops for the pigs, Lanie?

LANIE. They's some pot liquor there by the stove. [*He disappears into the kitchen. The voice at the left is quiet and* LANIE *goes to the door and calls.*] Supper's 'bout ready, Brother Simpkins.

VOICE. Thankee, sister, thankee. . . .

WALT. [*Reappearing with his bucket.*] How long 'fore you're ready to eat?

LANIE. Soon's the coffee boils.

WALT. I'll be back in a minute then. [*He starts out at the right and then stops.*] Won't he be too late for service?

LANIE. [*Working rapidly about the table.*] Brother Jackson preaches first tonight.

WALT. Ah! [*He goes out, but immediately returns and sits down in a chair near the door.*]

LANIE. Ain't you going to feed the pigs?

WALT. Are you going to the church tonight?

LANIE. I cain't miss the last meeting.

BROTHER SIMPKINS. [*Within.*] Hallelujah, hallelujah, glory! [*He begins singing and clapping his hands.*]

WALT. Makes more racket than usual.

LANIE. [*Quickly.*] He's thinking of all the sinners that'll not be saved. [*With a catch in her voice.*] Might be singing with you in his mind, Walt.

WALT. Better change his tune then.

LANIE. Oh, Walt!

WALT. Yeh, and he had.

LANIE. All of them preachers and them prayers ain't made no impression on you.

WALT. Made a' impression on my smokehouse all right. Been feeding Brother Simpkins for the last week. That's a' eating white man, I'm here to tell you.

LANIE. We'd ort to count it a privilege to feed him. [WALT *sits looking at the floor, pondering.*] Ain't you going tonight?

WALT. No.

[BROTHER SIMPKINS *is heard washing himself in a basin, splashing and blowing the water through his hands.*]

LANIE. All the evening I been thinking about that song— "Why not tonight?" [*Chanting in a childlike voice.*]

"Tomorrow's sun may never rise,
     To bless thy long deluded sight" . . .

WALT. Don't worry about me.

LANIE. But I cain't help it.

WALT. And I'm worried about a heap of other folks myself. [*He gives* LANIE *a sharp look.*]

LANIE. You're 'bout the only sinner in the neighborhood not saved.

WALT. Naw, your daddy'll keep me company.

LANIE. He got saved this evening, and went home shouting.

WALT. Good gracious!

LANIE. And he stood up in the church and testified every single mean thing he'd ever done.

WALT. He couldn't a-done that.

LANIE. Oh, Walt, tonight's the last night and won't you go?

WALT. [*A bit sharply.*] You've been enough for both of us.

LANIE. And two weeks ago I was lost to God and the world and now— [*She raises her face to heaven.*]

WALT. Ah!

[*He sits looking at her mournfully and then picks up his bucket and goes quickly out and down the steps.*]

[BROTHER SIMPKINS *comes through the door at the left carrying a Bible in his hand. He is a dark bearded man of middle age, heavy-set, with a bloated ignorant face, but somewhat kindly withal. He is dressed in a thin black seersucker suit, a celluloid collar with an enormous white tie.*]

BROTHER SIMPKINS. [*In a deep throaty voice, hoarse from thundering in the pulpit.*] Ah, sister, he's unworthy.

LANIE. I dunno—

BROTHER SIMPKINS. [*Coming close to her.*] I've told you— [*Suddenly opening the Bible and pointing to a verse.*] Read there—it's the message again, coming another way—plain— plain. [*Reading in a low vehement voice.*] "For both he that sanctifieth and they who are sanctified are of one." [*His eyes bore into hers and he lays his hand on her shoulder.*]

LANIE. Yes, yes.

BROTHER SIMPKINS. Ah, you are sanctified—the seal is on your forehead—pure and holy.

[*He bends quickly and kisses her.*]

LANIE. Oh—I—

BROTHER SIMPKINS. It is written in Corinthians, one, one and two, "They that are sanctified are called the saints." And the saints are those saved forever, sealed for the rapture, and they can do no harm.

LANIE. I know it, I feel it—

BROTHER SIMPKINS. Amen!

[WALT *comes abruptly in again with his bucket.*]

WALT. Forgot to put any meal in these slops.

[*He brings a dipper of meal from the kitchen, pours it into the bucket and stirs it.*]

BROTHER SIMPKINS. How ye tonight, Brother Ennis?

WALT. Tired—How're you?

BROTHER SIMPKINS. Bless God I'm carrying on happy towards the Glory Land. [LANIE *moves around the table arranging supper, now and then looking at* WALT *with a puzzled expression.*]

WALT. [*With sudden admiration in his voice.*] You *are* a big strong man, ain't you?

BROTHER SIMPKINS. Nothing but sinful clay. [LANIE *looks at him with undisguised admiration.* WALT'S *eyes narrow a bit.*] God gave me a big voice and a big body to use in his vineyard and I've brung him big harvest for twenty year.

WALT. He's proud of you, I bet.

BROTHER SIMPKINS. [*Softly.*] Hanh— And the biggest harvest of all has been gathered here in this neighborhood these two weeks. . . .

,WALT. Kin you shoulder a sack of guano?

BROTHER SIMPKINS. Well, I dunno—I ain't—

WALT. They don't have guano 'way off yonder where you come from, do they?

BROTHER SIMPKINS. I dunno. . . . My work has been in the church.

WALT. You was talking 'bout a vineyard.

BROTHER SIMPKINS. [*Perplexed.*] The Lord's Vineyard.

WALT. Brother Simpkins, let me tell you something.

BROTHER SIMPKINS. Yes.

WALT. I can shoulder a sack of guano.

LANIE. Yes, he can.

BROTHER SIMPKINS. Yes.

WALT. Two hundred pounds.

BROTHER SIMPKINS. That's a right smart weight.

WALT. Yeh, it is. And that ain't all. I can shoulder it standing in a half bushel peck-measure.

BROTHER SIMPKINS. [*Looking around him uncertainly.*] Yes, yes.

WALT. [*Pleasantly.*] I weigh a hundred and fifteen pounds. How much do you weigh, Brother Simpkins?

BROTHER SIMPKINS. Two hundred and twenty.

WALT. A right smart weight. Lanie, you and Brother Simpkins better go ahead with your supper. I hear the folks starting their music over at the church.

[*He gets up and goes out with his bucket.*]

BROTHER SIMPKINS. Seemed like your husband was making fun.

LANIE. No, he won't thinking of that.

BROTHER SIMPKINS. I fear he'll never turn from his ways.

LANIE. We must do all we can this last night.

BROTHER SIMPKINS. [*After a moment, sternly.*] No. He's refused again and again, and there's nothing to be done.

LANIE. [*Nervously.*] I dunno . . . I've tried to get him to the meeting tonight.

BROTHER SIMPKINS. It's better for him not to be there.

LANIE. Yes—

BROTHER SIMPKINS. We'll go straight on from the church.

LANIE. [*Sitting down in her chair by the table.*] Oh, I don't see how I can do it.

BROTHER SIMPKINS. It's the hand of God behind it. He's sending us forth to labor together for bringing souls to the anxious seat, and set them forth in the morning light.

LANIE. [*Standing up, as he puts his arm around her.*] Yes, yes. . . .

BROTHER SIMPKINS. Like a lily of the valley, a sister of mercy. . . . [*He kisses her and strokes her hair.*] Unto such glory thou wilt go.

LANIE. [*Her face shining.*] Wonderful, wonderful!—Is it fine there where we're going?

BROTHER SIMPKINS. Fine, fine, but sinful. The wastefulness of the rich, the pride of the haughty, the sweating and groaning of the poor and oppressed, injustice and crime, sin—sin —sin. The houses lift themselves up high to heaven, their chimneys spit dust and ashes in God's face, silk and finery, lights and crowds and moving, moving, moving down the devil's sinful road. I've stood on the streets there and cried: Repent, repent, remember Sodom and Gomorrah! Like them sunken cities they pay no heed—but you and me'll go back there, go back there and keep crying: Repent!

LANIE. Keep crying repent, and they will repent. [*Slipping out of his arms.*] Oh, but people will think hard of me, I'm afraid.

BROTHER SIMPKINS. They hadn't ought to.

LANIE. No, they can't, they won't, and me going with you, will they? [*Looking up at him suddenly.*] But I ain't told him yet.

BROTHER SIMPKINS. You mustn't tell him . . . maybe.

LANIE. But you've preached about deceiving.

BROTHER SIMPKINS. I don't know. I been thinking . . . while ago he talked funny, like he already knew something.

LANIE. You will explain everything, I know you will. There they go singing at the church.

[*Far off across the fields comes the pulsating rhythm of the meeting's song.* BROTHER SIMPKINS *raises his face in a ragged smile.*]

BROTHER SIMPKINS. Hear Brother Jackson's voice—hallelujah, amen!

LANIE. [*Softly.*] Amen.

BROTHER SIMPKINS. [*Moving up and down the room.*] That great old song, how they sing it! [*Listening.*] There's Sister Eason's alto, and Sister Jernigan's soprano rising to heaven in the night. Amen, amen, give 'em power, hold up Brother Jackson's arms, touch his tongue with fire, amen, amen. Let him prepare the way, for tonight I come with the power.

LANIE. [*Watching him in loving terror.*] Hallelujah!

BROTHER SIMPKINS. [*Joining in the far-away song with a roar.*]

"As I journey thro' the land, singing as I go,
Pointing souls to Calvary—to the crimson flow,
Many arrows pierce my soul—from without, within—"

[*He suddenly flings out his arms, turning upon* LANIE.] Yes, tell him everything. He cain't stand out against me, nothing can. I'll sweep on, move everything before me with you at my side.

LANIE. [*Her gestures hypnotically beginning to resemble his.*] Yes, yes.

BROTHER SIMPKINS. [*Singing.*]

"On the streets of Glory let me lift my voice,
Cares all past,

Home at last,
Ever to rejoice."

LANIE. [*Joining in with a high piping voice.*] "When in valleys low I look towards the mountain height."

BROTHER SIMPKINS. Yea, yea, sealed for the rapture. [*Brokenly.*] Lanie, Lanie! Hurt not the earth, neither the sea nor the trees, till we have sealed the servants of God in their foreheads.

LANIE, [*Chanting and staring at him wide-eyed.*] Sealed and set unto the day of redemption.

BROTHER SIMPKINS. Glory!

LANIE. [*With a sharp hysterical giggle.*] Hallelujah.

BROTHER SIMPKINS. [*Shouting.*] The power, the blessing coming down!

LANIE. [*Moaning.*] I cain't stand it no more, I cain't stand it—

BROTHER SIMPKINS. Pour out, pour it out on us, God. Let it come down like buckets of water, let it come down, let it come down drenching us, flooding us.

LANIE. [*Springing up and down in the room, her face set in a sort of mask.*] Let it come down, let it come down—give it to me, give it to me—give—give—give—

BROTHER SIMPKINS. [*Jumping to his feet and prancing back and forth as he throws his hands above his head.*] Glory—glory—glory—glory. Give it to us—gloryglorygloryglory—rrry. [*His words pass into a frenzy of senseless sounds.*] Meeny-meeny-meeny-eeny-eeny- yari-yari-yari-hi-hi-hi-ee-ee-ee-ee— [*He shudders, closes his eyes, swings his head from side to side, his lip fluttering in a flood of sound.*] Hic-y-hic-y-hic-hree-hree—whizzem-whizzem—loki-loki—

LANIE. [*Fluttering towards him and stretching out her arms before her.*] Manny-yan-manny-yan—kari-kari-manny-yan-

yan-manny-yan-yan. [*She dances into his arms, and wrapped in each other's embrace they dance up and down, skip back and forth, all the while with their faces lifted towards the sky as if peering directly at a blinding light.*]

BROTHER SIMPKINS. Hah-hah-hah.

LANIE. [*Laughing in oblivion.*] Hee-hee-hee.

[BROTHER SIMPKINS *closes his eyes, a smile spreads over his face, and he falls to whistling a thumping barbaric tune to which their heels click rhythmically against the floor.* LANIE *closes her eyes and abandons herself to him. They whirl up and down the floor faster and faster. Now and then the whistled tune is punctuated by a shout or scream.*]

BROTHER SIMPKINS. [*With a blood-curdling yell.*] Yee-ee-ee-h!

LANIE. Glory-glory-glorrrryyyrryyrryy!

[*Presently* WALT *rushes in at the right and stops thunderstruck.*]

WALT. [*Shouting.*] Heigh, you! Stop that!

BROTHER SIMPKINS. Give it—give it—give it—

WALT. Great God A'mighty!

BROTHER SIMPKINS. The blessing—the blessing—it's come—it's here—here—

LANIE. Hallelujah—hallelujah!

BROTHER SIMPKINS. Hallelujah—glory—hoofey-beigh—hoofey-beigh—loki—loki—

WALT. [*Running up and snatching* LANIE *from him.*] Stop it, stop it! [*He spins* LANIE *around and shakes her like a rag.*]

BROTHER SIMPKINS. [*Slapping himself as if trying to beat off a spell.*] Brother Ennis, Brother Ennis!

WALT. Don't "Brother Ennis" me. [*He flings* LANIE *down in a chair by the table.*] I thought you'd done enough o' that unknown tongue business at the church without doing it here.

LANIE. Everything looks so purty. Walt, Walt, I love everybody. Your face is so purty. [*She springs up and throws her arms around his neck. He fights her away from him.*] Oh, I wisht you could see how purty this room is.

WALT. Have you gone plumb crazy?

[LANIE *drops into her chair and begins to cry softly, her body quivering and jerking.*]

BROTHER SIMPKINS. [*Twisting and looking around him.*] I must get on to the church—we must get on.

WALT. Yeh, and I reckon so. From the sound of it they's a big outpouring over there and you'd do better to spill yours there. [BROTHER SIMPKINS *rushes into the room at the left and reappears with a worn derby hat. He crams it on his head and stands looking down at* LANIE.]

BROTHER SIMPKINS. Sister, le's be going on.

WALT. She ain't fitten to go nowheres till she's had some supper.

LANIE. [*Quavering.*] Le's all set down and eat.

[WALT *furtively sits down; the preacher hesitates a moment and then sits to the table without removing his derby.*]

BROTHER SIMPKINS. [*Regretfully.*] And this is my last supper here.

WALT. Ah!

LANIE. I'll get the coffee. [*She rises to her feet and then falls weakly back in her chair.*]

WALT. I will for you. [*He goes into the kitchen.*]

LANIE. I'm so h—happy—happy. [*Her hands writhe and twist uncontrollably in her lap.* BROTHER SIMPKINS *bends over and strokes her head, and she suddenly grasps his hand and covers it with crazy, hysterical kisses.*]

BROTHER SIMPKINS. Let your tears be joyful at your deliverance.

LANIE. [*Shivering.*] Yes, yes.

BROTHER SIMPKINS. Now you can tell him— [*Turning from the table.*] Listen, listen, a second day of Pentecost—but wait—wait, when I get there— [*Lifting up his eyes.*] And when the day of Pentecost was fully come, they were all with one accord in one place. And suddenly there came a sound from heaven as of a rushing mighty wind, and it filled all the house where they were sitting. And there appeared unto them cloven tongues like as of fire and it sat upon each of them. [*Raising his voice.*] Yea, yea, hear my prayer! [WALT *comes in with the coffee.*] Let me bring the wind to them and fetch tongues of fire for them when I do come. Go on, go on, Brother Jackson,—make ready—make ready! [*Looking through the door at the right.*] I can almost see the fire now.

WALT. [*Looking out.*] What's that—where?

BROTHER SIMPKINS. The fire from heaven!

WALT. [*Pouring out the coffee.*] Le's eat something.

BROTHER SIMPKINS. [*Bowing his head.*] Now may— [*He remembers and snatches off his hat.*]

WALT. [*His face suddenly hard.*] Lemme ask the blessing.

BROTHER SIMPKINS. You! . . . hallelujah . . . amen!

WALT. Bow yer heads.

BROTHER SIMPKINS. Him, Sister Lanie!

WALT.

> Bless the bread and damn the meat,
> Great God, le's eat!

[*He falls to eating.*]

BROTHER SIMPKINS. [*Starting back.*] Blasphemy! [WALT *goes on eating, watching them with a hard face.*]

WALT. Have some bread, Brother Simpkins.

BROTHER SIMPKINS. Ah! [*He bows his head in inaudible prayer a moment and then begins to eat.*]

WALT. Help yourself, Lanie.

LANIE. I cain't eat nothing. [*She drops her head weeping on the table.*]

BROTHER SIMPKINS. A man blessed with such a wife as yours, and such blasphemy!

WALT. Yeh, two weeks ago they won't no better nowhere.

BROTHER SIMPKINS. Two weeks ago!

LANIE. No, I was lost then, Walt.

BROTHER SIMPKINS. Now look into her face and see the hand of God. Today she was consecrated and sanctified.

WALT. Was! Didn't look like it while ago.

LANIE. Oh, Walt, everything is specially peaceful and happy now. Used to I'd set here and be so lonesome, the house all so quiet and you off in the field. They was a great emptiness in here around my heart. Now I'm full, full. I feel like crying all the time, I'm so happy.

BROTHER SIMPKINS. Bless God! You hear her, Brother.

LANIE. I feel like I'll never be lonesome no more, never no more. [WALT *bends his head over his plate eating heavily and saying nothing. There is a step on the porch at the right and* JODIE, *a country boy about sixteen years old, comes in carrying a rope in his hand.*]

JODIE. You all seen Pa?

WALT. No. Ain't he at the church?

JODIE. He ain't.

BROTHER SIMPKINS. Is that Brother Sut Maynard's boy?

JODIE. Yessir. [*He eyes the preacher rather boldly.*]

BROTHER SIMPKINS. In all my twenty years of toiling in the vineyard I ain't seen a happier man than your Pa was when the power come on him.

JODIE. Wisht you'd tell me where he is now. Muh's jest about crazy.

BROTHER SIMPKINS. No doubt he's in some quiet place offering up prayers on bended knee.

JODIE. Reckon his knees are bended, but I'm mis-doubtful 'bout the prayers.

WALT. When'd you see him last?

JODIE. About sunset. [*Bursting out.*] He's been like a wild man every since he got home this evening from the church. I started off to git the cow in the pasture a while ago, and Muh run out and said Pa was gone. We couldn't find him nowhere. I been all down in the pasture but I cain't find him.

WALT. I spect he's at the church then. And who would a-thought it?

JODIE. He come home from church talking them old unknown tongues, and then he took off near'bout all his clothes and got down on his all-fours and run about the house like a dog.

BROTHER SIMPKINS. He's humbling himself. Tomorrow he'll come out clothed in his right mind and praising God.

JODIE. [*Almost whimpering.*] He's run mad or something.

WALT. You know how yer Pa is, Jodie. When he gits a thing he gits it good.

LANIE. [*Sharply.*] It's what'll keep Pa's soul out'n the clutches of the old Bad Boy.

BROTHER SIMPKINS. [*With a fond look.*] Ah, Sister. Go home,—no, go to the church and pray for your father.

JODIE. Something bad has happened to him?

BROTHER SIMPKINS. Cain't nothing bad happen to him. He's one of the consecrated now. I told him what to do to test his faith. Romans eight, twenty-eight.

JODIE. Pa's been talking about that man in the Bible that went around on his all-fours.

BROTHER SIMPKINS. [*His mouth full of food.*] Nebuchadnezzar. But afterwards he returned to the fold a wiser and a better man.

JODIE. Ma says she bets he's off eating grass like a cow somewhere, and he out in the damp without his shoes.

BROTHER SIMPKINS. He needs no shoes to protect him.

JODIE. [*Pleadingly.*] Walt, come help me ketch him.

WALT. [*Jumping up from the table.*] Yeh, I'll go. [*He starts out through the door, looks back at* LANIE *and the preacher and hesitates.*]

JODIE. Come on, he'll mind you if we find him.

WALT. [*Coming back to the table.*] No, I cain't go now, Jodie. I'm needed here.

JODIE. Cain't you come, Walt?

WALT. Not tonight. If you ain't found him in the morning, I'll help you. I jest cain't leave tonight.

JODIE. If your folks was in such a fix I'd help you. [JODIE *suddenly goes off in a huff.*]

LANIE. I'm glad you didn't go, Walt.

WALT. Yah.

LANIE. Now tell him, Brother Simpkins, please do.

BROTHER SIMPKINS. No, you'd better tell it like the message come to you. [LANIE *looks down and says nothing.*]

WALT. Well, go ahead. [*He waits and they are silent.*] But I already know what you're gonna tell.

LANIE. Then I won't have to tell it?

WALT. Brother Simpkins spoke about it while ago. And I reckon I got eyes to see what I saw when I come in.

BROTHER SIMPKINS. [*Hurriedly.*] I don't remember it.

LANIE. Are you willing to it, Walt?

WALT. I ain't willing, but I don't see what I kin do about it.

BROTHER SIMPKINS. No, no, they's nothing you can do about it. We cain't go against the will of the Almighty.

LANIE. It'll be hard, I know, but it's all come so clear to me. And Brother Simpkins has had a vision from above.

WALT. I know it. No, I ain't willing, but the whole country's turned upside down from Rocky Mount to Fayetteville, and I cain't blame you entirely. [*Nodding his head at* BROTHER SIMPKINS.] He's the one to be blamed most.

LANIE. Both of us have received the command.

WALT. I thought you had more sense, Lanie, than to get all wropped up in such.

LANIE. I don't know how you'll get along at first. I suppose after while you'll get used to it.

WALT. I betcha Sut Maynard'll be back cussing and chewing tobacco as bad as ever in a month. And you'll soon forgit it all too, Lanie.

LANIE. No, I won't, no I won't. I'd druther die.

BROTHER SIMPKINS. Never. She's stamped and sealed, and the mark will never pass away.

LANIE. Reckon you'll mind after a month or two, Walt?

WALT. It'll all be passed out'n my mind. [BROTHER SIMP-KINS *smiles broadly and looks at* LANIE *happily.*]

BROTHER SIMPKINS. Hallelujah.

LANIE. Brother Simpkins said at first you might try to get the law on him.

WALT. [*Staring at her.*] Law on him—not me. I got more sense than that.

BROTHER SIMPKINS. Amen!

LANIE. [*Piteously.*] I got everything fixed where you can find it.

WALT. Hanh?

LANIE. And be sure to feed the chickens regular. And don't you let the flowers dry up. [*Wringing her hands.*] Oh, I don't see how you can git along without me.

WALT. Git along without you?

LANIE. I know it'll be lonesome for you.

WALT. I ain't gonna be here by myself.

LANIE. Would you git somebody else to come and stay with you? No, no, I couldn't let you do that.

WALT. [*Bounding out of his chair.*] You mean you're think-ing of going away?

LANIE. Yes, yes, I got to go off and leave you.

WALT. Lanie!

LANIE. [*Wretchedly.*] I cain't help it, it's got to be done.

WALT. [*Sitting down with a gasp.*] Where you going?

LANIE. [*Beginning to sob.*] Oh, 'way off some'r's.

WALT. Are you mixed up in her wild idees 'bout leaving?

BROTHER SIMPKINS. It's a power beyond either of us.

WALT. What power?

BROTHER SIMPKINS. [*Gesturing.*] Up there.

WALT. And what does the power up there say?

BROTHER SIMPKINS. That she shall go out and labor in the vineyard with me.

WALT. [*Springing out of his chair again.*] Great God! I thought she's talking about all that gitting sanctified and filled with tongues. [*He moves towards the preacher who pushes himself behind his chair.*] You old goat, I'll—

BROTHER SIMPKINS. Ask her, ask her about it.

WALT. Lanie, what'n the world you mean by all this?

LANIE. I cain't help it, I cain't help it. Don't blame me.

WALT. I ain't blaming you completely.

LANIE. I been feeling the call all the week to do something, to go out and work and help spread the message. It's got stronger all the time. Oh, I've just got to go.

WALT. Has he been talking to you about it?

LANIE. He's sympathized with me all the time.

WALT. [*Gripping his chair.*] 'Y God, I reckon so.

LANIE. Don't think he's the fault, I am. I've been having dreams about it and several times a voice has come to me telling me I had to give up home and everything— Yes, it said I'd have to give up you—and go forth.

WALT. Did that voice say for you to go with him?

LANIE. [*Weeping.*] Yes. It said, "Lanie Ennis, go with Brother Simpkins."

WALT. [*Looking helplessly around him a moment and then sitting down in his chair.*] What else did it say?

LANIE. That's about all it said to me. But I might have still stayed with you if it hadn't a-been for the vision?

WALT. What did the vision say?

LANIE. He's the one had it; he'll tell you. It was so beautiful. He'll tell you.

WALT. I ain't interested in what he had, ner how beautiful. If you didn't have no vision, why you want to put dependence in his?

BROTHER SIMPKINS. What you do is done at the call of your own sinful self, the movement of man. What I do is in obedience to a higher power. Without him I am nothing; with him I am everything.

WALT. Then why you want her if he's everything to you?

BROTHER SIMPKINS. He will work with me through her.

WALT. Will he?

BROTHER SIMPKINS. He will—glory!

WALT. [*Suddenly turning upon* LANIE.] What's that you got around your neck?

LANIE. [*Covering her throat with her hands.*] A little chain.

WALT. I been watching that. Who give it to you?

LANIE. He done it.

WALT. Did God tell you to give that to her, Brother?

LANIE. It was so purty I thought I'd wear it.

BROTHER SIMPKINS. I asked you not to.

WALT. [*Sharply.*] Thought you'd wait till you toled her off with it, did you?

BROTHER SIMPKINS. [*With childlike sullenness.*] You never give her nothing.

LANIE. [*Plaintively.*] He don't make a lot of money the way you do.

WALT. No, 'y God, I don't. I don't go around preaching and begging the folks and taking up collections in dishpans. By God, I ain't got that low yit. I work for my living.

BROTHER SIMPKINS. [*Breaking out.*] I had the vision and I'll heed the vision. If she's willing we will go.

WALT. Are you willing, Lanie?

LANIE. They ain't nothing else to do. [*She buries her face in her arms weeping.*]

BROTHER SIMPKINS. Come, come, and we'll go forth to new fields, to new labors.

WALT. [*Imploringly.*] Lanie, you cain't go off thataway. [*Helplessly.*] You ain't got your clothes fixed.

LANIE. They're all packed in the suitcase. Brother Simpkins will take 'em up the road. We're gonna leave from the church. Oh, I cain't go off and leave all this. [*She begins smoothing a pattern in the tablecloth affectionately.*] Aunt Rachel give me that tablecloth. [*She bursts into sobs again.* WALT *looks at her in consternation, beating his hands together. Presently he stands up.*]

WALT. [*Threateningly.*] Brother Simpkins, you'd better go on by yourself, and you better go mighty quick.

BROTHER SIMPKINS. [*Staring ahead of him and booming.*] It come to me in the night clear as the broad daytime, an angel, the angel Gabriel. He brung a message to me like the messages of old to the prophets. I was in that room there; he come in through that door [*Gesturing to the left and the right.*] and stood with a flood of glory around him. He spoke to me in a loud voice and said he'd choosed one of the fairest daughters of men to be an aid to me on my way. [LANIE *looks at him with shining face.*] And no sooner had he said she was fair than I knowed it was Sister Lanie, for they's none fairer than her, like a pearl, like a dewdrop on the mountain, like a diamond lost among swine. He said stoop down and lift her up, and she will hold up your arms in times of trouble. Your powers will be multiplied, your labors will be fruitful under the sun. Then to make sure

I bowed my head and asked who the chosen one was and he said it was her, Sister Lanie. It was a message. And then I slept and behold she appeared to me in a dream and said that whither thou goest I will go and whither thou lodgest I will lodge. Then I awoke and praised God, hallelujah! Next morning she told me she'd had a dream telling her to go with me. [*Glaring at* WALT *who sits hunched in his chair taken aback.*] Before the angel Gabriel left, he told me to let no man put his message astray. And no man can. [LANIE *moves towards him and takes his outstretched hand.*]

WALT. Lanie!

LANIE. I wisht it could be different, but it cain't. I could never stay here no more. The lonesomeness would eat my heart out. They's something calling me off—calling me on towards it. I don't know what it is, but I know its wonderful and great.

WALT. [*In a low voice.*] Suppose the vision hadn't come, Brother Simpkins, would you a' wanted her anyhow?

BROTHER SIMPKINS. But it did come, and that settles it for me.

WALT. [*Softly.*] Does it?

BROTHER SIMPKINS. I am nothing but a weak and empty vessel. As I am filled I am powerful and give forth the waters of salvation in his name—hallelujah!

LANIE. [*Weeping.*] Hallelujah!

BROTHER SIMPKINS. [*Looking down at* LANIE.] The gift of tongues will come upon the multitude, the sick will be healed, and such an outpouring of the blessing this night as these old fields and woods have never seen. [*He leads her towards the door at the Right.*] Listen there, listen there at the children of the Lord. [*The singing and shouting from the church rise clear and strong, punctuated by high screams.*]

LANIE. Good-by, Walt, good-by. [*She runs up to him and throws her arms around him, weeping over him.*]

WALT. [*Suddenly convulsed as if with an electric shock.*] What's that, what's that, what's got hold of me? [*Springing from his chair and whirling around in the room, his eyes set like one seized with a fit.*] Turn me loose, turn me loose!

LANIE. [*Aghast.*] They's something happened to him!

WALT. [*Staring before him and beginning to talk as if to some person immediately before him.*] Who's that? Is that you? Who? [*He answers himself in a strange far-away voice.*] It's me, the angel Michael.

BROTHER SIMPKINS. The power's coming on him—hallelujah.

LANIE. Glory, glory!

WALT. [*Beginning to jabber.*] Yimmy-yam-yimmy-yam. [*He skips up and down the floor.*] Yee-yee-yee. Yamm-yamm-yamm. [*His voice lowers into a growl, like an animal mouthing something.*] Hanh—hanh—hanh—we—we—we—we—whee—ee—h!

BROTHER SIMPKINS. It's come on him like a flood. Glory, glory to God!

LANIE. [*Clapping her hands.*] Glory—glory—glory!

WALT. [*Stopping and speaking as if to an unseen person.*] Yes, yes, yes, I hear you. [*His voice coming faint and funereally.*] Go towards him, come to him. [*He moves like a blind man towards the preacher.*]

BROTHER SIMPKINS. He's seeing a vision.

WALT. I see an angel with a rod and staff in his hand.

BROTHER SIMPKINS. Glory!

LANIE. He's saved.

WALT. [*Speaking in the voice of the angel.*] He's a liar, he's a dirty low-down suck-egg dog. [*In his own voice.*] No, he's a servant of God. I'm willing for her to go with him. Let her go. [*With the angel's voice.*] Step up to him, choke his liver out, crucify him. [*He draws nearer the preacher.*] Oh, the angel Michael's killing·a man with a stick!

BROTHER SIMPKINS. What is it, Brother? What is it?

WALT. [*In the angel's voice.*] He's a dirty scoundrel trying to ruin your wife. Scratch his eyes out. [*Shuddering and speaking in his own voice.*] No, no, I can't hurt him; don't make me hurt him. [*In the voice of the angel.*] He's led women off before; don't let him do it again. [*With the fury of a wildcat he suddenly flies on the preacher, clawing and biting him.*]

BROTHER SIMPKINS. [*Screaming.*] Help! Help! Keep him off'n me, sister!

LANIE. Walt, Walt, don't you know what you're doing? [*She throws up her hands and drops in a chair. The preacher is helpless before the attack of* WALT *who is all over him, around him.*]

WALT. [*On top of* BROTHER SIMPKINS *and tearing him in the face.*] I hate to do it; I hate to do it!

BROTHER SIMPKINS. [*Roaring.*] Mercy. Mercy!

WALT. [*Astride of the preacher as he crawls about the room squealing in pain.*] Tear him all to pieces! [*He rips the preacher's coat and shirt from him leaving him almost bare above the waist.*]

BROTHER SIMPKINS. [*Falling exhausted on the floor.*] So was the prophets persecuted before me. [*He lays himself out on the floor whimpering.*]

WALT. [*Standing up presently and shaking himself as if coming out from a dream.*] Lord 'a mercy, what I been doing! [*He stares at the prone figure amazed.*]

LANIE. You done beat him near 'bout to death.

WALT. Is that you, Brother Simpkins? Is that you on the floor there?

BROTHER SIMPKINS. [*Gasping.*] Help, mercy.

WALT. Bring a towel and some water quick, Lanie, they's something happened. [LANIE *runs into the kitchen and returns with a basin of water and a towel.*]

LANIE. Oh, me, look how his face is bleeding.

WALT. It's his nose, ain't it? Worse'n a butchered yearling. [*Bending over him and bathing his face.*] Who in the world done it, Brother?

BROTHER SIMPKINS. Lemme leave this place; lemme git away.

WALT. [*Pushing him down and pouring water over him.*] Did I do it? I couldn't 'a done it.

LANIE. Yes, you did, you sailed on him like a run-mad man, a-biting and a-scratching.

WALT. [*Contritely.*] Good gracious me! A sort of spell come over me—I seen a vision. It won't my fault, don't blame me. I can't help it. It was a power from above. The angel Michael stood out all of a suddent with a pile o' glory around him and he told me what to do. He give my arm power. He come in through that door there.

BROTHER SIMPKINS. [*Sitting up.*] Git me some clothes, I'm going from here.

LANIE. [*Coming up to him.*] I'll help you.

BROTHER SIMPKINS. [*Snarling.*] You ain't gonna help me nothing. Get back from here, you sinful creature.

LANIE. Oh, Lord have mercy! [*She begins to sob again.*]

BROTHER SIMPKINS. May a curse come on this household for so persecuting a servant of the Lord! [WALT *runs into the kitchen and returns with a bottle.*]

WALT. Here's something that'll take the burn out'n them raw

places. Put some on your face. [*He shoots the bottle to him.*]

BROTHER SIMPKINS. [*Knocking it from him with a shout.*] That's liniment! You're trying to kill me!

WALT. Lord, I didn't mean no harm.

[*There is a stir on the porch at the right, and old man* SUT MAYNARD *creeps in on his all-fours, dressed in an old shirt and a torn pair of drawers. A mop of gray hair hangs down over his eyes. His face is swollen, and one eye closed. He has a rope around his neck by which* JODIE *tries to pull him back.*]

JODIE. Pa, ain't you got no shame about ye? Gracious, what you all been doing to the preacher?

WALT. We all had a spell of unknown tongues a while back. Where'd you find him?

JODIE. Down there in the edge o' the br'ar patch. The yellow jackets got after him down there and I heard him hollering. Make him come on home with me, Walt.

LANIE. Pa, what ails you?

WALT. Go on home, Sut. You and the preacher ain't fitten to be seen in public. [BROTHER SIMPKINS *sits up nursing his head in his arms.*]

SUT. [*Going up to* BROTHER SIMPKINS *and whining.*] Brother Simpkins, ain't I been humble enough?

BROTHER SIMPKINS. [*Growling.*] I dunno. . . .

SUT. You told me to go a day and night. I cain't do it. . . .

BROTHER SIMPKINS. Go on and do what you want to.

SUT. I'm a' old man and I cain't stand much o' the night air. [*He waits and the preacher makes no reply.*]

JODIE. No, he cain't.

SUT. I done suffered my shur. About a hundred o' them yellow jackets stung me.

BROTHER SIMPKINS. [*Angrily.*] I wisht a thousand of 'em had popped their tails into you.

SUT. Hanh?

JODIE. Now you see. [*Looking around the room.*] I couldn't do a thing with him till I'd put the rope around his neck. Then he made me drive him up the road here to see the preacher.

SUT. Brother Simpkins, I done been humbled in the dirt. Nebusadnezzar didn't suffer like me. Lemme quit now.

BROTHER SIMPKINS. Quit then. [*Flinging out his arms.*] Damn all of you, damn all of you!

LANIE. Lord 'a' mercy!

JODIE. He's gone to cussing.

SUT. [*Rearing himself up on his haunches*]. Hanh? What you say?

WALT. Knowed he's a cussing man and a humbug. Sut, he's been trying to steal Lanie from me and git her to run off with him.

BROTHER SIMPKINS. [*Staggering to his feet.*] Let me git some clothes; I'm going to the church.

SUT. [*Jerking loose from* JODIE.] Air ye that kind o' man, air ye, suh?

WALT. A vision come to us here in the room and a' angel said he was a low suck-egg dog.

SUT. [*Running around the room looking for a weapon.*] And they stung me till my eye's plumb closed. [*He trots into the kitchen.*]

WALT. [*Going up to* LANIE *and snatching the locket from her neck.*] Here's yer little purty, mister preacher. [*He throws it to him.*]

SUT. [*Coming through the kitchen door with a hunk of wood*

in his hand and squealing.] Lemme git to that there devil and I'll fix him.

BROTHER SIMPKINS. [*Yelling.*] Keep that man off!

WALT. Go to him, Sut. [SUT *makes a dash for the preacher who flees through the door at the right and into the darkness, trying to hold up the shreds of his trousers as he goes.*]

SUT. Come on, Jodie; come on. We'll ketch him and beat hell out'n him. [*Old* SUT *dashes out after him, the rope dangling behind.*]

JODIE. Run him down. [*He follows after, yelling in pursuit.*]

WALT. [*Standing in the door.*] Sic 'im, boys; sic 'im. [*They are heard running and shouting down the road.* LANIE *rocks herself back and forth in a storm of grief. After a moment* WALT *returns to the table.*] They'll never ketch that man. He'll be to Benson in twenty minutes.

LANIE. Oh, Lordy, Lordy. . . .

WALT. You want some hot coffee. [*She makes no answer.*] All right then. [*He pours himself a cup and sips it from the saucer slowly.*] Don't you cry. I'll git you a locket a whole heap purtier'n that 'un. . . . [*But* LANIE *rocks on.*]

THE NO 'COUNT BOY

CHARACTERS

PHEELIE
ENOS, *her beau.*
THE NO'COUNT BOY
AN OLD NEGRO WOMAN

TIME—*Several years ago.*
PLACE—*Before a farmhouse in eastern North Carolina.*

THE NO 'COUNT BOY

THE *scene is the small yard immediately before a Negro cabin. At the right front is a thick lilac bush with a bench beside it, and to the left from this a clumpy china tree with a rocking-chair under it. At the left rear is a well, roughly boarded up, a chain and battered tin bucket hanging from a cross-piece above. In the back is the cabin. Rickety steps lead up to the door in the center. It is an afternoon late in summer.*

PHEELIE, *a neat Negro girl of seventeen, is sitting on the bench by the lilac tree looking through a book. She is dressed in cheap clothes—a white dress, white shoes and stockings. Presently there is the sound of an approaching buggy in the lane off at the left and a voice calls, "Whoa!"* PHEELIE *listens a moment, and then, without turning her head, gives it a toss and goes on fingering the leaves of her book.* ENOS *comes in at the left and stands watching her. He is a short stocky Negro of twenty or more, dressed in a faded gray suit and black felt hat. His celluloid collar and scarlet tie shine out brilliantly against the black of his face.*

ENOS. [*In a drawling voice that now and then drops into a stammer.*] Well, Pheelie, heah I is.

PHEELIE. [*Looking up casually.*] I see you is, and you's 'bout a hour early.

ENOS. But ain't you all dressed up to go?

PHEELIE. I's dressed up, but I ain't ready to go.

ENOS. [*Dubiously.*] Well, suh, now—I—I—

PHEELIE. I des' put on dese heah clothes 'caze it was so hot in de house wid my work duds on. [*He takes off his hat.*
177

and discloses his naturally kinky hair combed back in a straight pompadour. He waits for her to notice it, but she keeps looking straight before her.] Set down and rest yo'se'f. [*Somewhat ill at ease he sits down in the rocking-chair and watches her.*]

ENOS. I drapped by a little early hoping—a—mebbe you'd lak to take a small drive befo' church begun.

PHEELIE. [*In the same cold voice.*] Thanky, I don't believe I wants to take no drive. [*She becomes absorbed in her book.*]

ENOS. [*Picking at the lining of his hat.*] And I thought we mought stop by Buie's Creek and git some ice cream. [*He watches her narrowly.*]

PHEELIE. [*After a moment.*] Dat'd be nice, I reckon, but I don't want no ice cream nuther. [*She is silent again. He pulls nervously at his fingers, making the joints pop.*] And I'd be much obliged if you'd quit popping yo' finger j'ints.

ENOS. [*Jerking his hands apart and running his fingers over his greased hair.*] 'Scuse me, Pheelie. [*Somewhat timidly, but with a hidden touch of spirit.*] You—you don't seem glad to see me much.

PHEELIE. You didn't have no date to come over heah a hour befo' time.

ENOS. [*Worried.*] I knows it. But whut's de matter wid you? You ain't mad at me, is you?

PHEELIE. No, I ain't mad.

ENOS. Seems lak you'd druther look at dat old book dan talk to me.

PHEELIE. Mebbe I had. [*He feels his tie, twirls his hat, and spits softly through his teeth off to one side.*]

ENOS. Whut sorter book is it, Pheelie?

PHEELIE. Whut difference do it make to you? You ain't int'rested in no book.

ENOS. 'Speck dat's right. But you sho' seems mo' tuk wid it dan anything I ever seed you have befo'.

PHEELIE. It's a fine pitchture book.

ENOS. Whah'd you get it?

PHEELIE. Dis mawning I was up to Mis' Ella's helping her hoe out de gyarden, and she told me a whole heap 'bout de places she and Mr. Jack went when dey was merried. And she give me dis book dat showed a passel of things.

ENOS. Hunh, dey had money to travel wid and enjoy deirselves.

PHEELIE. She said one place dey went to was some sorter Falls or something lak dat, whah de water poured over in a great river and made a racket same as de world was busting up.

ENOS. Dat ain't nothing—mostly talk, I bet a dollar.

PHEELIE. [*Closing the book with a bang.*] Dat's whut you allus says. You don't care a straw 'bout gwine off and seeing things.

ENOS. [*Sharply.*] Ain't I done told you, honey bunch, we ain't gwine have no money to be traipsing round de world, not yit nohow.

PHEELIE. Don't you honey me no mo', I tells you.

ENOS. [*Amazed.*] Whut'n de name of Old Scratch ails you? Ain't I gut a right to honey you? and you engaged to me!

PHEELIE. Engaged to you! It's you engaged to me.

ENOS. Aw right, I's engaged to you den, and you knows mighty drot'n well I's glad to be too. Dey ain't no put-on wid me.

PHEELIE. I reckon you is glad. But mess wid me and you won't be engaged to nothing.

ENOS. [*Pleadingly.*] Now, Pheelie, you better th'ow dat book in de far and come on and le's go foh a drive, it's stirred you all up. Come on, I's gut a mess of news to tell you.

PHEELIE. I ain't gwine on no drive. And I's 'bout decided not to go wid you to no meeting tonight nuther.

ENOS. [*Alarmed.*] Lawd, don't talk lak dat. Heah I's been waiting all de week foh dis Saddy night, and you ain't gwine back on me, is you?

PHEELIE. [*Softening.*] But, Enos, you's so samey, allus satisfied wid whut you has. You des' gits my goat.

ENOS. [*Humbly.*] If you means I ain't tuk wid no wild idees or sich 'bout trips way off yonder to see folks making fools of deirselves, den I is samey. But you listen heah, chile, dey ain't no meracles and sich off dere lak what you thinks. Onct I spent a good five dollars gwine on a 'scursion to Wilmington, and dey wa'nt a thing to see, not ha'f as much as dey is on dis heah farm.

PHEELIE. You gut to have eyes to see things. Some folks is natchly bawn blind.

ENOS. [*Placatingly.*] Well, mebbe when we's married we'll take a little trip to Raleigh or Durham and see de street cyars and big buildings.

PHEELIE. But I wants to go furder, clean to de mountains, and right on den mebbe.

ENOS. 'Y craps, must think I gut a can of money buried somewhah.

PHEELIE. I don't nuther. Us could hobo, or walk part de way, des' fool along.

ENOS. [*Laughing.*] Hobo! Us'd hobo right into some white man's jail, dat's whut. And dey ain't nothing to dat walking business. We'd be a purty sight wid our feet blistered and somebody's bulldog tearing plugs out'n—well, you knows whut.

PHEELIE. [*Ignoring his reply.*] Setting dere looking through dat book I gut plumb sick and tar'd of you and all dis farming and sweating and gitting nowhah—sick of everything. And des' looking at old lazy Lawrence dancing over the fields made me want to puke.

ENOS. [*Eyeing her.*] Honey chile, de last time I was heah you said you'd lak it working in de fields wid me and keeping de house and sich.

PHEELIE. I will, Enos, I reckons I will. But dat dere book set me to wanting to go off and git away.

ENOS. [*Moving his chair over to her.*] Listen to me. I knows I ain't fitten to breave on you, but I's gwine do my best by you. And whut you reckon? Mr. Pearson done told me today dat he's having de lumber sawed to build our house. September she'll be done, den you'n me kin have business—kin see de preacher.

PHEELIE. Mr. Pearson's good to you awright.

ENOS. Ain't he! Dat's a man whut is a man. And it ain't all foh me he's building dat house. He laks you and says he'll be glad to have you on his place.

PHEELIE. [*With signs of interest.*] Whut kind of house is it—des' a shack wid a stick-and-dirt chimley?

ENOS. [*Jubilantly.*] Now I was des' a-hoping you'd ax dat. No, suh, it ain't no cow-shed you could th'ow a dog through de cracks—nunh—unh. It's gwine be a nice frame house wid a wide po'ch, and it'll be ceiled. And listen heah, it's gwine have wallpaper. And, honey, Mr. Pearson said he wanted you to come up a-Monday and help choose de pattern. [*He looks at her delightedly.*]

PHEELIE. [*Her face brightening somewhat.*] Oh, dat's so nice of you and him! [*She bows her head.*]

ENOS. Whut's de matter now?

PHEELIE. [*Looking up with tears in her eyes.*] You's too

good to me, Enos, and I hadn't ort to allus be so onsatisfied.

ENOS. Sho', never mind now. [*He puts his arm around her.*]

PHEELIE. [*Letting her hand rest on his hair.*] Grannys alive! you done spent money to git yo' hair straightened.

ENOS. [*With a kind of shamed joy.*] Yeh, yeh, I has. But it was to celebrate a little.

PHEELIE. Dat's th'owing away a dollar and a half. In a little bit it'll be kinky ag'in.

ENOS. Course it will, but I thought you'd lak it while it lasts.

PHEELIE. [*Laughing.*] You sho' is a proud nigger. [*She kisses him quickly and stands away from him.*] Nunh—unh, I ain't gwine do it no mo'. [*He drops reluctantly back into his seat, and she sits again on the bench.*]

ENOS. [*After a moment.*] You want to take dat little drive now?

PHEELIE. I mought, I guess.

ENOS. [*Slapping himself.*] Hot dog, den le's go, honey!

PHEELIE. [*Brightly.*] Lemme shet up de house and we'll be ready. Muh and Pap and all de kids is over to de ice cream supper at Uncle Haywood's befo' preaching. [*She starts up.*]

ENOS. [*Standing up.*] Aw right, honey babe. I sho' laks to see you jollied up. And I's gut anudder surprise foh you too.

PHEELIE. [*Stopping.*] You has?

ENOS. [*Mysteriously.*] Unh—hunh. But I'll tell you a little later.

PHEELIE. Naw, suh, tell me now—please.

ENOS. [*Anxious to tell it.*] In course I cain't stand out ag'in' you. Well, we ain't gwine drive behime no flop-yured mule dis time.

PHEELIE. We ain't! [*She starts towards the left to look out.*]

ENOS. Naw, suh, I's driving Egyp' today.

PHEELIE. Mr. Pearson's fine hoss!

ENOS. [*Grinning.*] Yeh, yeh, sho' is. I worked hard all de week, and dis mawning he come to me and axed me if I didn't want Egyp' to haul you wid tonight.

PHEELIE. [*Looking off.*] Dere he is. Ain't dat fine, and is he safe?

ENOS. Safe! Safe as a cellar. But, Lawd, he kin burn de wind!

PHEELIE. Goody-good. Now come help me shet de house.

ENOS. [*As they go off at the left rear.*] Mr. Pearson knows I ain't gwine beat his stock and bellows 'em lak some de niggers. I tells you, sugar lump, if we stays wid him and do right, some dese days we gwine have money to take dem dere trips you wants to.

[*They have hardly disappeared when a slender Negro youth of sixteen or seventeen, barefooted and raggedly dressed in an old pair of overalls, shirt and torn straw hat, comes in at the right front and stands staring after them. He is whittling a green walking-stick. In a moment he pulls out a small mouth organ and begins playing a whirling jig.*]

ENOS. [*Coming back around the corner.*] Who's dat playing to beat de band? [*He and* PHEELIE *come back into the yard.* PHEELIE *stares at the boy in delighted astonishment. Suddenly he winds upon a high note. As he beats the saliva out of the harp against his thigh, he bursts into a loud joyous laugh.*]

PHEELIE. Lawd, you kin play. Who is you?

ENOS. [*With a touch of authority in his voice.*] Whut you want heah? I ain't never seed you befo'.

BOY. [*In a clear childish voice, as he looks at* PHEELIE.] You ain't?

ENOS. Naw, I ain't. Whut you mean walking up in people's yards and acting lak you was home?

BOY. I thought I mought get me a drink from de well dere.

PHEELIE. Help yo'se'f. [*He draws water and drinks.* ENOS *and* PHEELIE *watch him.*]

ENOS. [*In a low voice.*] I bet he's some boy run away from home. Mebbe a tramp, I dunno.

PHEELIE. Dat boy a tramp! Hunh, he ain't no sich.

ENOS. I bet you on it. Looks s'picious to me.

BOY. [*Returning from the well and wiping his mouth with his sleeve.*] I thought I mought git a bite to eat heah mebbe. [*He looks from one to the other, a lurking smile in his eyes.*]

PHEELIE. [*Uncertainly.*] You mought.

ENOS. Lak as not de lady wants to know whah you come from and whut yo' business is befo' she 'gins to feed you.

BOY. [*Looking at* PHEELIE.] Would you?

PHEELIE. Yeh. Whut's yo' name?

BOY. [*Laughing and blowing out a whiff of music.*] Mostly I ain't gut no name. [*Beating the harp in his hand and scratching his leg with his toe.*] 'Way 'way back down dere—[*Pointing indefinitely behind him.*]—whah I come from some of 'em calls me Pete, but mostly dey calls me de No 'Count Boy.

ENOS. Why dey call you dat fo'?

BOY. [*Laughing again.*] 'Caze I don't lak to work in de fields.

ENOS. Unh—hunh, unh—hunh, I s'picioned it.

BOY. S'picioned whut?

ENOS. Aw, nothing. Anyhow dat's a good name foh you, I bet. Whose boy is you and whah'd you come from 'way back down dere as you calls it?

BOY. [*Quickly.*] Cuts no wool whose boy I is. As foh whah

I come from, I cain't tell you, bo, 'caze I dunno hardly. [*Hesitating and pointing off to the right.*] You see whah de sky come down to de earf—'way, 'way yonder?

ENOS. I sees it.

BOY. [*Grinning to himself.*] Well, I come from miles and miles beyont it. [*A kind of awe creeping into his words.*] Lawd, Lawd, how fuh has I come?

PHEELIE. You been all dat distance by yo'se'f?

BOY. Sho' has. And whut's mo' I walked it every jump. [*Again he draws the harp across his lips in a breath of music, all the while watching them with bright eyes.*]

ENOS. Whah you gwine?

BOY. Des' gwine.

PHEELIE. You mean you ain't gut no special place in mind—you des' hoboing along?

BOY. Dat's it, I reckon.

ENOS. How does you git yo' rations—beg foh it?

BOY. I pays foh it when I kin git 'em. Times I goes hongry.

ENOS. [*Looking at him keenly.*] You ain't gut no money, has you?

BOY. [*Cunningly.*] Dat's awright. I pays foh it des' de same. [*He stops and looks at* PHEELIE *with big eyes.*] You's purty as a pink, ain't you?

PHEELIE. [*Turning away her head.*] Why you ax dat?

ENOS. [*Sharply.*] You needn't be thinking you gwine git yo' supper on soft talk, hoss-cake.

BOY. [*Still looking at* PHEELIE.] Whut's yo' name?

PHEELIE. My name's Ophelia, but dey calls me Pheelie.

BOY. [*Staring at her admiringly and cracking his palm against his thigh.*] Dawg-gone! des' lak me foh de world. I's named one thing and dey calls me anudder.

ENOS. [*With a hint of uneasiness.*] Heah, I 'specks you better be gwine on up de road. Me'n Miss Pheelie's des' ready to go out foh our afternoon drive, and we don't want to be bothered wid nobody's no 'count boy.

BOY. [*His face falling.*] I hates to hinder you, Miss Pheelie, and cain't I git nothing t'eat—a 'tater or anything?

PHEELIE. I 'speck I could give you a snack in yo' hand right quick.

BOY. No sooner said'n done, I hopes. And I pays you foh it too.

ENOS. [*Almost sarcastically.*] Gut yo' pockets full of silver and gold, apt as not.

BOY. Naw, suh, I gut something better 'n new money. Heah she is. [*Holding up his harp.*] I plays you a piece or two pieces or three, and you gives me a bite and whut you pleases. [*In mock seriousness he pulls off his hat and addresses them.*] Ladies and ge'men, de fust piece I renders is called "De Dark-eyed 'Oman." It's music 'bout a 'oman whut had three little boys, and dey tuk sick and died one June night whilst de mockingbirds was singing. And allus adder dat dey said she had a dark shadow in her dark eyes. [*He clears his throat, spits once or twice and lays the harp gently to his lips. Closing his eyes, he begins to play.* ENOS *stirs about him as the notes flood from the boy's mouth, and now and then he looks questioningly at* PHEELIE'S *averted face. The boy's nostrils quiver, and he makes a sobbing sound in his throat. Tears begin to pour down his cheeks. After a moment he winds up with a flourish.*]

ENOS. [*Gruffly.*] Lawd Jesus, dat rascal kin blow!

BOY. [*Looking at* PHEELIE *as he wipes his eyes.*] I hope you don't mind. Every time I blows dat piece I cries. [PHEELIE *glances up with moist eyes.*]

PHEELIE. I sho' don't mind. Whah you learn dat?

BOY. It's a made piece.

ENOS. Who made it?

BOY. Me.

ENOS. [*Ironically.*] Hunh, you mought!

BOY. [*His face troubled.*] You believes I made it, don't you, Miss Pheelie?

PHEELIE. Dat I do.

BOY. [*His face clearing.*] Aw right den. And I'll play you anudder piece foh dat snack of grub.

PHEELIE. Dat one's enough to pay.

ENOS. You sho' you didn't git no rations down de road?

BOY. Not nary a chaw.

PHEELIE. Ain't you had nothing all day?

BOY. Nothing but some branch water and a little bitsy bird I killed wid a rock and fried. [*His face takes on a sober look, and tears again glisten in his eyes.*]

ENOS. [*Looking at him in astonishment.*] You sho' is a quare fellow.

BOY. [*Staring up at the sky.*] Dat little bird was singing so sweet and ruffling his breast in de wind, and I picked up a rock an des th'owed devilish lak, never thought I'd hit him. But dat's de way it is—when you thinks you won't, you does, and I kilt him.

PHEELIE. And den you et him?

BOY. [*Wiping his eyes on his sleeves.*] I was so hongry den, and I built a speck of fire and baked him. [*Wretchedly.*] Won't it better foh me to eat him dan foh maggits to git at him?

PHEELIE. 'Twas dat.

BOY. [*Mournfully.*] But I sho felt bad 'bout dat little bird. I cain't git his chune out'n my haid. He sot on dat limb and would give a long call and den a short one—[*Imitating on his harmonica*]—des lak dat.

ENOS. You's a mighty big fellow to be crying over a bird, seems lak to me.

PHEELIE. Enos, you quit dat making fun.

BOY. When I come through de creek back dere, a good-god was pecking in a high daid tree, and he turnt his haid sideways and hickered at me. I heahd him say he gwine ha'nt me foh killing dat bird.

ENOS. I swear! [PHEELIE *gives him a cutting look, and he stops his laughing.*]

BOY. I've hearn dat dem good-gods is old women turnt to birds 'caze dey was weeked. And you see dey's still gut on little old red caps.

PHEELIE. Dey won't hurt you.

ENOS. Pshaw, dey ain't nothing but great big sapsuckers.

BOY. How you know? Des' de same dis'n scolded me foh th'owing dat rock. I could tell it in his talk and de way he looked at me.

PHEELIE. You didn't mean to do it nohow, and you was hongry too. Now play us some mo'.

BOY. I 'speck mebbe den it's aw right, I 'speck so. Now I plays you my udder piece to pay you plenty foh my eatings.

PHEELIE. 'Tain't dat, 'tain't dat. We laks to heah you. I'll feed you foh nothing.

BOY. Well, listen to dis, folkses, dis moan song. [*He again pulls off his hat and makes his stage bow.*] Ladies and ge'men, dis is a talking piece I's gwin render. It's 'titled "De Coffin Song," and tells 'bout a nice gal whut went away from home all dressed out in white and died, and

dey sont her body back to her Muh and Pap. Dis heah's de
Coast-Line coming down de track on a dark and rainy night
wid her coffin on boa'd. [*He closes his eyes and begins blowing the choo-kerr-choo of a starting train. He intersperses
his blowing with short speeches.*]
De rain is beating on de window panes and everybody is
mo'nful.
[*The choo-kerr-chooing takes on a sobbing note, and the
speed of the train increase.*]
De old man and de 'oman is at de station waiting foh deir
daughter's body, her dey loved so well, oh, her dey loved
so well. "Don't cry, honey, she gone to heaven," de old man
say, Lawd, Lawd, de old man say. Den he heah dat coffin-
blow.
[*A long mournful wail of the engine's whistle follows, swal-
lowed up in the growing speed of the locomotive. He opens
his eyes and begins to chant forth his bits of dialogue.*]
Now she's balling de jack 'cross de river trustle.
[*He quivers and sings with the straining timbers of the
bridge.*]
Heah she is passing by de gravel-pit. How she goes by, how
she goes by! Lak a great black hoss, a great black hoss! And
now she's blowing foh de crossing.
[*The whistle moans again.*]
Her Muh and Pap's on de flatform at de station and dey
feel deir hearts in deir moufs at de crying of dat train,
Lawd, Lawd, de crying of dat train!
[*Again he gives the coffin-blow, long and heart-breaking.*]
De train she slow up.
[*The choo-kerr-chooing slowly stops.*]
Dey takes out de coffin and flowers and puts her in a huss,
and dey all drives off slow, slow, lak dis.
[*He plays a sort of dead march and stalks back and forth.
across the yard.*]
Den de next day dey takes her to de graveyard, de lonesome
graveyard. And de preacher preach—shout hallelujah—de

preacher preach and de people sing, shouting glory to de
lamb. And den dey 'gin th'ow dirt in on her.
[*He imitates the thump, thump of clods falling on the coffin.*]
Den de favver and muvver and sisters and bruvvers all
cry out loud. Her Pap cries lak dis.
[*He gives forth a long deep groan.*]
And de sisters and bruvvers lak dis.
[*A medley of weeping sounds.*]
And de muvver cry lak dis.
[*A high piercing shriek.*]
And den dey roach up de grave and de preacher make prayer
—"Lawd, Lawd Jesus, have mercy upon us!" Den dey all
go off and dey ain't nothing left 'cepting a crow in a high
scraggly pine a-saying:
[*He mingles his music with a raucous h-a-r-r-c-k,
h-a-r-r-c-k.*]
Den adder dat when night come, dark and rainy night, de
last thing is a small wind in de bushes lak dis:

[*A trembling flute-like note rises, bubbles and disappears. He
beats the harp against his hand and looks uncertainly at* ENOS
and PHEELIE, *the tears wetting his cheeks.*]

ENOS. [*Presently.*] I cain't deny you gut de world beat
handling dat baby, but whut'n de name o' God makes you
cry so much?

BOY. [*Watching* PHEELIE'S *bowed head.*] When I plays dat
piece I feel so lonesome lak I cain't help crying, I allus cries.

ENOS. I's seed folks cry when deir people died, but, Lawd,
I never seed no sich cry-baby as you.

BOY. You's hard-hearted. Look at Miss Pheelie, she's crying.

ENOS. Help my life! Whut ails you, Pheelie?

PHEELIE. [*Hurriedly drying her eyes.*] Don't make no fun
of me, Enos. I des' had de blues ag'in.

ENOS. [*Patting his hat anxiously.*] Heah, don't you git to

feeling dat a-way no mo', honey. Le's go on wid our drive.

BOY. You calls her honey!

ENOS. Dat I do. She's my gal, dat's whut. And listen to me
—I don't want no no 'count fellow come piddling by wid
a harp and wild talk to git her upsot.

BOY. [*Unhappily.*] I didn't know you was her man. I—I
thought she was too purty and lak a angel foh dat. [PHEELIE
looks at him tearfully and he gazes back warmly.]

ENOS. [*Angrily.*] Look out, nigger, mind whut you's up to!

PHEELIE. Enos, you quit talking to dat boy lak dat.

ENOS. [*Coming up to her and catching her by the arm.*] Come
on now and let dat fellow go on whah he's started.

PHEELIE. [*Springing up.*] Turn me a-loose. He's gwine stay
right heah if he wants to and eat and sleep to boot.

ENOS. [*Hesitating a moment and then flaring out, his timid-
ity and slowness gone.*] De hell you say! [*He turns suddenly
towards the boy and points off to the left.*] You see 'way,
'way yonder in de west whah de sun is setting in de tops
of dem long-straw pines?

BOY. [*Questioningly.*] Yeh, yeh, I sees it.

ENOS. [*Moving towards him.*] Well, I wants you to git in
dat road and in three minutes start dere.

PHEELIE. [*Putting herself quickly before him.*] He ain't,
I tells you.

BOY. [*Emboldened by* PHEELIE'S *protection.*] You means you
wants to run me off befo' I gits any rations?

ENOS. I don't keer whedder you gits any rations or not. I
wants you to leave heah befo' you gits Pheelie all tore up
wid yo' foolish notions. [*Snapping.*] You better git from
heah!

BOY. [*Swinging his stick before him and smiling with weak
grimness.*] Ah—hah—I ain't gwine. [ENOS *makes another*

step towards him.] Don't you come towards me. I'll split yo' haid open wid dis heah stick. [ENOS *stops and eyes him cautiously. The boy holds his stick in trembling readiness.*]

PHEELIE. [*Getting between them.*] I tells you, Enos Atkins, you ain't gwine harm nary a hair of dis boy's head. You do and I'll scratch yo' eyes out apt as not.

ENOS. God A'mighty! done hyp'otized wid him a'ready, is you? [*In a wheedling tone.*] Now, boy, cain't you see how 'tis wid me? We was des' ready to go off to church, and heah you pops up and sets yo'se'f in 'twixt us. [*He feels in his pockets and pulls out a dollar.*] Heah, take dis dollar and go on. You kin buy enough grub wid it to last you a week.

BOY. [*Breaking into a loud derisive laugh.*] Ain't he a sight trying to har me off from his gal!

ENOS. Dem dere laughs is lakely gwine be tacks in yo' coffin. [*The boy closes his eyes in merriment. With a quick movement* ENOS *snatches his stick from him.*] Now see'f you don't strak a trot up dat road. [*He puts out his arm and pushes* PHEELIE *back. Egypt is heard off the left pawing the ground and shaking his bridle.*] Whoa, Egyp'!

BOY. [*Half whimpering.*] Don't hit me wid dat stick.

ENOS. I ain't gwine hit you if you lights a rag out'n heah dis minute. Scat, or I'll wring yo' neck. Make yo'se'f sca'ce, nigger.

PHEELIE. Let him 'lone, let him 'lone, I tells you!

BOY. You better go tend to yo' hoss, bo. I heah him trying to git loose.

ENOS. [*Looking appealing at* PHEELIE.] Egyp's gitting restless, Pheelie. You 'bout ready to be driving now? [*He steps to the left and calls.*] Whoa! whoa dere, Egyp'! Come on, Pheelie, and le's go.

PHEELIE. [*Shaking her head determinedly.*] I ain't gwine on no drive wid you, and dat's my last say.

ENOS. Oh, hell fiah! [*He lowers his stick. At the left he turns and speaks.*] You des wait heah, you little pole-cat, and I'll fix you yit. [*He hurries out.*]

BOY. [*Turning boldly back into the yard.*] Hunh, dat nigger ain't nothing but bluff.

PHEELIE. And he ain't gwine make you leave nuther. You stay right wid him.

BOY. He thinks you's gitting to laking me, dat's whut he thinks. [*He falls to staring at her intently.*]

PHEELIE. Why you look at me lak dat?

BOY. [*Shyly.*] How old is you?

PHEELIE. Seventeen.

BOY. [*Joyously.*] Is? Den we's des' de same age. Cain't— cain't I call you Pheelie?

PHEELIE. [*Looking at the ground.*] Yeh, yeh, you kin.

BOY. I feels des' lak I knowed you all my life, and I ain't never seed nobody lak you in all my progueings, nobody— and I's travelled a heap too.

PHEELIE. And you's seed a monstrous lot whah you travelled, ain't you? Yeh, you has, I bet.

BOY. I has dat—Lawd, Lawd!

PHEELIE. [*Dropping into the rocking-chair.*] Has you seed any big rivers and waters and sich?

BOY. Rivers! Lawd, yeh!

PHEELIE. Has you been by a place whah a great river pours over a steep hill roaring lak de judgment day?

BOY. [*Dropping on his knees and marking in the dirt as he*

ponders.] I dunno— Yeh, yeh, dat river was two miles wide and you had to stop yo' yurs in a mile of it.

PHEELIE. Go on, go on, tell me some mo'. Has you been in any big towns?

BOY. Has I? I's been in towns dat had streets so long dey won't no coming to de end of 'em.

PHEELIE. Was dey many people dere?

BOY. People! People! [*He rolls over on the ground at the remembrance of it and then sits up.*] All kinds and sizes. People running, people walking, some wearing diamont dresses and gold shoes. Rich, my, my, how rich! Ortymobiles as big as dat house wid hawns dat jar lak a earfquake and b'iler busting all at onct.

PHEELIE. [*A little dubiously.*] Aw—

BOY. Hit's so. And street cyars running wid nothing pulling or pushing 'em. And buildings so high dat de moon breshes de top. High! Lawd, Lawd, how high! And people hauling money wid trains, big train loads whah dey keeps it in a big house wid a school breaking of folks to gyard it.

PHEELIE. I been looking at pitchtures in dis book, but nothing fine as dat. [*She brings the book and shows it to him.*]

BOY. [*Somewhat disturbed.*] Yeh, I's gut a book lak dat. [*He begins picking his teeth meditatively with a straw.*] It was give to me by a peddling man. [*Smiling wisely.*] But dat was befo' I went out travelling foh myself. Lawd, Lawd, 'pared to what I's seed in New Yawk dat book ain't nothing.

PHEELIE. New Yawk! You been dere?

BOY. Dat I has. She's a long ways yonder too, mebbe two hundred miles, who knows? But, Pheelie, dat's de place to go, everything easy, people good to you, nothing to do but eat ice cream and mebbe now and den drink lemonade—and see people, people! worse'n de fair at Dunn. Never seed sich a mess of people. [ENOS *is heard quieting his horse.*]

PHEELIE. How'd you travel so fuh and pay yo' way? Must take a lot of money.

BOY. I walked, dat's how, bum my way. And when I gits hongry I plays my harp.

PHEELIE. Whah you sleep?

BOY. You don't know nothing 'bout travelling, does you? I sleeps on de warm ground. Come sunset, I stops in a hollow and breaks down bushes and rakes up pinestraw and sleeps lak a log. And in de mawning I wakes and sees de jew on everything and heahs de birds singing, and I lies dere a while and practice on my harp. Den I's off down de road breaving de fine air and feeling des' as happy as I kin.

PHEELIE. [*Vehemently.*] I done told Enos we could do lak dat. I sho' has told him time and ag'in.

BOY. Would you lak to live dat a-way?

PHEELIE. Unh—hunh, yeh, oh, yeh, I would.

BOY. [*Earnestly.*] Why cain't you, Pheelie?

PHEELIE. [*Twisting her hands nervously.*] I dunno—I wants to—I do wants to go and keep on gwine.

BOY. [*Leaning quickly forward.*] Pheelie, Pheelie, come on wid me and go tromping through de world. You kin leave dat bench-leg Enos behime.

PHEELIE. [*Turning impulsively towards him and then dropping her head.*] I cain't do it, I's 'fraid to. [ENOS. *slips in at the left rear and watches them.*]

BOY. I tell you we would have de best time gwine. Come on and go wid me.

PHEELIE. [*Hesitating.*] I—mought do it—I's half tempted to do it.

BOY. [*Catching her hand.*] I tells you whut—how 'bout me waiting out in de woods dere till dark comes down and den you kin put on a old dress and j'ine me?

PHEELIE. [*Pulling her hand unwillingly from him.*] Dat'd be fine—fine, but wouldn't folks raise cain?

BOY. Let 'em. Whut you'n me keer? We'll be splashing in de rain and shouting in de sun. And we'll step along togedder, and I'll hold yo' purty little hand and you'll hold mine, and I'll teach you to sing songs. I knows a bushel of purty ones. And den I'll learn you how to blow my harp. And we'll slip down de roads at sunrise and sunset, singing and blowing de finest chunes dey is. Please'm say you'll go wid me.

PHEELIE. [*With shining eyes.*] You has de purtiest talk of any man or boy I ever seed, and, oh, I wish—wish—— [*With sudden abandon.*] Yeh, yeh, I will—I will, I'll go. [*Ecstatically he touches her arm and looks straight into her eyes.*]

BOY. [*Cooingly.*] Birdie mine, birdie mine. [*He stands up and bends over her chair.*]

PHEELIE. [*Her face alight as she leans her head against him.*] Oh, it makes my haid swim to think of all we's gwine see and heah. [*He timidly puts his arm over her shoulder.* ENOS *throws his stick behind him, springs forward and snatches the* BOY *away from* PHEELIE.]

ENOS. Heah, you low-down rascal, trying to steal my gal, is you? Oh, yeh, I been heahing whut you said. [*His nostrils dilating.*] And I's gwine give you a kick in de seat of yo' britches dat'll send you whah you's gwine.

BOY. [*Retreating behind* PHEELIE.] I ain't trying to steal her nuther. She don't keer nothing foh you and wants to go on wid me.

ENOS. Dat's a lie, you little ficey fool, and you better look out befo' I gives you de lock-jaw.   .

BOY. She much as said she don't love you, now den.

ENOS. You didn't say dat, did you, Pheelie?

PHEELIE. I dunno whah I loves you or not.

ENOS. [*Turning savagely upon the boy.*] Damn yo' soul, I gut a notion to ham-string you. [*He makes a movement towards the boy, who darts over to the left, sees his walking-stick, and seizes it.*] You des' come heah rolling off yo' lies by de yard and tear up everything! Why don't you leave? Want me to bring out a fedder bed and wash yo' feet and sing to you and fan you and put you to sleep, does you? [*Jumping forward.*] I'll put you to sleep!

BOY. [*Falling quickly behind* PHEELIE *and drawing his stick.*] You make anudder move at me and I'll scrush yo' skull.

PHEELIE. [*Crying out.*] Enos, stop dat, stop dat!

ENOS. [*Sarcastically.*] Yeh, and who's you to order me—you lost every ray of sense you ever had! Wouldn't you be a purty fool running off wid dis heah woods-colt and sleeping in de jambs of fences and old hawg beds and scratching fleas lak a mangy hound! [*His voice rising high in wrath.*] Dat you would. And in winter weather you'd have yo' shirt-tail friz to you hard as arn. You'd be a sight for sore eyes!

PHEELIE. Shet up.—Boy, I wouldn't let him call me no woods-colt.

BOY. [*Weakly.*] Don't you call me dat.

ENOS. [*Taking off his coat.*] Call you dat! I ain't started yit. I's gwine twist off bofe yo' yurs and make you eat 'em widdout no salt. Hell, you ain't gut no mo' backbone dan a ground-puppy.

BOY. [*Trembling and clinging to his stick.*] Pheelie, Pheelie, don't let him git at me.

PHEELIE. Don't you hurt dat boy, I tells you ag'in.

ENOS. [*Laughing brutally.*] Hurt him! I's gwine crucify him. [*He begins circling* PHEELIE. *The* BOY *keeps on the opposite side.* ENOS *reaches out and pulls* PHEELIE *behind him.*] Now, my little son of a gun, whah is you?

BOY. [*In desperation raising his stick.*] Don't you come neah me. [ENOS *makes a dart at him. The* BOY *starts to flee, but as* ENOS *clutches him, he turns and brings his stick awkwardly down on his head.* ENOS *staggers and falls to his knees.*]

PHEELIE. [*Looking on in amazement a moment and then screaming.*] Lawd, you's kilt Enos! [*She stands in uncertainty, and then runs and holds him to her.*]

BOY. [*In a scared voice as he drops his stick.*] Muhcy, whut's I gwine do? Is—is you hurt, Enos? [ENOS *groans.*]

PHEELIE. Git out'n heah, you, you. You's murdered my husband. Enos, Enos, honey baby, is you hurt bad? [*He groans again and she helps him to a chair.*]

ENOS. [*Twisting his head from side to side.*] Hurt? Nothing but a little crack. Dat lizard ain't strong enough to kill a flea wid a sledge hammer. [*He suddenly whirls around and runs his tongue out, snarling at the* BOY.] Ya-a-a-h! [*The* BOY *bounds backwards and, tripping over the bench, falls sprawling on the ground.*] See dere, blowing my breaf on him th'ows him into fits.. [*The* BOY *lies stretched out still.*]

PHEELIE. Oh, my Lawdy, you—I believes he's daid or something!

ENOS. [*Trying to hide his fear.*] Sho' nothing but de breaf knocked out'n him.

PHEELIE. [*Shrilly, as she bends above the boy.*] He's hurt, I tells you. Po' boy. [*Turning towards* ENOS.] Whut if you's kilt him?

ENOS. [*Rubbing his head.*] Shet up, he ain't hurt bad.

PHEELIE. You hateful mule-beating rascal, he is hurt. [*Moaning over him.*] Oh, my sweet honey-boy.

BOY. [*Sitting up.*] Jesus, dat fall jarred de wind out'n my stomach. [*Suddenly getting to his feet and eyeing* ENOS *fearfully.*] Don't let dat man make at me.

PHEELIE. I don't reckon he will. You gi'n him a dost to last foh a while.

ENOS. [*Standing up.*] A dost! Hunh, he cain't faze me wid no little tap on de skull. [*He begins rolling up his sleeves. There is a hail off at the right front.*] And now I rolls up my sleeves foh de hawg-killing.

PHEELIE. You all stop dat rowing now. Yonder comes some-body. [*The* BOY *reaches down and gets his harp out of the dirt.*]

ENOS. Who is dat? Some old 'oman in a steer cyart.

BOY. [*Looking up hastily.*] Lawd Jesus, dat's—who's dat! Hide me, people, hide me quick so's she cain't get to me. [*He looks around him in terror.*] Whah must I go?

PHEELIE. Why you scared of her?

BOY. Pheelie, put me somewhah, civer me quick!

PHEELIE. Drap down on yo' knees, she's coming up de paf. Better git behime de house mebbe.

BOY. [*On his all-fours.*] And if she axes foh me, don't you tell her.

PHEELIE. We'll tell her we ain't seed hair nor hide of you. But I cain't see why you so tore up. [*He crawls rapidly off at the left rear around the house.*] Now, Enos, you keep yo' mouf closed. Dey's something up—dat boy 'fraid so.

ENOS. Dey is something up, and my s'picions is coming to de top.

OLD WOMAN. [*Calling off the right front.*] Heigho!

PHEELIE. Heigho! [*A stout old negress, dressed in rough working clothes, comes in at the right. She carries a long heavy switch in her hand with which she cuts at the ground as she talks.*]

OLD WOMAN. How you all come on?

PHEELIE. Well as common, and how does you?

OLD WOMAN. Well, I thanky. I's looking my boy—seen anything of him?

PHEELIE. [*Slowly.*] Whut sorter boy?

OLD WOMAN. Lawd, take me all day to gi'n you a pitchture of him. He's des' de no'countest fellow ever was bawn. He goes round playing a harp, and he's not des' right in his haid. He talks wild 'bout being off and travelling everywhah, and he ain't never been out'n Hornett County. Gut all dat mess out'n pitchture books and sich. [*A delighted grin begins to pass over* ENOS' *face.* PHEELIE *looks dejectedly at the ground.*]

PHEELIE. [*In a choked voice.*] I ain't seed him nowhah.

OLD WOMAN. [*Watching her closely.*] I whupped him t'udder day 'caze he so sorry, and he run off. And when I ketches him dis time I's gwine cyore him foh good and all. You say you ain't seed him?

PHEELIE. [*Looking up.*] Naw'm.

OLD WOMAN. [*Eyeing her.*] Dat's quare. I thought I seed somebody lak him standing heah in de yard. Last house down de road said he passed dere a hour ago, and dey ain't no road to turn off.

PHEELIE. [*Persistently.*] Naw'm, I ain't seed him. [*Unseen by* PHEELIE, ENOS *makes a signal to the* WOMAN *that the* BOY *is behind the house. Looking off.*] Mebbe he went by when we won't looking. [*The* WOMAN *darts around the house and is heard crying out.*]

OLD WOMAN. Ah—hah—heah you is, heah you is!

PHEELIE. How'd she find out he's dere? [*There is the sound of blows followed by loud crying.*]

ENOS. Listen at him cry, de baby!

PHEELIE. [*Who has started towards the rear.*] Quit yo'
laughing. [*She chokes with sobs.*] You set her on him, dat's
whut you done. And I'll help him out, she shain't beat him
so. [*She meets the* OLD WOMAN *coming in leading the* BOY
by the collar. He is crying like a child.]

OLD WOMAN. [*Yelling at him.*] Dry up! [*He stops his sobbing and looks off ashamed.*] Now ain't you a mess to be
running off and leaving me all de cotton to chop! [*Looking
around her.*] Well, we's gut to be moving, and I's gwine
gi'n you a beating whut is a beating when you gits home.

ENOS. Whah you live?

OLD WOMAN. Down neah Dukes.

ENOS. Oh-ho, I thought mebbe from yo' boy's talk you was
from New Yawk or de moon or somewhah.

OLD WOMAN. I be bound he's been lying to you. He cain't tell
de truf. De devil must a gut him in de dark of de moon.
[*She brings the switch across his legs. He shouts with pain.*]
Step on now! [*He struggles against her and holds back.*]

BOY. Pheelie, Pheelie, help me, cain't you?

PHEELIE. [*Raising a face filled with wrath.*] Help you! Dat
I won't. [*Coming up to him and glaring in his face.*] You
dirty stinking rascal, why you fool me so?

OLD WOMAN. [*Giving him another cut.*] You put a move
on you or I'll frail de stuffing out'n you. [*They move off
towards the right front, he looking back and holding out his
hands to* PHEELIE.]

BOY. Pheelie, don't turn ag'in me so. Pheelie! [*They go out.*]

ENOS. [*Going up to* PHEELIE.] Honey, don't—don't be mad
now. See, if it hadn't been foh me, apt as not you'd a-let dat
little fool gut you to gwine off wid him. [PHEELIE *bursts
into wild sobs. He pulls her head against his breast, but she*

shakes herself from him. The loud voice of the OLD WOMAN *is heard outside.*]

OLD WOMAN. You git in dat cyart or I'll Pheelie you!

PHEELIE. I don't want—I ain't never gwine to speak to you ag'in! Oh, he's done gone! [*She runs to the right and calls down the road.*] Heigh, Boy! Boy!

BOY. [*His voice coming back high and faint.*] Pheelie-ee-ee! [PHEELIE *falls on the bench, sobbing in uncontrollable grief.* ENOS *stands looking at her with a wry smile while he gingerly rubs his bruised head. After a moment he goes over to her and puts his arms around her. They are still around her when the curtain falls.*]

THE MAN ON THE HOUSE

CHARACTERS

OSCAR GRAHAM, *a farmer.*
JULIE GRAHAM, *his wife.*
LORA GRAHAM, *his daughter.*
EDWARD GRAHAM, *his son.*
TAPLEY JONES, *an old farm laborer.*
COLIN SPENCE, *a young farm laborer.*
A PREACHER.
A SOLDIER.
NEIGHBORS, *men, women, and children.*
NEGRO MOURNERS.

TIME—*Several years ago.*
PLACE—*A farm in eastern North Carolina.*

THE MAN ON THE HOUSE

An *illumination of the darkness discloses the edge of a tobacco field on a late afternoon in spring. At the back is a hedgerow of dogwood bushes, sassafras shrubs and wild flowers glowing with a medley of colors in the slanting sun. A sandy road runs parallel beyond the hedge, and farther back a forest of lob-lolly pines stretches away. Inside the hedge a narrow wired-off plot encloses two graves marked by small white tombstones. The wire fence is half-buried in honeysuckle and trumpet vine, and the ground before is carpeted with a thick growth of green broomstraw.*
LORA GRAHAM *comes in from the right, dressed in the rough outdoor clothes of a farm girl. She is about seventeen years old.*

LORA. [*Calling softly behind her.*] I'm going down the hedge to pick some flowers! [*She moves up to the wire fence with a peculiar gliding grace and stands looking down at the graves.*] They fade quick with the days getting hot. I'll put some fresh ones here. Violets are coming out as thick as specks on the wall, and the bluets on that road bank now— [*She goes toward the left as old* TAPLEY *and* COLIN *come in from the right.* TAPLEY *is a stout old farmer with a round red face;* COLIN *a lanky farm youth, freckled and serious. They talk in drawling monotones.*]

COLIN. [*Timidly.*] Want me to help you git some flowers, Lora?

LORA. [*With a startled movement.*] I know where they are—
best. [*She goes off quickly.* COLIN *sighs.*]

TAPLEY. Mought as well give it up, boy.

COLIN. Hanh?

205

TAPLEY. Quit thinking of it, I tell you. . . . Wisht our tobacco plants hadn't give out right here. [*He stares solemnly at the two graves.*]

COLIN. I don't mind,—if the dead don't—too tired to mind.

TAPLEY. And this stump is a good place to rest. [*He sits down on a stump at the right and leans his head in his arms.* COLIN *stretches himself out on the ground.*]

COLIN. I'm so sleepy!

TAPLEY. You'll ketch yer death on that wet ground, you will.

COLIN. Could sleep in a mudhole—about.

TAPLEY. All night there at Mack's?

COLIN. All night.

TAPLEY. How do they take it?

COLIN. Wailed and moaned till daybreak.

TAPLEY. I don't blame 'em, pore niggers!

COLIN. Ner I don't neither. [*In a moment* COLIN *staggers to his feet.*] I better go down to the plant bed and help him.

TAPLEY. He'll be back in a minute, I tell you.

COLIN. I don't know!

TAPLEY. He'll be back in a minute.

COLIN. The sun's about hid behind the trees already. I better go.

TAPLEY. [*Softly.*] Colin.

COLIN. Unh?

TAPLEY. What's on your mind?

COLIN. Nothing on my mind.

TAPLEY. I mean about him.

COLIN. [*Hurriedly.*] Nothing.

TAPLEY. Noticed nothing quare about him today?

COLIN. Seems sorter worried.

TAPLEY. Know why?

COLIN. [*Shortly.*] No.

TAPLEY. I do.

COLIN. Hanh?

TAPLEY. He's got sump'n in his pocket too.

COLIN. Unh?

TAPLEY. [*Looking carefully around him.*] He bent over onct and I saw the handle of a pistol in his pocket.

COLIN. I seen it—this morning myself.

TAPLEY. Whyn't you tell me?

COLIN. I dunno. . . .

TAPLEY. A preacher in the church!

COLIN. What's he 'fraid of, you reckon?

TAPLEY. [*Throwing out his hands.*] That's just it.

COLIN. Must be sump'n.

TAPLEY. Always sump'n.

COLIN. He wouldn't hurt a fly.

TAPLEY. How do you know?

COLIN. A good religious man.

TAPLEY. Religion works in a man's head sometimes—ferments like.

COLIN. [*Dully.*] In his head. [LORA *wanders up the road behind the hedge from the left.*]

LORA. [*Singing as she turns in the forest.*]

> "There may be a change in the mountain
>   There may be a change in the sea,

There may be a change in your heart
But there is no change in me."

[*She disappears among the trees.*]

TAPLEY. Anh, she will sing!

COLIN. [*Softly.*] Right purty.

TAPLEY. Oh, yes—purty.

COLIN. What's he toting that pistol for?

TAPLEY. [*Looking at him hard.*] His boy's coming back. [*Snickering grimly.*] Sump'n.

COLIN. Unh?

TAPLEY. That Edward.

COLIN. Why Mis' Julie and all of 'em's fixing and cooking at the house for him . . . and gitting ready.

TAPLEY. Don't make no difference. Ever since he got the news, Mr. Oscar's been like a man lost, a-skeared.

COLIN. Dunno—

TAPLEY. You've hearn whispers, ain't you, [*Nodding towards the graves.*] about it all?

COLIN. Jest whispering—

TAPLEY. Hanh. Six years ago today they pulled them two out'n the millpond dead and they holding hands. 'T'ain't whispering. I holp git 'em out myself.

COLIN. They was quare was why they drownded theyselves.

TAPLEY. Quare! . . . And he ain't been seen since.

COLIN. Couldn't be right in their upper-story— Nothing but whispers.

TAPLEY. *All* empty upstairs.

COLIN. [*Angrily.*] Hunh?

TAPLEY. Course, all but that 'un.

COLIN. Talk, I tell you.

TAPLEY. [*Ironically*.] Course.

COLIN. I'm going now. . . .

TAPLEY. You needn't for there he comes. . . .

COLIN. [*Lowering his voice*.] And he ain't got no plants.

TAPLEY. Gimme a chew o' tobacco. Doctor says I better quit it or . . . [*Singing*.]

> Oh the mens for the women
> And the womens for the men
> The doctor said it'll kill you,
> But he didn't say when—

Yeh, that there Apple is hard to beat.

COLIN. It don't hurt you.

TAPLEY. Does, I'd a-been dead long ago. Chewed it since I was knee-high to a duck. Bet I got a coat of it on my insides thick at this hyuh finger.

[*He holds up a stuffy, gnarled forefinger.* OSCAR GRAHAM *comes in along the hedgerow from the right. He is a tall, raw-boned farmer of fifty or more, with the suggestion of something fierce and proud in his bearing.*]

GRAHAM. [*In a husky voice*.] I'm back.

TAPLEY. Yessuh.

GRAHAM. [*Looking up and down the hedge*.] Where is she?

TAPLEY. Out there in the woods picking vi'lets. Hear her singing?

GRAHAM. Aye. [*He sits down on a stump and stares across the field*.] Always fooling wi' flowers.

TAPLEY. She said she'd be right back.

GRAHAM. [*Looking behind him*.] The woods'll be dark soon

and its dangerous in the cool places where moccasins and adders sleep.

COLIN. Want me to go git her?

GRAHAM. Never heard about her great-grandmother, did ye, Tapley?

TAPLEY. Never heard, I ain't.

GRAHAM. Ah, it's been handed down and on down. She was a flower-girl to the queen.

TAPLEY. A puore queen?

GRAHAM. In a great castle with a king and purty ladies and young men playing on harps. There must a-been great goings-on in them days, Tapley.

TAPLEY. [*Foolishly.*] Lordy, that must a-been time and time ago!

GRAHAM. Long before our folks come across the sea. [*He passes his hand over his head.*] She might a-been a flower-girl to a queen, aye, a queen herself.

TAPLEY. [*Blinking.*] Yessuh.

GRAHAM. Still they were evil folks in them days, fighting and cutting each other and breaking the Lord's command-ments. [*He stares morosely at the ground.*] One of our folks, they tell, was a hand for it—Sir Hughie Graham—they called it Grime then, and there was a song about him. Grandmuh knew it all by heart, more'n twenty verses. He fought ten men at once backed up against a tree and all because they accused him of stealing a mare. [*Reciting in a sing-song voice.*]

> "Sir Hugh of the Grime's condemned to die,
>   And of his friends he had no lack;
> Fourteen foot he leaped in his cell,
>   His hands tied fast on his back.

Then he looked over his left shoulder,
To see who he could see or spy;
Then was he aware of his father dear,
Come tearing his hair most pitifully. . . ."

[*He goes over to the plot, and stands looking down at the two graves.*]

COLIN. [*In a low voice.*] What in the world—

TAPLEY. Ah.

COLIN. Never seen him do like that before.

TAPLEY. You'll see worse.

COLIN. [*Violently.*] Hush, hush, I tell you.

TAPLEY. [*Angrily.*] Give respect where—the Almanac'll tell you. I'm a' old man.

GRAHAM. I am the resurrection and the life, saith the Lord.

COLIN. Mr. Graham.

GRAHAM. For the living know that they shall die, but the dead know not anything.

TAPLEY. What you want with him?

GRAHAM. For the race is not to the swift nor the battle to the strong.

COLIN. Mebbe I'd better go git the plants, Mr. Graham.

GRAHAM. [*Raising a haggard face.*] Hanh?

COLIN. The tobacco plants.

GRAHAM. Hanh?

TAPLEY. We'll go git 'em.

GRAHAM. [*Walking back and forth at the end of the rows.*] He's come—come back from the darkness and the grave. Seven years gone and no word from him—nothing. Across the field I saw him standing on the back-porch. The sun was shining on him. And then my dream come back to me.

TAPLEY. You go on home and rest. We'll finish.

GRAHAM. I cain't get the dream out'n my head. . . . I was coming up the lane with everything dark around me but the road. The road was like a furrow of light ploughed on before me. I come along near the house and I looked and the house was all black, and a thin frame of a woman all dressed in black was standing before it with her head hid under a great big black bonnet. Then I heard somebody wailing inside, and it was Lora. And away off in the wood back of the house I heard them two [*Throwing out his hand towards the graves*] calling so lonesome it'd eat your heart out. When I come up at the woodpile I asked the black woman what she was doing, but she wouldn't say nothing, just stood there high as a stake. And I heard the sparrows talking in the elm trees, fluttering and whispering and looking at me with big hollow eyes, and they were sorry. I heard 'em, Tapley. [*He shudders and turns away his head.*]

TAPLEY. [*Wonderingly.*] A dream—

GRAHAM. It skeared me, skeared me to death nearly. In the yard everything was dark, like the eclipse. The cow was lowing 'way off and the sound seemed to run across the sky like a roll of thunder in August. It died away and I heard my daddy calling the hogs up at the mulberry orchard the way he useter. Every time he called a kind of jarring run right through me into the ground. Then Florie and Minna begun to call the hogs with him. They'd call the little ones and he'd call the big ones. The calling changed from the hogs to me—"Oscar, where are you, Oscar?" he would say, and they'd say, "Father, father, come get us, we're lost up here under this big clay-root. We're stifling to death in the dirt." And all of a sudden my daddy hollered to me to let him come home, let him come back and set down in his chair at the table and eat some roas'n ears. He was a great hand for young corn. I was skeared to death, I tell ye, and called back and told him not to come. Then Lora run to the window and leant out and begged me to make Florie and Minna go back to their graves. "Make 'em go back, make 'em go back!" she'd say. And I looked at the thin woman in the yard, and she turned and went up the road to run 'em back in their graves. There come a mournful wailing up at the pasture when she put 'em back in the ground. All of a sudden I heard Lora screaming around the house. I run and met her and Edward was walking behind smiling, his lips pulled back from his teeth like a dog. And he'd took a hot iron and burnt Lora's face all black. [*Beating his hands together.*] I woke up and it was day.

TAPLEY. A nightmare.

GRAHAM. [*In an awestruck voice.*] Next morning a telegram come from him saying he'd be here soon. And he's here now, Tapley, there at the house.

TAPLEY. Then everybody'll be glad.

GRAHAM. Yeh—will she be glad, Tapley?

TAPLEY. After seven long years.

GRAHAM. Ah! Listen to her singing there. Aye, happy. Is anybody happy except the good?

TAPLEY. Don't see how they could be, I don't.

GRAHAM. Ye'll never find a better one, Colin.

COLIN. [*Starting.*] No sir, I won't.

GRAHAM. I wisht it was settled between ye.

COLIN. Yessir.

GRAHAM. Ye could take the farm after me, ye and her. [*Beseechingly.*] She's got to have somebody to protect her, Colin. I won't be here long to do it. She's got her God to help her, but she's got to have somebody to protect her, some man.

COLIN. [*Uncertainly.*] Yessir.

GRAHAM. [*Calling.*] Come here a minute wi' ye, Lora. [*She answers in the distance, and* GRAHAM *moves towards the hedge at the back and looks out at the forest. Far up the road to the right an intermittent wailing begins.*]

TAPLEY. [*Softly.*] Pore niggers!

COLIN. [*Shivering.*] Yeh.

TAPLEY. Started to the graveyard with little Tommy.

COLIN. Anh.

TAPLEY. Mack'll never have another boy kin side cotton like Tommy.

COLIN. No, he won't, never. [LORA *is seen entering the road from the forest. She stands listening to the wailing with a thoughtful face a moment and then comes on through the hedge, carrying an armful of late dogwood sprays and wild flowers.*]

LORA. [*Gently.*] Why do they do that?

GRAHAM. Sorrowing for their dead.

LORA. Tommy!—Can't you go down the road and make 'em stop it?

GRAHAM. [*Looking up at the sky.*] Grief is the way to be purified.

LORA. I'm ready to go back to work. [*Starting.*] Have you heard anything else from Brother? [*Clutching his arm.*] Has he come? Yes, he has come.

GRAHAM. That's not what I called to ye for.

LORA. [*Almost with a sob.*] Oh, I know he'll never come back! Why won't he come?

GRAHAM. In his time.

LORA. You promised he would come—and he never has.

GRAHAM. Lora, take them flowers out'n your hair.

LORA. I just—

GRAHAM. The Book says—

LORA. [*Removing the flowers.*] Vanity . . .

GRAHAM. Vanity of vanities saith the preacher.

LORA. I can't see—

GRAHAM. [*Softly.*] Minna and Florie done like that.

LORA. Oh!

GRAHAM. Ye're one of the redeemed now. . . .

LORA. Yes.

GRAHAM. And things that decorate and make ye purty, leave 'em alone, leave 'em all alone. Put not your heart in that.

LORA. [*Childishly.*] Put it in Jesus.

GRAHAM. In Jesus. He will save ye and protect ye from the adversary.

LORA. He is my hope and my salvation.

GRAHAM. And all the things of this world are vanity and vexation of spirit.

LORA. All is vanity.

GRAHAM. Like the wind. Aye, like man's poor life, [*A smile hovering on his lips.*], whirling about continually, no rest, no peace.

LORA. In the grave whither thou goest.

GRAHAM. Amen. [*They stand a moment silent.* TAPLEY *and* COLIN *move around in embarrassment.*]

LORA. What is it?

GRAHAM. [*Tearfully.*] Ye're so good, Lora. Ye are good, ain't ye, child?

LORA. I try to be.

GRAHAM. [*To himself.*] Let the dream go now, pass from my mind.

LORA. A dream?

GRAHAM. I've dreamed of ye in your white robes, like a saint of God.

LORA. With wings and all. . . .

GRAHAM. Lora, ye do feel saved and consecrated?

LORA. [*Putting her hand on her breast.*] I do, Father, you know I do.

GRAHAM. And ye do love the Lord?

LORA. And I always will . . .

GRAHAM. Through him we walk in the new Jerusalem and rest by the river of life.

LORA. [*Still repeating like a child.*] He set us free from the wages of sin and death.

GRAHAM. Aye.

LORA. [*Looking up at the sky, a smile fluttering in her face.*] I love the Lord better than everything. [*Her voice rising in a chant.*] He died for the sins of the world. He is the lamb whose blood was shed for sinful man. All of us so pitiful and black in the corruption of the world can be washed in that precious blood—like a great sea of blood the way the sunset is—all of us can be made as white as snow, white like these dogwood blossoms.

GRAHAM. Though our sins be as scarlet, they shall be as white as snow.

LORA. [*With lifted face.*] And we shall walk upon the mountain.

GRAHAM. Amen!

LORA. [*Bursting into sobs.*] I believe in him and love him

and worship him. I bow down and worship him. Father, don't talk so.

GRAHAM. Aye, aye, my daughter. [*He bends and kisses her and puts his hand on her head.*] May God be with thee like Jacob of old.

LORA. [*Like a child.*] Jesus will stay with me, for I'm afraid of God.

GRAHAM. [*Uncertainly.*] God is good, he is love.

LORA. I see him at night and he scares me—I'm afraid of God, with his beard.

GRAHAM. Then keep your little heart on his son. Hark!

LORA. [*Her face flushed.*]—He so young and beautiful hanging there on the cross and the mean people spitting on him. I close my eyes and see his face and the tears pouring down it, so wonderful and white, and it looks like brother's picture before 'twas burned up long ago.

GRAHAM. [*Sharply.*] He was not of this world.

LORA. Why did God let them drive nails through his soft hands? [*Shuddering.*] I dream about it till it gets all in my head. It was mean and cruel and I can see his long white fingers twisting and twisting.

[*The lamentation of the mourning Negroes draws nearer. The two farm helpers move over to the hedge and stare up the road to the right.*]

GRAHAM. Keep his suffering in your mind, poor child. So do it and ye'll hold the old Bad Boy away from your pure soul.

LORA. And I don't let him tempt me. Last night he came and begged me to go into a dark woods. He showed me the woods and said it was purty there. And flowers shone out like little new lamps—so beautiful. I wanted to go, but I was afraid and I began to say parts of the Bible by heart, and he went away. It was so strange. He looked ugly with hoofs and horns, and then he became beautiful like brother's picture, but older.

GRAHAM. Ah.

LORA. Oh, me!

GRAHAM. God may try ye soon, child.

LORA. He may!—

GRAHAM. He tries everyone, don't he, Tapley?

TAPLEY. Reckon he does, he does.

GRAHAM. Trying poor Mack and Jennie there with their dead boy. [*In a fierce voice.*] Ye've got to be strong, Lora!

LORA. [*Starting back and letting her bonnet fall.*] Father?

GRAHAM. [*Rubbing his forehead.*] Ah, gnawing and grinding!

LORA. Go home and rest. [*Gathering her flowers together.*] And now I'll put these flowers there for 'em. And I'll tell 'em to pray for us all to be saved, Colin and Tapley and everybody in the world.

GRAHAM. [*Twisting his hands.*] Will they answer ye, Lora?

LORA. I hear 'em in the air and sometimes behind the hedge-row.

GRAHAM. Ah . . . ye better quit coming up here at night. [*He turns and strides off to the left and then returns.*] . . . Colin . . . do ye ever pay any mind to what I asked ye about him?

LORA. Please . . .

GRAHAM. He'd be good to ye.

LORA. Please, please . . .

GRAHAM. He would—and that's all right.

COLIN. Sump'n moving in that bonnet.

TAPLEY. Hanh?

COLIN. [*Jumping back.*] Goodness, it's a snake! [*He reaches for his tobacco peg.*]

LORA. [*Snatching up the bonnet and revealing a small glittering green snake.*] I caught him on a vine out there. [*She caresses it.*]

GRAHAM. [*Shouting.*] Lora, throw that snake down! [*She drops the snake and watches it wriggle away in the grass.*]

TAPLEY. Great guns, she put her hands on him, she did!

LORA. [*Smiling naively.*] He was so purty and gentle playing there. He stuck out his little red tongue at me teasing.

GRAHAM. [*Whirling abruptly around.*] I'll be right back with the plants, Tapley. Ye all meet me up there at the other end of the rows . . . Oh, God! [*He puts his hands to his head and goes heavily out at the left.*]

LORA. [*In distress.*] Father . . .

TAPLEY. I dunno, I don't. [COLIN *suddenly begins beating in the grass with his tobacco peg.*]

LORA. [*Flying at him.*] Don't you hurt him, don't you hit that little snake! [*He holds the dead snake aloft.*]

COLIN. That thing bite you, and it'll kill you. [LORA *snatches the snake from him and falls on the ground, sobbing and crooning over it.*]

TAPLEY. Now . . .

COLIN. Hush! [*He takes the snake away from* LORA *and throws it far into the woods.*]

LORA. [*Gasping.*] Don't you put your ugly hands on me.

COLIN. But you do what your father said. [*With suppressed sobs she goes over to the hedge and stands leaning against a dogwood bush. The moaning and beating of the Negroes draw nearer.*]

TAPLEY. Holler like that all the way to the graveyard!

LORA. [*With sudden calmness.*] Do you believe in God?

TAPLEY. I reckon so.

LORA. Did God kill little Tommy—like the little snake?

TAPIEY. In a way he done it, he did. [*The funeral procession is heard near at hand, with a background of chanting and song, interspersed with moans and wails and the dull thud of beaten breasts. The mournful lamentation rises to the sky, led by a woman's piercing voice.*]

> "Dark was de night and cold de ground
>   In which my Saviour laid!"

COLIN. He stepped on a nail and the lockjaw killed him.

TAPLEY. Anh, he'd be in the field ploughing this very minute.

COLIN. [*Monotonously.*] We bring death on ourselves.

LORA. [*Vehemently.*] Then Jesus brought death on himself.

TAPLEY. He had to die for us all!

LORA. God wouldn't let it happen if he could.

COLIN. All's for a purpose!

LORA. He wouldn't let it happen if he could. [*Mockingly.*] Ha, I bet I know why he didn't help it.

> "De bones in de grave cried Calvary
>   De night my Jesus died."

[*The head of the cortège comes slowly in at the right, and the two men take off their hats. A Negro preacher goes before, beating on his breast with a Bible and swaying his bare head from side to side. Following him come four moaning Negro farmers carrying a rude pine box between them; then the parents, and behind, several turbaned Negro women, men and children. The slow procession shows above the hedge*]

*in a queer nodding minstrelsy, moving forward with the
jerky steps of instinctive puppets, their faces set in a wooden
stare.*]

> "In de resurrection, in de resurrection,
>   Gwine putt de new man on.
> King Jesus said it, King Jesus said,
>   Gwine putt de new man on."

[LORA *begins to sway like the Negroes. She snatches up an
armful of flowers and rushes through the hedge.*]

LORA. Tommy, Tommy! [*She falls in with the mourners,
throwing bouquets on the coffin. The wailing bursts forth
in a redoubled howl:*]

> "Dark was de night and cold de ground
>   In which my Saviour laid.
> De bones in de grave cried Calvary,
>   De night my Jesus died."

[LORA *flings herself down in the road rocking and weeping,
and the procession passes on.*]

TAPLEY. They carry on, they do.

COLIN. Niggers.

LORA. [*Behind the hedge.*] There's Tommy dead and stiff.

TAPLEY. Listen at her.

LORA. The little puppies I buried had worms in 'em three
days after. I dug 'em up and saw it.

COLIN. Lora!

TAPLEY. What's she saying?

COLIN. [*Sharply.*] Hush up. [*Presently a low cold laugh is
heard behind the hedge.*]

TAPLEY. For God's sake, she's laughing about it! [COLIN

steps quickly through the hedge and lifts LORA *from the ground.*]

COLIN. Come on and go home, Lora.

LORA. [*Breaking from him.*] Let me loose. Don't you put your cold hands on me! [*She turns upon them with a queer light in her eyes.*] The trees become gold and the field there turned like a great bowl of sunshine. I heard their wailing inside of my head and I could see little Tommy way off there like a little black stick, stretched out stiff, same as a black nail in a bed of coals. [*She breaks into a cold sardonic laugh.*]

TAPLEY. Merciful heavens!

LORA. [*Huskily.*] Jesus, and I love Jesus. They spit on him and put nails in him, nails like little Tommy stuck in his foot—rusty nails. [*She approaches* TAPLEY *and* COLIN, *staring at them.*] And Jesus cried to God and God didn't answer. They stuck a hole in his side and a black cloud came down to hide it all. He said let the cup pass—he prayed let the cup pass—[*She walks up and down with the steps of the Negro mourners*]—there in the garden—there on the mountain. But the cup couldn't pass—couldn't pass. God couldn't answer, nobody could answer—he had to die—had to suffer —everybody's got to die—got to suffer. [*Waving her hands over her head.*] Minna and Florie had to suffer and die—I have to suffer and die—

COLIN. [*Seizing her arm.*] Hush that.

LORA. [*Beating off his hands.*] I love Jesus but I hate God— I hate whatever it is . . .

COLIN. Stop that before the ground swallows you up. [*She drops her head and stands gazing down at the earth, shivering and seeming to shrink under her clothes.*] What has happened to her?

TAPLEY. The niggers passing mebbe.

COLIN. Good Mr. Graham didn't hear you, Lora.

LORA. [*Her face suddenly blanched with terror as she stares across the fields to the right.*] Look! I see something standing over the house. There's a sword in its hand.

TAPLEY. Lord a-mercy! Hanh, ain't nothing there . . . Colin?

COLIN. Ain't nothing. [LORA *drops down upon the grass hiding her face in her hands.*] Lora, Lora . . .

TAPLEY. [*Heaving a deep sigh.*] Look at them tobacco plants out there? They stand up proud and straight like little soldiers. The dew's begun to fall on 'em and started 'em growing.

COLIN. [*Softly.*] Yeh . . . Flea bugs short it in two, who knows?

TAPLEY. My rows look fresher'n yourn, they do. They ain't nothing better'n this old finger for putting 'em in the ground. [*Spitting.*] I wouldn't have one o' them there pegs.

COLIN. [*Monotonously.*] Yeh, wear your fingernail off to the roots if you want to.

TAPLEY. [*Shrugging his shoulders.*] We better git on up there to the other end.

COLIN. [*Bitterly.*] Yeh, let's go on.

TAPLEY. Be so dark in a minute you cain't see how to set. We're ready to go, Lora.

COLIN. Let her rest. [*They start off at the left.*]

TAPLEY. [*Jerking his thumb over his shoulder.*] Now what you got to say?

COLIN. [*Whining in smouldering fury.*] Don't you say another word about it, I tell you!

[*His shoulders heave with restrained sobs as he lurches off*

at the left. TAPLEY *gazes about him, blinking his eyes in stupefaction. With a grunt he goes off after him.*
[*By this time the sun has set and the thin mist of dusk has overspread the scene. Bullbats are braying in the sky and the whippoorwill is heard in the woods. Above the pines at the rear a thin new moon has come out. And from the neighboring countryside the sounds of evening move one after the other across the scene—farmers calling their pigs, the tinkle of cowbells, a country lad whistling to his dog, the high song of a laborer going home.*

[*Presently* LORA *gathers the scattered sprays and flowers in her arms, passes within the enclosure, and begins placing them on the graves.*]

LORA. These are purty flowers now, fresh and purty and they smell so sweet. I got 'em in the woods all around. You've never seen so many flowers—everywhere,—violets and pinks and bluets. I put some of 'em in my hair, but father made me take 'em out. It's wrong for me to wear 'em, but he don't care if you do. He's glad for you to, yes he is. It's vanity for me, but when I die it'll be all right. They'll put a lot of flowers on me and dress me in a white dress. [*Bending over the tombstones.*] And I caught a purty little green snake and Colin killed him. He killed him with a peg and threw him away in the woods. Minna and Florie, I don't like Colin, and his hands—I can't stand them. Little Tommy's gone now, they carried him by to the graveyard. You heard 'em all passing, I know you did. It was pitiful. Is it bad not to like God?—I believe God is the old Bad Boy—and I'm afraid of him. [*She takes up several trinkets from the graves—little glass slippers, cups, shells and the like—and refills them with fresh flowers. She bends her head to one of the tombstones and whispers.*] He's not come yet. They said he was coming back to us, but he's not come yet. Will he come, will he come to us? [*Jubilantly.*] I'm so glad, I'm so glad! [*A young man comes quietly along the road behind the hedge at the right. He is bareheaded, with a shock of yellow hair, and dressed in the uniform of an army lieutenant. He comes quietly up to the hedge and stands looking over at her, his face filled with a slumbrous brooding sadness.*] Let him come back to me, and then I'll die. I want to be with you, yes, yes. I'm afraid of father and mother, too. I want to go where you are. If brother could be there with us, we'd all be happy. Is it purty up there? The preacher says it is, and father says so. If you could tell me about Jesus, for he is there. You're there with him, I know. You didn't drown yourselves in the pond, I know you didn't. Why don't you tell me you didn't? It's not wrong if you did, is it? It's better to be in heaven, everybody says so. Let brother come back to me, and then I'll do it too, I'll hide under the water, I'm not afraid. Brother, brother!

EDWARD. [*In a low voice.*] Who is she?

LORA. Who is that?

EDWARD. Lora?

LORA. [*Coming slowly towards him through the gate.*] I'm Lora and this is Minna and Florie.

EDWARD. [*Bowing his head over the hedge.*] You're happy in this quiet place.

LORA. Where did you come from?

EDWARD. Seven years, and I've come back.

LORA. [*With a cry.*] It's brother! [*She suddenly stops and retreats from him.*] Go away, go on back,—leave us alone.

EDWARD. [*With a low bitter laugh.*] Mother's at the house by the window crying.

LORA. [*Staring at him.*] He's come, Minna and Florie, come back to you. And his face is pitiful! He's like Jesus. [*She drops down on her knees and bows her head in her lap.*] Edward, Edward— [*Laughing.*] Think of my saying that name out loud to him . . . and he's standing there hearing my words.

EDWARD. Say it again.

LORA. Hide quick, father's up yonder in the field.

EDWARD. Father—

LORA. I think he will . . . I don't know . . . I think he will. [*Putting her hands over her eyes.*] There's nobody there. I knew he'd never come back.

EDWARD. Lora.

LORA. It *is* brother too, they told me he was coming back.

EDWARD. I have.

LORA. They all said you were wicked. I've been baptized and I'm a Christian now. [*She stretches out her fingers as if to touch him.*]

EDWARD. Ha.

LORA. No, not like that.

EDWARD. My soul is lost.

LORA. You're good and beautiful, and you will be saved in the great day.

EDWARD. [*Stepping through the hedge.*] Their hand is upon me. [*Gesturing.*] Down the road, back into the seven years. [*He stands near to her.*] Lost—everything cold and black around me.

LORA. Oh me!

EDWARD. [*Starting.*] I'll tell you about them.

LORA. I know.

EDWARD. [*Sharply.*] Draw your hand back.

LORA. I know—and I don't mind. [*He turns and walks away. She follows after him.*] I don't mind it.

EDWARD. I hear their voices night by night,—when I lie

down . . . I come back. And now all is ashes, chokes me like dust and ashes.

LORA. [*Flinging herself down and embracing his feet.*] Let me wipe it away from your heart. Let's pray to Jesus to help you.

EDWARD. The years and years they called to me—called me to come back—[*Touching his head with his hand.*]—louder than the firing of the guns—queer—queer. And now two mounds and the grass and vines.

LORA. They've not forgot.

EDWARD. [*In a low vehement voice.*] You made them forget.

LORA. No.

EDWARD. Kiss me good-bye. [*He slowly pulls her up from the ground.*]

LORA. Then stay here.

EDWARD. And I will leave you.

LORA. [*Her face shining out in the dusk.*] I'm not afraid, not like them. I would die and not mind it. . . .

EDWARD. There's a tree in the forest and the pinks and violets grew there under our feet. [*Pointing over his shoulder.*] When the moon was there, we'd meet. And round and round, their hair flying behind them . . .

LORA. [*Holding up her hand.*] I found Florie's ring there.

EDWARD. Their hair was dark and their cheeks like maple buds.

LORA. [*Somewhat defiantly.*] But mine is yellow as gold, like yours and long—longer than theirs. [*She loosens her hair and lets it roll down over her shoulders.*] And I could dance and run faster than they. I go there alone in the moonlight sometimes. And I've seen them peeping at me behind the big poplar.

EDWARD. They were too beautiful to die, and you . . . And so good-bye.

LORA. You shan't go away. I'll go with you.

EDWARD. You're beautiful, Lora, more beautiful than they.

LORA. If you leave me I will go and be with them.

EDWARD. And the moon would not come up tomorrow night, the sun and the stars would go out forever. [*She leans against him and he touches her hair gently with his lips.' Presently he draws his shoulders back and lifts his head in a military posture.*] Can you hear it?

LORA. I hear the crickets in the hedge, and everything drowsy like.

EDWARD. It comes in at my ears and beats behind my eyes.

LORA. [*Whispering.*] Look at all the trees there swimming back and back and going behind the sky somewhere, everything lifting up like a yellow curtain and leaving us alone in the world. [*In a queer hypnotic voice.*] You are the world somehow.

EDWARD. It beats behind my eyes. The air is full of honeysuckle, coming through the roots out of their graves, and going up to the moon. [*Softly as if seeing a scene far off.*] One-two-three-four— One-two-three-four.

LORA. [*Wildly.*] You'll not leave me— Now you're here, you've come back. I can hardly believe it but it's true, you're here with me. You'll never leave me any more. [*Seizing his hands and kissing them.*] Your hands are wonderful and sad like your poor face, they're like his hands where they drove the nails. His face was like yours. They burned the picture to keep me from seeing you, but I saw you in my mind, more wonderful than he was. And they nailed him on the cross, and made him suffer. Make me suffer like him, like you. Don't be pitiful and lonely and lost. Let me be near to you, oh do!—Little boy, little boy! My love is more than theirs. Ha, they were afraid and went away from it. I am not afraid. Jesus was not afraid and you're like him—you are the light of the world. [*Her breath comes through her lips like a gasp as she clings to him. He kisses her shyly, then pushes her from him.*]

EDWARD. Good-bye . . . [*His face set and hard, he turns away.*]

LORA. At first I couldn't understand, and now I do.

EDWARD. Lora!

[GRAHAM's *voice is heard calling her in the fields.*]

LORA. [*Snatching up handsful of flowers.*] You said I was—their eyes and their hair was black but you said—say it again—

EDWARD. You are, you are.

LORA. We'll go there under the tree and they'll come too—we'll all be together. They'll not peep maybe—[*She starts out through the hedge at the back.*]

EDWARD. [*Raising an anguished face.*] New moon, new moon, Mr. New Moon!

LORA. Crazy moon.

EDWARD. We'll put out your light, yellow moon.

LORA. [*Wildly.*] Yellow moon, funny moon!" [*She hurries through the hedge and he follows her.*]

GRAHAM. [*Coming in from the left.*] God have mercy! [*They are engulfed in the shadow of the forest. For a moment he stands crushed and stupefied, and then raises his head towards the sky.*] Thy will not mine be done. [*He runs through the hedge after them. Presently a pistol shot is fired, followed by a scream. In a few minutes he returns leading LORA by the hand. She walks stiffly and mechanically like a puppet. GRAHAM is babbling idiotically.*] He done it hisself, he snatched it out'n my hand and stuck it in his breast. He done it, I didn't do it. . . . He killed hisself. [*Old* TAPLEY *and* COLIN *hurry in.*]

TAPLEY. [*Wetting his lips.*] Now jest look—

GRAHAM. There he lies in the woods dead—The slayed—weltering in his own blood, as it was foretold about the beast under seven seals. [*Leading* LORA *off towards the right.*] Let's go home, supper is ready. [*Smacking his lips.*] Supper—eat—eat.—Let the ants and flies tear him off bit by bit. Let him rot—and the buzzards hollow his heart and eyes out. . . .

TAPLEY. [*Striking himself with his hat.*] Great God!

GRAHAM. [*Going off at the right with* LORA.] Turn the earth dark with shame. God said destroy, destroy utterly. The adversary is abroad in the land—kill him, kill him. . . . A blight come into the world. Like him of old I curse my mother now. For let that day perish wherein I was born, and the night in which it is said there is a man child conceived . . . [*They pass out at the right, his voice dying away.*] Let that day be darkness; let not God regard it from above, neither let the light . . .

TAPLEY. [*Fearfully.*] We got to go there in the woods and see . . .

COLIN. [*Bursting into sobs.*] I'm gonna leave here. . . . [*He dashes through the hedge and down the road at the left. Old* TAPLEY *hesitates a moment and them stumbles after him. . . . The scene disappears in darkness. . . . Several minutes pass, and then the light comes up again, showing a bedroom in the Graham farmhouse.*

[*It is a cloudy late afternoon three days later. The light that trickles in from the doorway to the right leaves the room to the left shadowed in a gray semi-darkness. Above the mantel is a faded oil portrait of a courtier in the time of Elizabeth. A coffin draped in a United States flag is placed in the center of the room before the fireplace, its two ends rest-*

ing on chairs. A YOUNG PREACHER *stands at the head reading from a Bible; and at the foot, a* SOLDIER, *erect and stiff, looks before him with unseeing eyes.* GRAHAM *and his wife, dressed in crude mourning, sit on the edge of the bed to the left.* LORA *dressed in black sits nearby, her head slightly bent, with a white flower on her breast. Her clenched hands continually beat a tattoo on her knees. Near the door at the right* COLIN *and* TAPLEY *with several other farmers stand bowed in an attitude of respect. Through the door the faces of neighbors are seen, curious and reverent.*]

PREACHER. [*Reading.*] Wilt thou hide thyself forever? Shall thy wrath burn like fire? Remember how short my time is: wherefore hast thou made all men in vain? What man is he that liveth and shall not see death? Shall he deliver his soul from the hand of the grave? Lord, where are thy former loving-kindnesses, which thou swarest unto David in thy truth? Remember, Lord, the reproach of thy servants; how I do bear in my bosom the reproach of all the mighty people; wherewith thine enemies have reproached, O Lord; wherewith they have reproached the footsteps of thine anointed. Blessed be the name of the Lord forever. Amen and Amen. [*Closing the book.*] So endeth the reading of the lesson according to the Psalms. [*Wiping his face with his handkerchief.*] I passed a cornfield in the spring and near the road a hill of corn was withered and dead. A mole ploughed under it. It put forth its strength in the sun and dew to die in the early days of its life. Death is everywhere and we don't understand it. Books tell us how one nation has to kill off neighboring nations in order to live. And still God says thou shalt not kill. I don't understand it. We see the morning and the evening go by, the trees and plants around us die, and it makes us feel the tragedy of this young man's passing away. The old man like a ripening apple fulfills his season, lives out his years and goes to his everlasting home. But this young man was cut down in the bloom of his days, in the very budding of his spring—cut down without knowing what it is to live to the sweet and peaceful setting of the sun. . . . [*His voice chokes, and* MRS. GRAHAM *sobs in her handkerchief.*] The atheist and the infidel say yes there is no God and there is no hope. A man is no more than a flower, a beast of the field led to slaughter, a leaf flickering down under the winter snow. [*Laying his hand reverently on the Bible.*] But blessed be the name of the Lord, we have a hope. Let the days and seasons change and man's poor life be forfeit, we still have a hope in the Word. It says all things are possible with God. His ways are not like our ways, and everything works for the good of those who love him. Even in the case of this young man who so suddenly took his own life—there is a hope. And I say to the father and mother and the dear sister, let not your hearts be troubled, for I know the Redeemer liveth and he will not desert his own. [*He closes his eyes a moment and is silent.*] Now as the choir sings, those who wish may look at the dead. The service will be concluded at the grave. [*There is a low murmur and stirring in the hall as the* SOLDIER *lifts back the flag and raises the lid. Presently a chorus of rough untrained voices, men and women, begin singing.*]

> "In the land of fadeless day
>   Lies a city four-square,
>   And it ne'er shall pass away,
>   For there is no night there."

[*Neighbors begin to go slowly by the coffin, their faces heavy and sad. A country woman comes in with her little son and lifts him up.*]

WOMAN. [*Softly.*] Kin ye see, sonny?

BOY. [*Loudly.*] He's got curly hair, mammy! [*They pass on and out through a door at the right rear. Others come in as the music continues—farmers and their wives, and children, some young and others bent and toilworn. A little girl and her small brother come in.*]

LITTLE GIRL. [*Whispering loudly.*] He's the purtiest corpse

I ever seen, Buddie. [*Two young women. come by. They stare down in the coffin a moment and then with a poignant look at each other stuff their handkerchiefs to their lips and go out weeping. The music from the hall hesitates and drags as some of the singers enter and go by—*]

> "God shall wipe away all tears,
>   There's no death, no pain nor tears—
> And they count not time by years,
>   For there is no night there."

[*The farmers at the door pass by.*]

TAPLEY. Wanter see him, Colin?

COLIN. Don't want to. [TAPLEY *goes, the last of the procession, looks and returns quietly to his place, tapping his fingers against his trousers.*]

PREACHER. If there's no one else, I'll ask that the lid be closed.

LORA. [*Suddenly starting up from the bed.*] I'll put a flower on his lips, a little flower. [*There is a stir of craning necks and faces in the hall.*]

TAPLEY. [*To the men around him.*] Anh, she does thataway. [*They nod their heads.*]

WOMAN'S VOICE. [*In the hall.*] She's a good Christian girl.

MAN'S VOICE. Like her father and mother.

A GIRL. The best one of 'em all.

WOMAN'S VOICE. Her pore mind's cracked about wi' grief.

LORA. I'll put a flower on him to remember me by. [*She moves across the room with the steps of the Negro mourners, and taking the flower from her breast places it in the coffin. She turns and looks strangely around her.*] I will arise now and go about the city in the streets, and in the broad ways I will seek him.

PREACHER. [*Taking her kindly by the shoulders.*] Don't cry, child, don't cry.

FARMER. Anh, her heart's broke in two.

PREACHER. [*Leading her back to her seat.*] You can put it all on Jesus. He is waiting to bear our griefs . . . he understands . . . Ask God . . . to . . .

LORA. [*Dully.*] There is no God. There's no one but Jesus. He is Jesus and they killed him. Brother was Jesus.

FARMER. Her pore face!

TAPLEY. Anh. [*The* SOLDIER *closes down the lid.*]

GRAHAM. [*Crying out.*] Hide that sinful woman from me!

PREACHER. Our Father—

GRAHAM. [*Standing up as a murmur of horror runs down the hall.*] I shot him and killed him there in the woods. Take me away, put my eyes out, cut my tongue from its roots and bury me in the ground. [MRS. GRAHAM *screams and stares at him in terror.* GRAHAM *points at* LORA.] Out of my loins has come forth the seed of hell. Neighbors will rise up and curse me while the world do stand. Take me away and kill me! [*He rushes out and is heard crying and cursing himself in the distance.*]

THIRD FARMER. [*Awestruck.*] They must be a curse on 'em all.

FOURTH FARMER. He said he killed him.

THIRD FARMER. Too good a man fer that. [*The* SOLDIER *as if unconcerned removes the flowers from the coffin, hands them to several girls, and motions to the men to bear the body out. With the exception of* TAPLEY *and* COLIN *the men at the door move forward and take up the coffin.* LORA *breaks away from the preacher and rushes toward them.*]

LORA. They shan't take you away from me, never as long as I live.

TAPLEY. [*Lifting her firmly to her seat.*] Be quiet now.

LORA. Don't give him to them!

TAPLEY. [*Pushing her back.*] Stop and be easy. [MRS. GRAHAM *gets up and totters into the hall. Hands are stretched through the door to support her. The men go out slowly with the body, the* PREACHER *walking ahead and the* SOLDIER *behind. The crowd follows through the hall and the noise of their going gradually dies up the road.* TAPLEY *and* COLIN *remain by the door, as* LORA *crouches moaning in her chair.*]

COLIN. [*Coming up to her.*] Let me help you to lie down now, you're sick. [*They pick her up and place her on the bed.* COLIN *bends tenderly over her, in a catchy voice.*] Lora, Lora, you jest wring my heart to pieces.

LORA. I can see you there.

COLIN. Oh, please let me do something, Lora.

LORA. And I'll come to you.

TAPLEY. Colin, we better go look for him, his face was quare . . .

COLIN. She's about to go to sleep.

TAPLEY. [*Nervously.*] So much has happened I'm all foolish. Colin, he mought harm hisself . . .

COLIN. I got to watch her. [TAPLEY *goes out at the right.*]

LORA. [*Starting up in the bed, her face transfigured.*] I can see you!

COLIN. [*Laying her gently back.*] Sleep now, sleep right quiet and easy.

LORA. [*In a happy voice.*] They won't ever be able to part us again. . . .

COLIN. [*Bending over her a moment and then sitting down by the bed.*] Oh, I wisht you could sleep till day after tomorrow. Ye ain't slept a wink since it happened. Pore thing—worry, worry, worry! Rest yourself, please rest yourself. Oh, Lora Lora, honey child! [*Several minutes pass and then* TAPLEY *comes in on his tiptoes.*]

TAPLEY. [*Huskily.*] Is she better?

COLIN. Asleep—ssh!

TAPLEY. [*In a hushed voice.*] Before God, Colin, he's gone and done it.

COLIN. Ss-h!

TAPLEY. There he is in the crib hung by a rafter.

COLIN. Lord A'mighty, he couldn't!

TAPLEY. Dead as a wedge. [*Tapping his fingers against his trousers.*] Never was sech a day in the world.

COLIN. [*Standing sharply up.*] My God A'mighty!

TAPLEY. Hunh?

COLIN. Ah, it's been eating in hyuh since that night there in the field. [*Half-whispering.*] I been saying all the time to myself they won't nothing to it. But it was all that made him do it . . .

TAPLEY. [*Peering at him.*] What you saying? . . .

COLIN. [*With an abandoned gesture.*] Him and her there. . .

TAPLEY. I've knowed her from a baby.· . . .

COLIN. [*Staring at him with bright eyes.*] Hanh? . . .

TAPLEY. I dunno . . .

COLIN. [*His shoulders shaking with sobs.*] I ain't gonna believe nothing!

TAPLEY. She's quiet . . . [*He bends closer over her and then steps back, gently removing his hat. His gaze travels around the room as if he wanted to ask somebody a question. Finally his eyes stop on* COLIN.] She's gone, Colin, dead!

COLIN. Lora! [*Burying his face in the bed beside her.*] She was purty as a' angel and now she's dead, that's what she is. [*He seizes her hands and kisses them crazily—softly.*] You useter work in the fields with me, and at night when I'd lay down I thought about you. And when I got up in the morning the sky was purty when I thought about you. [*Rocking himself in grief.*] I didn't treat you right. I killed your little snake and made you feel bad. [*He springs up and seizes* TAPLEY *by the arms.*] You didn't like her, you talked about her mean.

TAPLEY. Lordy mercy!

COLIN. [*Helplessly.*] Now I won't have nothing to think on, nothing no more. [*His agony pouring itself out in words.*] I got to ketch my mule in the morning and go to the fields and plough and plough, row after row. And they won't be no pleasure in watching the crops now. I got to pull the fodder and pick the cotton and feed the stock all through the summer and all through the fall. And the lonesome winter's coming. . . . [*Shuddering.*] I'm gonna quit, gonna go away to public work. I'll leave here. . . . I'm gonna leave—

TAPLEY. [*Looking at the walls queerly.*] They's a hand somewhere. . . . [*He stares fearfully around him.*] Nothing else kin happen. . . . [*He touches* COLIN *on the shoulder and they go slowly out at the right. In the distance a bugle blows. The courtier above the mantel whose face resembles Edward's looks quietly before him as if he had nothing at all to do, with such things, nothing at all.*]

THE PICNIC

CHARACTERS

MISS CHARLOTTE ⎫
MISS ANNIE ⎭ *Sunday School teachers.*

NANCY NELSON, *a tenant farm girl.*

JESSE NELSON, *her brother.*

ED ROBERTS, *a rich young landowner, their landlord.*

ANDERSON COPELAND, *a poor white farmer.*

FLOYD COPELAND, *his young son.*

ETHEL, *a girl.*

BOYS AND GIRLS.

TIME—*A Sunday afternoon, several years ago.*
PLACE—*The slope of a hill in eastern North Carolina.*

THE PICNIC

ON *a late afternoon in summer the Sunday School picnic from Little Bethel Church is nearing an end. Children are playing their last game of hide-and-seek in the woods close upon the grassy slope of a gently descending hill. Their home base is over there where the tops of three or four tall post-oaks and water oaks mark the sudden declivity of a spring ravine. Now and then a country child, calling to his fellows, rushes across the slope. In the background a haphazard worm-fence enclosing a pasture straggles in from the right, crossing the hill and disappearing through a thick growth of old-field pines, sassafras bushes and underbrush at the left rear. The fence is half-hid at the back with a hedge of plum bushes and trumpet vines in full bloom. Beyond and across a field heavy with ripening corn the sun, red as an angry eye-ball, is setting behind a low wall of cloud. In the immediate foreground is a large mossy boulder with a mark on the earth running back to the fence and separating two piles of sticks. The ground is torn and scuffed from the children's recent game of stealing pawns. Down in the depths of the pasture a farmer is heard calling his hogs. He calls softly, for it is on a Sunday, "Whoa—ah, pig! Who-ah, pig!"*

The two teachers come up the hill from the spring.

MISS CHARLOTTE. [*Somewhat prim and nearing fifty.*] They've had a nice day, haven't they? And we have too.

MISS ANNIE. [*Considerably younger and somewhat plump.*] Seems a shame to make 'em stop to eat supper.

MISS CHARLOTTE. But I reckon they're hungry by this time. And see, the sun is setting for bad weather.

MISS ANNIE. Rain on a picnic day or near it. Yes, they ought to be out of the woods. [*Calling.*] Chil—dren!

MISS CHARLOTTE. Tell them to play here in the open till we get supper fixed.

MISS ANNIE. Children! [*One or two answering shouts are heard in the woods.*] You'll have to come play here now!

MISS CHARLOTTE. [*Raising her more timid voice.*] Come along, it's late!

A CHILD. [*Running across the rear.*] Going to the spring for a drink. I'll be right back.

MISS ANNIE. They're following that tomboy Nancy Nelson still.

MISS CHARLOTTE. She does seem a bit that for a girl of twenty. [*Quickly.*] I'm not saying it's harmful in her.

MISS ANNIE. Oh, no, it's all right of course. She just feels good. [*She smiles at* MISS CHARLOTTE.] Chil—dren!

MISS CHARLOTTE. Come along!

MISS ANNIE. There's Nancy's brother out there and that Ethel child. Come on, chil—dren!

MISS CHARLOTTE. They're a job to look after, aren't they?

MISS ANNIE. Oh, I don't mind it so much.

MISS CHARLOTTE. One picnic a summer is enough. No, I don't mind it, but still—

MISS ANNIE. [*Looking at her straight.*] I don't mind children . . . Wear out, rust out . . . No, I don't mind the children.

MISS CHARLOTTE. Yes. Excuse me but, but do you mean something about Mr. Copeland?

MISS ANNIE. [*Moving off towards the right.*] Let's go lay out the supper. Everybody come on up the hill! We did talk some about things down at the spring. [ED ROBERTS *comes down along the fence at the rear*.]

MISS CHARLOTTE. Please don't think I wanted you to tell me. [*Sighing*.] I'd be glad.

MISS ANNIE. Well, everything's so strange. [*Also sighing*.] Nothing's settled of course. [*Timidly*.] We were talking— [*Her voice trails off*.]

MISS CHARLOTTE. Good evening, Mr. Roberts.

ROBERTS. [*Awkwardly*.] Good evening. [*He is a nice-looking, well-built man of thirty, but shy and ungainly in his actions*.]

MISS ANNIE. A surprise to see you.

ROBERTS. I—yes I don't go around much. [*Fooling with his hat*.] Passing on the road—thought I'd stop and get a drink at the spring.

MISS ANNIE. Help yourself. [*He tips his hat and goes off at the left. The two teachers look at each other*.]

MISS CHARLOTTE. That's about the first time I've ever seen him dressed up and away from his farm.

MISS ANNIE. Mr. Copeland—Anderson—said he was at Nancy's party last night.

MISS CHARLOTTE. Umh.

MISS ANNIE. He's about the loneliest person I ever saw. Another man with all his land would be—be different.

MISS CHARLOTTE. Nancy—[*Regretfully*.] I was about to gossip.

MISS ANNIE. What is it about Nancy?

MISS CHARLOTTE. He wants to see Nancy then.

MISS ANNIE. He ought to go out with the girls more. He'd get over his queerness.

MISS CHARLOTTE. Let's go spread supper.

MISS ANNIE. Nancy, come bring the children on!

A VOICE. All right 'm! [*They go off up the hill to the right. Presently there is a scamper at the left and* NANCY NELSON *comes running in, pursued by little* FLOYD COPELAND, *a boy of seven or eight. She flings herself down on the boulder as the boy runs up and touches her.*]

FLOYD. I got yer tag and you cain't git mine. [*He darts away from her and stands waiting.*]

NANCY. [*A raven-haired girl with a lithe, full figure.*] Yes, you got it. Keep it then till the next August. [*Fanning herself with her handkerchief.*] Whew, I'm run to death!

FLOYD. [*Gleefully.*] I knowed we could tar you down. Aw, but come try to ketch me.

NANCY. We got to stop now.

FLOYD. [*Whining.*] We wanter play some more—jest a little bit more.

NANCY. Tell 'em all to come up here and maybe you can play another game of stealing sticks.

FLOYD. [*Dashing off.*] Come on, everybody, we're gonna steal sticks ag'in! [*After a moment,* ED ROBERTS *comes in at the rear and stands watching her.* NANCY *glances stealthily behind her and begins folding her handkerchief aimlessly back and forth across her knees.*]

ROBERTS. How're you today?

NANCY. [*Laughing softly.*] All right, I reckon, about as usual. How're you, Mr. Ed?

ROBERTS. All right. [*Presently.*] What you laughing at?

NANCY. [*Turning and looking at him.*] I wan't laughing. [*He stands awkwardly before her, rolling and unrolling his hat in his hands.*] Maybe it seemed funny to see you at a foolish picnic. [*Suddenly embarrassed.*] I was just a-laughing.

ROBERTS. [*Throwing his hand out with an ungainly gesture.*] Seems funny to me.

NANCY. Thank you, thank you for coming to the party last night.

ROBERTS. [*Staring around at the sky.*] I liked some of it. Fruit-basket I reckon you called it. I was glad to come.

NANCY. [*Doubling over with laughter and yet watching him closely.*] I just about sat in your lap once in the scramble.

ROBERTS. I don't mean—well—I dunno. [*He continues staring at the heavens.*] Sorry I had to leave so early.

NANCY. That was all right. The sky's purty at sundown, ain't it?

ROBERTS. [*Spontaneously.*] All the time. Maybe it's purtier this time of day than any other. [*Hastily.*] It looks purty nice most of the time.

NANCY. [*Standing up.*] It does! That's a purty sunset.

ROBERTS. [*Almost gruffly.*] Yes.

NANCY. [*After a long while.*] How do you like Pa's crop, Mr. Ed?

ROBERTS. Fine . . . Sure—anything. He works hard, you do too—he's a good farmer.

NANCY. He gets discouraged sometimes. [*Timidly.*] You see you never tell him one way or the other.

ROBERTS. Great goodness!

NANCY. We never had such a good crop in Georgy, not the twenty years we stayed there.

ROBERTS. His crop's good. You might keep the dikes built up a little better.

NANCY. I'll tell him.

ROBERTS. [*In alarm.*] I'm not finding fault. He's all right— he's good—you all are good—all right.

NANCY. Thank you. . . . He'll be glad of that.

ROBERTS. The children are coming up this way now.

NANCY. You won't think I'm brassy if I ask you something, Mr. Ed?

ROBERTS. [*Startled.*] No—oh, no.

NANCY. What made you leave so early last night?

ROBERTS. I just had to go. I had to go back home.

NANCY. I thought maybe—well—.

ROBERTS. What in the world is it?

NANCY. I thought maybe [*Confused*] maybe you didn't feel just right being in our house.

ROBERTS. I don't understand all this.

NANCY. I thought once or twice you looked like you were ashamed to be there. [*Looking directly at him.*] That's what I mean.

ROBERTS. Lord a-mercy!

NANCY. [*In a low voice.*] I don't mind being poor, Mr. Ed. I mean it don't make me feel bad.

ROBERTS. [*Starting forward.*] Great goodness, you must be crazy. [*Foolishly.*] No, I mean you're wrong. [*He eyes her in perplexity a moment and then turns and goes off towards the fence at the rear as the children come pouring up the hill.*]

NANCY. [*Starting after him and then stopping.*] That's all right. I didn't mean a thing.

[*A dozen or more boys and girls come pushing and scrouging in, squealing and arguing with one another as they near the game's line. Among them are JESSE NELSON, NANCY'S brother, the ETHEL child, a girl of fifteen and FLOYD ANDER-*]

SON. *The children range from seven or eight up to* JESSE *who is the largest. Some of them are buoyant and light-footed, others thin, undernourished and toil-worn, resembling timid little old men and women browned and burnt by slavery in the fields.*]

CHILDREN. Le's play, le's play!

JESSE. Let Nance be the empire.

NANCY. [*Business like.*] Let everybody get on the side they were before.

[*The children arrange themselves on either side of the line, and soon the game begins.*]

CHILDREN. Dare you to come over, dare you to come over! Coward, coward! We ain't! Yah, yah, we got one. [*A little bent wizened fellow of nine or ten goes across the line and is caught*] Hah, hah—hee, hee. We gotcha.

[*Smiling wanly, he takes his place in the prison ring and stares out with the sad reflective eyes of a monkey in a cage. Another is caught on the opposite side. He looks pleadingly across at* JESSE.]

BOY. Come git me out, Jesse. See, here's my hand reached out.

[*After a moment* JESSE *shoots across the line and seizes a stick, paying no attention to the pleading prisoner. He raises the piece defiantly in his hand.*]

JESSE. Now we'll see who'll git broke up first.

ETHEL. I touched him, I touched him! He's got to go to jail.

JESSE. [*Angrily beating off her hand.*] You didn't neither. I had the stick first. Nancy, you seen me. I was there first.

ETHEL. Was he, Nancy?

NANCY. [*Who has been looking out where* ROBERTS *stands gazing at the field of corn.*] I didn't see it.

CHILDREN ON THE RIGHT. Yah, yah, yah, she didn't see him.

CHILDREN ON THE LEFT. You got to put that stick back. We seen her touch him.

CHILDREN ON THE RIGHT. You're 'bout to git broke up, that's what makes you so ill.

CHILDREN ON THE LEFT. Tain't nuther. But you gotta play fair.

[JESSE *breaks loose from the little girl and marches triumphantly across the line to his party's nest of sticks at the right.*]

ETHEL. [*Sobbing.*] He does it 'cause he's biggest. He's a plumb hawg.

JESSE. [*Glaring back at the enemy.*] Don't neither. I stole it fair.

CHILDREN ON THE LEFT. Make him put it back, Nancy.

NANCY. Jesse, put it back and start again. I didn't see that.

JESSE. Well, where's yer mind?

NANCY. Put it back.

CHILDREN ON THE LEFT. Yah, yah, yah!

JESSE. Well, take the old stick then.

[*He throws it sullenly across to them and the game is renewed.* FLOYD *darts across the line from the left, suddenly stops and hobbles over to the boulder where he sits down nursing his foot in his hands.*]

NANCY. [*Turning around.*] Hurt yourself, Floyd?

FLOYD. [*Gulping.*] Not much.

[*A yell of triumph breaks from the group at the right as one of their number succeeds in stealing a stick.*]

A BOY. Come on now, we got 'em going.

A GIRL. Smarty, smarty, think you done sump'n' 'cause you got one old stick.

[JESSE *watches his chance and shoots across. But this time* ETHEL *is lying in wait for him.*]

NANCY. She got you, Jesse.

[*With a growl he goes and sits in jail with the sticks. Screams of joy burst forth from the conquerors.* MISS ANNIE *comes in from the right and goes to* FLOYD *who is sitting on the boulder picking at his foot.*]

MISS ANNIE. What's the matter, Floyd?

FLOYD. I stepped on a' old plumb thorn.

[*He manfully tries to keep back the tears. She kneels down on the ground by him and draws back with a gasp.*]

MISS ANNIE. You've hurt yourself bad.

[*The game goes on in the rear with shouts and a flood of verbal assaults.*]

FLOYD. If Pa'd come he'd git it out with his knife.

[MISS ANNIE *hurries off down the hill at the left.*]

NANCY. Want me to help you, Floyd?

FLOYD. You go on watch 'em. Pa's coming and 'll fix it.

NANCY. [*Smiling.*] Don't it hurt you mighty bad?

FLOYD. It don't nuther.

CHILDREN ON THE RIGHT. Hah, hah, we got two that time!

JESSE. [*From his prison.*] Some of you let the sticks go and come git me.

A LITTLE GIRL. I got my eye on you all right.

[MISS ANNIE *comes up the hill and behind her* ANDERSON COPELAND, *a tall lean-faced man of about forty-five.*]

COPELAND. [*Dropping down and taking* FLOYD's *foot in his hand.*] Well, looks like you had bad luck, buster.

[*He takes out his knife and with his thumb against the blade finally extracts the thorn.*]

MISS ANNIE. [*Shuddering.*] My, it's an inch long.

FLOYD. [*Smiling grimly at her.*] Pshaw, onct I stuck the pitchfork clean through my foot—that same foot and I didn't cry, did I, Pa?

COPELAND. [*Patting him.*] Purty brave man.

MISS ANNIE. [*Kneeling and wiping the blood from his foot.*] Yes, you are a brave man.

[*She bends and kisses him.*]

FLOYD. [*His lips twisting.*] Don't do that, don't you.

[*With a wail he suddenly buries his head against her breast.*]

CHILDREN ON THE LEFT. Jesse reached out so they could touch him.

JESSE. I didn't do it, I tell you.

[*The two groups rush pellmell across to each other's pile of sticks and seize what they can in angry confusion.* NANCY *moves among them trying to restore peace.*]

COPELAND. [*Bending timidly over* MISS ANNIE *and* FLOYD.] Le's take him up there to the buggy.

MISS ANNIE. Give me your handkerchief.

[*She ties up* FLOYD'S *foot and they take him off to the right.*]

FLOYD. I didn't cry 'bout that thorn—I jest—jest cried.

[MISS ANNIE *and* COPELAND *look at each other fleetingly and move on.* MISS CHARLOTTE *comes down the hill meeting them.*]

MISS ANNIE. [*Hurriedly.*] He hurt his foot, Miss Charlotte, and we're taking him to the buggy.

MISS CHARLOTTE. Bad?

COPELAND. [*Mumbling.*] Not much, he'll be all right.

[*They go out.*]

MISS CHARLOTTE. [*Coming up to* NANCY.] Supper's ready, everybody.

NANCY. Children, supper's about ready up at the wagons.

BOYS AND GIRLS. You said we could play some more, you said so!

A GIRL. You said we'd play King William.

BOYS AND GIRLS. Yes you did, yes you did! King William, King William!

NANCY. Just a little then. [*Timidly.*] Wouldn't you like to play, Miss Charlotte?

MISS CHARLOTTE. No, thank you. [*She goes off up the hill again.* NANCY *takes the hand of the child nearest her and the children form a ring around the boulder.*]

BOYS AND GIRLS. Who'll be in the middle?

NANCY. [*Reflecting.*] Oh, well let Ethel be it. She wan't choosed before. [*The little yellow-haired girl runs into the center of the ring and stands on the boulder. The boys and girls then begin marching around in a circle singing, as they watch her expectantly.*]

> King William was King George's son
> And round the royal race he run,
> He wore a star upon his breast,
>   Points to the east and points to the west.

[ETHEL *turns along with the wheeling marchers, her eyes picking them over.*]

> Go choose your east, go choose your west,
> Choose the one that you love best.

[*The music is punctuated by snickers and muttered gibes as she bashfully chooses* JESSE.]

> If he's not here to take your part,
> Choose another with all your heart.

[*He marches sheepishly into the ring and stands with her.*]

> Down on this carpet you must kneel
> Sure as the grass grows in the field.

[*They kneel down in shy embarrassment.*]

> And when you rise upon your feet,
> Salute your bride and kiss her sweet.

[ETHEL *suddenly terrified, springs up and flees around the ring with* JESSE *in pursuit.*]

A BOY. Skeered of him—hee—hee!

A GIRL. Ketch her, Jesse, ketch her and kiss her. [JESSE *overtakes her and after a brief struggle kisses her. Then she takes her place among the marchers, her face burning with blushes, leaving him in the ring. The music begins again.*]

> King William was King George's son—

[ROBERTS *turns and leans against the fence looking on.* NANCY *glances up and sees him, hesitates a moment, and then moves on with a more nervous step.*]

JESSE. [*Spying him and speaking respectfully.*] Come on play, Mr. Ed.

BOYS AND GIRLS. [*As they march and sing.*] Yes, do, come on! We don't mind grown folks, Nancy's playing. Come on play!

ROBERTS. [*Coming over and standing near the circle.*] Go on, I'm too old for that. [*He stares at them, a smile breaking through his moody countenance.*]

> Go choose your east, go choose your west,
> Choose the one that you love best.

[JESSE *chooses a little tot of a girl amid gales of derision.*]

BOYS AND GIRLS. Ha, ha, ha, he's afraid to choose a big girl. 'Shamed! 'Shamed!

> Down on this carpet you must kneel,
> Sure as the grass grows in the field.

[*When they arise from their knees* JESSE *touches the little girl's hair with his lips and returns to a place next the yellow-haired girl. He bends and whispers something to her. As they pass* ROBERTS *she reaches out and grasps his hand.*]

ETHEL. [*Pulling him.*] Come on, Mr. Ed. and play. [*He pulls back a moment and then joins them.*]

BOYS AND GIRLS. Mr. Ed's gonna play.

ETHEL. Who'll kiss Mr. Ed? [*The children scream with laughter.*]

> King William was King George's son . . .

[*The tiny girl in the center stands confused as the song passes on to the moment of choosing.*]

A BOY. Choose somebody, foolish. [*The little girl bends her head whimpering.*]

JESSE. [*After whispering to* ETHEL.] Choose Nancy. [*The little girl goes and plucks at* NANCY'S *dress.* NANCY, *as if sensing a conspiracy, hesitates, then after a moment follows her in. A sort of jubilation comes over the children and they sing faster, winking and nodding among themselves. The little girl is kissed, and returns to her place.*]

> Go choose your east, go choose your west . . .

[NANCY *looks everywhere along the line except at* ROBERTS.]

A GIRL. She's got to choose somebody.

A BOY. Choose Mr. Ed.

A CHORUS OF VOICES. Choose Mr. Ed, choose Mr. Ed!

BOY. She's ashamed to choose. [*With a desperate movement* NANCY *reaches out and chooses the speaker.*]

NANCY. I choose you.

BOY. [*Pulling back and hurrying on the singers.*] No you don't. I ain't gonna go in, you got to choose him.

VOICES. Yes you have, yes you have! She wants to choose him and she's 'shamed.

NANCY. [*Defiantly.*] I'm not . . . [*Stepping up to* ROBERTS.] I choose you. [*He draws back but the children push him awkwardly into the ring.*]

ROBERTS. [*Waiting a moment and then drawing up his shoulders with a touch of recklessness.*] All right then—go on, go on.

> Down on this carpet you must kneel,
> Sure as the grass grows in the field.

[ROBERTS *kneels down and finally* NANCY *sinks beside him. The children double over in expectancy.*]

> And when you rise upon your feet,
> Salute your bride and kiss her sweet.

[ROBERTS *stands up, but* NANCY *refuses to rise. The chil-dren let go hands and crowd up in a clamorous gang about them.*]

GIRLS AND BOYS. Kiss her, kiss her! Fraidy, fraidy. We dare her to be kissed. [MISS CHARLOTTE *comes down the hill and stops in the background.*]

ROBERTS. [*With a strained laugh.*] Stand up, Nancy. [*But she keeps her head bent down.* ROBERTS *hesitates a moment and then catching her under the chin bends low and kisses*

*her full on the lips. Several of the boys roll over on the
ground squealing with laughter.*]

VOICES. He kissed her.

OTHER VOICES. She kissed him.

OTHER VOICES. Twict!

A BOY. They kissed, I heard it pop.

MISS CHARLOTTE. [*Shrilly as if suddenly exasperated.*]
Everybody come on to supper! [*The children gather themselves together and stampede up the hill at the right, their
voices coming back in merry gibes and catcalls.*]

VOICES. We made 'em kiss—hooray!

MISS CHARLOTTE. Mr. Roberts, you'd better come on to supper . . . [*He stands with his back to her saying nothing.
As if a sob were in her throat.*] I was surprised to . . .

[*She turns abruptly and goes off after the children.* NANCY
looks at ROBERTS *and then hurries off at the right. Left alone,
he sits down on the boulder staring before him.*]

ROBERTS. Now, my Lord. [*He starts and seems to be wondering at his own words.* NANCY *comes quietly back and
stands watching him.*]

NANCY. [*Softly.*] Mr. Ed.

ROBERTS. [*Without turning.*] Yes.

NANCY. Won't you come on?

ROBERTS. I don't want anything, thanky.

NANCY. [*Drawing nearer.*] I'd ought not to asked you in the
ring.

ROBERTS. That's all right. [*She waits and he says no more.
By this time the gray of twilight has drifted down over the
scene. Presently* NANCY *moves nearer to him and reaches
out her hand as if to touch him.*] That's all right, you better
go on eat your supper.

NANCY. [*Her dark eyes glowing over him.*] Mr. Ed.

ROBERTS. [*As if with a warding gesture behind him.*] I'm thinking about something now. Go along. [*She looks back up the hill a moment and then flings herself down at his feet.*]

NANCY. What is it?

ROBERTS. [*Drawing back from her.*] Don't . . . [*He raises his eyes and gazes intently at her as if she were gradually undergoing a change before him.*]

NANCY. [*The sombre strength of her face softening into a warm yearning look.*] What is it?

ROBERTS. Go on now, go on.

NANCY. [*A soft purring throaty note in her voice.*] What have I done?

ROBERTS. You've done a lot.

NANCY. [*Leaning towards him.*] Tell me, Mr. Ed.

ROBERTS. [*With a sharp malevolent laugh.*] Oh, my God! [*Softly.*] Goodness?

NANCY. [*Her eyes falling.*] I don't know.

ROBERTS. [*Leaning over her, his voice coming in a gasp.*] I'm thirty years old and I ain't never been with women, ain't never kissed 'em.

NANCY. Oh, oh—that's all right.

ROBERTS. Ho, you're making fun, are you?

NANCY. No sir.

ROBERTS. By God, you'd better not. [*Fiercely.*] You'd better not if you know what's good for you.

NANCY. Lord, Mr. Ed, I wouldn't never dream of it.

ROBERTS. I've never cussed a word in my life, never used strong words till now.

NANCY. That wasn't bad.

ROBERTS. It won't half as bad as I thought in my mind. [*He shudders and strikes the boulder with his naked fist.*]

NANCY. Don't.

ROBERTS. That's the way I feel in here somehow.

NANCY. What makes you feel like that?

ROBERTS. Yeh, what?

NANCY. [*After a moment.*] I don't know.

ROBERTS. I do.

NANCY. [*Softly.*] Please tell me.

ROBERTS. [*Staring at her with burning eyes.*] Nancy, Nancy! [*She turns her head away with a startled movement and wiggles her feet up and down in her shoes. Once or twice she raises her eyes fleetingly to his and lowers them again.* ROBERTS *glances stealthily around him, hesitates and then snatches her to him and kisses her. Then he pushes her from him and bows his head on his knees.* NANCY *looks up at his bowed form, her face a mixture of hurt and triumph. She waits and waits but he keeps his head bowed.*]

NANCY. Mr. Ed.

ROBERTS. Hush.

NANCY. You, you—why did you do that? Please don't, don't play like that.

ROBERTS. [*Jerking up his head and glaring at her.*] I ain't playing! [*Laughing.*] It's funny!

NANCY. [*Starting.*] Oh—

ROBERTS. [*Struggling for words*]. I'm ashamed of myself. I feel like I'd turned and done something mean—feel all queer. By God, it's your fault. [*Trying to laugh again.*] I didn't mean it, it was fun. [*Now he does laugh, low and sardonically.*] You thought you'd trick me by getting me into the ring, didn't you? Common!

NANCY. Oh, Mr. Ed—

ROBERTS. [*Triumphantly.*] Ha, I know you now. I saw that look in your eyes. I know you.

NANCY. Lord—

ROBERTS. Well, you can forget it. Forget I kissed you that way, if you want to. It didn't mean anything.

NANCY. I know it didn't.

ROBERTS. I told you a lie. Of course I've kissed other women, plenty of 'em, thousands of times, kissed 'em when the moon was shining and all. Don't you believe it?

NANCY. I reckon you've done all them things.

ROBERTS. [*Recklessly.*] I have. People think I'm nothing but a house-boy, something tied, brought-up with apronstrings. I've heard 'em talk, I know. [*Wildly.*] But if they just knew what's in here now—ah—ah. [MISS ANNIE *comes down the hill at the right.*]

MISS ANNIE. Miss Charlotte said it was getting late, Nancy.

ROBERTS. Tell 'em to go ahead.

NANCY. I'm coming. [MISS ANNIE *turns and disappears.*]

ROBERTS. [*Ironically.*] Why don't you go?

NANCY. [*With a sob.*] I'm going now—I'm—I'm sorry about it all. [*But still she sits looking before her.*] Mr. Ed—

ROBERTS. All right.

NANCY. I could tell you something too.

ROBERTS. Tell me.

NANCY. I ain't never kissed anybody before either, whether

there was a moon or no matter what there was.—I mean not
that way.

ROBERTS. [*Coldly.*] You haven't?

NANCY. Never before, but boys have wanted to—

ROBERTS. My tenant Steve?

NANCY. [*Starting.*] He'd want to but wouldn't say so—your
tenant!

ROBERTS. You're going to marry him, ain't you?

NANCY. Father said it, not me. I've got a will of my own—
no, not Steve.

ROBERTS. Who then? Who is he?

NANCY. Nobody.

ROBERTS. Hunh, some of these days I'll be passing on the
road and 'll hear you singing to your, to your children.

NANCY. No.

ROBERTS. They always say that, don't they? And look how it
turns out.

NANCY. [*Sharply.*] Why do you say that to me like that?

ROBERTS. [*Bitterly.*] Go ahead and do it, I'll not stop you.

NANCY. Do what?

ROBERTS. Anything you want to—marry of course—whoever
it is. You can live on my land.

NANCY. [*Furiously.*] Stop it. Oh, Mr. Ed, don't hurt my
feelings.

ROBERTS. [*With a sullen growl.*] All right, if you're so
proud. [*He sits rocking back and forth, his hands locked
around his knees.*]

NANCY. Why do you hurt yourself, hurt yourself so?

ROBERTS. I don't hurt myself. It's my self if I do. [*They sit *saying nothing and the twilight deepens, with now and then a flash of lightning low on the horizon.*]

NANCY. Now I've—[*She turns her head away and tries to hide her tears.*]

ROBERTS. Lord, I've hurt your feelings, haven't I?

NANCY. No, no.

ROBERTS. It's because I'm so torn up and hurt inside myself that I hurt you.

NANCY. [*With a touch of coldness.*] But there's nothing to do about it now. [*She starts to rise.*]

ROBERTS. [*Flinging himself down by her with his arms across her knees.*] Nancy, Nancy, I'm proud and mean. I don't know what makes everything so. I hardly know what I'm saying, but I can't stand to hurt you and see you cry. Nancy, I think a lot of you I do, I wouldn't feel this way if I didn't. [*Hesitating.*] I—I believe I just about love you.

NANCY. [*Pushing him away.*] Oh, please, please, you're sorry for me.

ROBERTS. It's not that. [*Vehemently.*] I swear I love you. Be sorry for me, then.

NANCY. Mr. Ed—Mr. Ed—

ROBERTS. I told you a lie. I've never kissed anybody like that but you. I've been a fraidy like they said up to now. Lord, last night I couldn't get you out of my mind. I run off from your party, for I felt like my heart would break or something. It was queer. I went home and couldn't sleep, and I walked in the fields. And all today I been like in a dream, fighting against coming down here where I knowed you were. And deep down all the time I knew I would come and see you. The children asked me to play and before they asked me I knowed I would and I knew you'd choose me in and I'd kiss you and I knew somehow I'd never go from here till I told you I loved you.

NANCY. [*With a sob.*] Don't say it, I'm not fit to hear it all.

ROBERTS. Nobody is as good as you.

NANCY. I don't know. [*Looking around her in alarm.*] We— we better stop now.

ROBERTS. Don't you like me some?

NANCY. I do. [*Impetuously.*] I don't just about. I do love you. [*Hiding her face in her hand.*] Oh, I'm the foolishest thing ever was! [ROBERTS *draws his arm away and rests on his knees staring at her.*]

ROBERTS. Maybe it'd be better for you not to.

NANCY. Now I don't care since I've said it. I do and have long, long—for months. There's never been anybody but you in my mind since I learned to know you. [*Her words coming out with a rush.*] I used to speak your name and call you Ed to myself, "Ed Roberts" I've said to myself over and over, "Ed, I love you." I knew you were so lonely.

ROBERTS. Did you like that?

NANCY. [*Looking up and smiling at him.*] Yes, I said it, I'm not afraid, and I know what I'm doing.

ROBERTS. Ah, last night and today you've waked up something in me—something in me—something maybe I've never had. [*He leans towards her, and puts his hand against her face.*]

NANCY. [*Shivering.*] You almost make me afraid. [*Holding her hands tight against her breast.*] But I'm not, I'm not afraid of you, Mr. Ed.

ROBERTS. I know you're not.

NANCY. I know you wouldn't— [*Bitterly.*] I'm crazy, like you said.

ROBERTS. [*Uneasily.*] Nancy . . . [*Suddenly on his guard.*] What you mean?

NANCY. [*Smiling.*] That's all right, I haven't asked you. I wouldn't ask you. Let's go now. Oh, they'll see us.

ROBERTS. What were you going to say?

NANCY. But I don't care, I don't, I do love you. [*Looking at him piteously.*] And anything you ask of me I'll give it to you. [*She suddenly throws her arms around his neck and kisses him.*] I do love you.

ROBERTS. [*Springing to his feet.*] Come on with me. We'll go driving down the river road. I've got a fast horse out there and we'll ride, we'll ride all night if you say so. [*Throwing out his arms.*] I'm happy, so happy I wish it would never stop—wish we could ride on forever and ever together. [*He lifts her up.*]

NANCY. I'll go with you.

ROBERTS. [*Rapturously.*] And I don't care what people will say. I don't, by God I don't.

NANCY. People.

ROBERTS. I just thought of—of it.

NANCY. People talk about—

ROBERTS. [*Letting his hands drop away from her, his mood beginning to change.*] People will talk!

NANCY. [*Waiting a moment and then flaring out angrily.*] You're not, you're not worth it. [*She evades his outreached hand and looks at him coldly.*] When will you get any sense?

ROBERTS. [*Amazed.*] I've got sense, I reckon. [*Stingingly.*] Maybe I haven't acted like it. I'd just begun—

NANCY. You'd just begun to act like it and now you're crazy again.

ROBERTS. Granny's alive!

NANCY. Swear like a man. [*Recklessly.*] God damn!

ROBERTS. What ails you?

NANCY. What ails you? [*Furiously.*] I tell you, you don't have to marry me. No, I wouldn't marry you.

ROBERTS. Now don't fire up.

NANCY. [*Straightening her hair and laughing bitterly.*] I'm a crazy fool. [*Quietly.*] I've got a lot of pride too. *Almost sweetly.*] I've loved you for months— [*Quickly.*] Not your money and land.

ROBERTS. [*His face tender again.*] Nancy, I knew you were fine—and straight. I've known all the time you were, were worth it.

NANCY. Worth what? Oh—I know what's wrong with you. [*Now eyeing him as a stranger.*]

ROBERTS. There's nothing wrong. Oh yes, a lot maybe.

NANCY. You been like God in your own mind, set up so high over us all. And always you've been afraid some girl was trying to steal you, and there with your mother in your big house you got queer. Now that she's dead you ought to marry. [*More sweetly still.*] I would make a good wife for you, make a man out of you. [*Laughing again.*] But you're afraid.

ROBERTS. No. Great goodness, Nancy, it's same as if you're somebody all of a sudden I've never known.

NANCY. [*Forlornly.*] Yes.

ROBERTS. You talk so funny. What's come over you?

NANCY. I'm not asking you to marry me. But together we could do a lot in this neighborhood. I've thought about it. I've been to school. I've got as much book sense as you. I can play the piano—[*Her words coming faster and faster.*] My family goes back a long way. We're poor, you're rich. One thing is sure and that is I'm no coward.

ROBERTS. [*Amazed.*] Stop that! and I'm not a coward either, my girl.

NANCY. You're a coward and wrapped up in your narrow self, you lie asleep, hide your rusty money in the bank and don't know what it is to be alive. [*Pushing her body up to his.*] Yes, I'll go driving with you in the night there down on the river, into the dark woods. [*Daringly.*] I'll give you everything. [*Staring at him.*] And you're afraid I'll hurt your good name—[*Bitterly*] or cost you two hundred and fifty dollars in court.

ROBERTS. Get away! [*Wonderingly.*] There's something wrong with her. [*He turns himself about, looks at her, and finally puts on his hat. Presently, as if both ashamed and afraid, he hurries off to the right, his steps quickening into a trot.*]

NANCY. [*Tauntingly.*] Coward, fool—[*She falls down in a heap on the boulder, weeping.*]

JESSE. [*Coming in after a moment with the* ETHEL *child.*] What 'n the world, Sis?

NANCY. You just go on back. Go right on back and leave me alone.

ETHEL. [*Catching* JERRY'S *hand.*] Don't tease her.

JESSE. I ain't. [*He stands watching her, perplexed. Then he pulls* ETHEL *down the hill to the spring, even daring to put his arm stealthily around her.*]

ETHEL. Don't pull me so, Jesse.

JESSE. [*Disappearing over the slope.*] Come on, fraidy, it ain't even dark there. Here we go—run!

IN AUNT MAHALY'S CABIN

CHARACTERS

BLUE-GUM ED
BOLL-WEEVIL } *two Negro murderers.*

AUNT MAHALY, *an old witch-woman from beyond the grave.*

THE BLACK DOG
THE LITTLE GIRL
JACK-MUH-LANTERN
THE IRON-FACED MAN
RAW-HEAD-AND-BLOODY-BONES
THE MOONACK
THE GHOST OF A MURDERED MAN
A MAN WITH A SATCHEL
THE SHERIFF
HIS DEPUTY } *goblins of the swamp who do* AUNT MAHALY'S *bidding.*

TIME—*Several years ago.*
PLACE—*A Cape Fear River swamp in eastern North Carolina.*

IN AUNT MAHALY'S CABIN

THE *scene is* AUNT MAHALY'S *deserted one-room cabin in a deep cypress swamp along the Cape Fear River late one August afternoon. In the center back is a heavy door partly swung open, letting in the sickly bluish light of gathering dusk. High up in the left wall, cut through the heavy logs, is a small opening serving for a window. A wooden shutter made of one width of plank swings from it. Through this window a sort of funnel-shaped column of light comes down, meeting the light from the door near the center of the room, and revealing an old black rusty wash-pot. Brambles and all sorts of puny creepers have grown up through the clay floor, some raising themselves up and falling back in great bows, others clasping the walls with their damp frail hands and running up into the rafters, sticking their heads out towards the window and the door and bending back to hang down in the room like long thin reptiles. A tall clump of willows and jimson weeds has grown up near the right front. As the eye grows accustomed to the gloom, it discovers a sort of low bed in the right rear, partly overgrown with briars and tall large-leaved reeds. Here and there on the floor are broken boards, a box or two, an old chair and, near the center front, a small pile of dry firewood. Further gazing into the thickening shadows reveals an old dress and strings of dried herbs hanging on the left rear wall, and above the door a wide-spreading pair of cowhorns. The sough of the wind in the cypress trees outside moans and whispers, mingled with the long cool notes of calling swamp thrushes. As the dusk grows deeper and deeper, an owl begins hooting far off, and another screams out his ear-splitting reply close by the haunted cabin.*

The thump of running footsteps draws near. It stops, and

then two low hushed voices are heard. After a moment a' tall muscular Negro of twenty-five or thirty, wearing a cap, with torn clothes, peers in through the door. Panting hard, he beckons to someone behind him. Another Negro, short and stocky, about forty, his clothes in shreds, staggers forward into the light. He carries a small satchel.

FIRST NEGRO. [*Almost in a whisper.*] Le's lay low heah, till it's good an' dark. [*He steps into the room.*]

SECOND NEGRO. [*Hesitating, and catching his breath.*] I—I believe I' druther stick in de swamp, Blue-gum. [*He mops his face with his sleeve.*] Lawd, I's run to deaf!

BLUE-GUM. Boll-Weevil, you is a damn fool. We'd be ketched sho' as thunder, I tells you. Dey'll look foh us everywhah but heah in dis ha'nted house. Come on in an' le's rest. You needs it, man.

BOLL-WEEVIL. [*Slumping down on the sill.*] I sho' do.

BLUE-GUM. [*In alarm.*] Don' set dere in de light o' dat do'. Git furder in de room. [BOLL-WEEVIL *rises wearily and reels into the room.*] Gimme dat satchel. I'll take keer of it whiles you rest. [*He reaches out for it.*]

BOLL-WEEVIL. [*Snatching it back and speaking in a hard voice.*] Nunh-unh, no you don't, hoss-cake. I's on to you. Dis satchel stays in my hands till we's safe in Fayetteville.

BLUE-GUM. [*With a sudden fire in his eyes.*] You damn runt, how come you so 'spicious! Didn't I do de killin'?

BOLL-WEEVIL. [*Putting the satchel on the ground and sitting on it.*] You stobbed de white man aw right, but I was de fust one to git claws on de dough, an' I's gwine hold to it till we gits away safe whah we kin split 'er up. I's gwine be sho' o' my ha'f.

BLUE-GUM. Why ain't I gut cause to 'spicion you den? How I know you ain' plannin' to skip wid de whole substance?

BOLL-WEEVIL. [*Calmly.*] You knows I ain't. I's stuck to you times befo', but I 'minds me o' one time you didn't stick to me. Unh-hunh—I's gut yo' number, baby.

BLUE-GUM. I done tol' you I had to run dat time. Dey was a-pushin' me clost.

BOLL-WEEVIL. Pushin' you clost! Well, how clost was dey pushin' o' me! Dat judge in Smithfield gi'n me th'ee yeah foh dat li'l scrap. An' den when I come out, you done spent all de jack, an' I ain't never seed a cent of it.

BLUE-GUM. [*Sullenly.*] Aw right, have it yo' way, li'l man— des' so I gits my shur. [*He moves among the brambles. There is a sudden whirr of wings and scrambling among the vines in the rafters.*]

BOLL-WEEVIL. [*Springing up.*] Lawd in heaben, what's dat!

BLUE-GUM. [*Hiding his fear and laughing quietly.*] Hee— hee—you's a brave man to be in a murder, an' a li'l bird roostin' in a ol' house to skeah hell out o' you!

BOLL-WEEVIL. [*With a grunt of relief.*] Oh, des' a bird! You needn't laugh. I bet it skeahd you.

BLUE-GUM. [*Lying down near the clump of willows.*] Not yo's truly, Boll-Weevil. I was des' listenin' foh one to fly out. I knowed dey'd be roostin' heah.

BOLL-WEEVIL. [*Scornfully.*] Thinks you's pow'ful smart, don't you? Allus prepared foh whut's gwine happen.

BLUE-GUM. Dat's me to a T. Takes mo'n dese heah Nawth Cahlina p'lice an' sher'ffs to ketch Blue-gum Ed. Ain't I been in more scrapes dan any nigger ever bawn in Johnson County, an' is I ever been ketched? Not onct.

BOLL-WEEVIL. Yeh, but you ain't never done murder befo'.

BLUE-GUM. [*With a sudden soberness.*] Dat's so, I ain't. [*He falls to pondering, half to himself.*] God, how dat man rolled his eyes at me when I souse my knife in him!

BOLL-WEEVIL. Whut's dat?

BLUE-GUM. [*Suddenly shaking himself.*] Nothin'. [*With conviction.*] But we's gut de stuff to pay foh it. A whole satchel full. Must be fo' or five thousan' in dere. Le's count an' see. [*He raises himself on his elbow.*]

BOLL-WEEVIL. [*Standing up quickly.*] Not yit, not yit. Wait till we's to Liza's place.

BLUE-GUM. You sho' is a stubborn fellow. [*He lies down again.*] Set down an' rest. I ain't gwine tech you. [BOLL-WEEVIL *sits down and finally stretches himself out with the satchel under his shoulder.*]

BOLL-WEEVIL. [*Threateningly.*] No, I reckon you ain't gwine tech me. You's already gut enough on you to send you to Raleigh to roost in dat big 'lectric cheer.

BLUE-GUM. You, too, nigger, don' you fo'git dat.

BOLL-WEEVIL. I didn't do de deed nohow.

BLUE-GUM. [*Laughing harshly.*] Dat's aw right 'bout de killin'. When I goes, you goes.

BOLL-WEEVIL. Dey says when dey strops you in an' turns on de juice, dat yo' hair des' quiles up an' dey kin smell yo' flush fryin'. I can't stand to think of it. Le's keep travelin'. [*He stands up.*]

BLUE-GUM. [*With forced bravado.*] Listen at dat skunk whimper! Shet yo' jaw an' take it easy. We'll be movin' fo' de moon's riz.

BOLL-WEEVIL. But seems lak to me de longer we stays heah, de mo' time dey has to ketch us.

BLUE-GUM. [*Lowering his voice.*] You's sharp, ain't you? Don' you know dat ten minutes adder de crime dem bank people was on to it an' de sher'ff had every road an' paf watched! Dat man made a hell of a racket de fust time I stobbed him, an' dey's boun' to git onto it quick. Whut chance we gut to git away till it's good an' dark?

BOLL-WEEVIL. But dey'll be all th'ough dis swamp adder us.

BLUE-GUM. Co'se dey will. [*Coolly.*] But dey won't look foh us heah.

BOLL-WEEVIL. Won't? How come?

BLUE-GUM. You sho' is a fool. Ca'se dis is Aunt Mahaly's ha'nted house, an' dey ain't nobody come 'in a mile of it in twelve yeah. Dat's de very reason we come heah. Dey ain't a nigger would come down to dis place adder dark to save his soul from de devil.

BOLL-WEEVIL. De niggers is skeahd aw right, but dem white men—dey'll not mind comin' to dis place.

BLUE-GUM. Yeh, but dey'll already say to deirselves—dey'll say lak dis: "Now every nigger in de country fights shy of dat ol' Mahaly House, and dese two will keep movin' on. Dey won't go dat way th'ough de swamp." And whiles dey is scourin' de creeks, heah you an' me lies safe as ticks.

BOLL-WEEVIL. [*Admiringly.*] You's smart, I'll ha' to hand it to you.

BLUE-GUM. I ain't no fool lak some folks. An' I figger dat later on when dey cain't find us, some of 'em'll say to search dis house. By dat time you an' me'll be clean gone.

BOLL-WEEVIL. [*After a moment.*] But de bloodhounds?

BLUE-GUM. Hain't you thought o' dem, befo'? Look heah, nigger, when you'n me splits up our dough dis time, we ain't pardners no longer. You's des' too simple.

BOLL-WEEVIL. Why foh?

BLUE-GUM. Listen at him! He axes me why foh! You reckon I ain't figgered on de bloodhounds? Co'se I has. An' so I says I gut des' forty minutes in dis house. Dark den. Lak dis: Dey ain't gut no bloodhounds at Smithfield. De nighest is at Fayetteville. In one mo' hour dey'll be heah. In forty minutes us'll be swimmin' down de creek, in fifty in de river, in sixty swum to de island and gut our boat. By two in de mawnin' we'll be sleepin' in Liza's cellar. Dere dat night, dat day an' de next—an' she out choppin' her beans an' milkin' de cows lak all times. Den from dere it's a cinch to make it Norf on de Coast-line.

BOLL-WEEVIL. Jesus Christ, you's de smartest nigger I ever see!

BLUE-GUM. I has to be.

BOLL-WEEVIL. Whyn't you tell me yo' plans befo'?

BLUE-GUM. Listen heah, Boll-Weevil, it don' do to talk too much an' too soon. Put dat in yo' hollow toof an' think on it. Now le's lie quiet an' rest. You's 'bout winded nohow.

BOLL-WEEVIL. I is dat. Lawd, dat was some race we put up. My legs is scratched to a frazzle, an' my insides is a-far foh water.

BLUE-GUM. Never mind yo' troubles. Shet up an' git yo' stren'th back. You ain't had no race a-tall lak whut you's gwine have.

BOLL-WEEVIL. Blue-Gum, you'll des' have to slow down on de next run. I's lot older an' flushier'n you is, an' my wind's short.

BLUE-GUM. [*Stretched out with his head on his arm.*] Pipe down, nigger, an' cool yo' tongue. [*They both are silent.*

BOLL-WEEVIL *arranges his head more comfortably on the satchel. By this time the shadows have deepened in the room. The thrushes have ceased calling, and only the wind is heard, with now and then the hoot of an owl. Presently* BOLL-WEEVIL *calls out in a tired voice.*]

BOLL-WEEVIL. Blue-Gum, if I gits so I cain't go fas' on de next lap, you'll stay by me, won't you?

BLUE-GUM. Whut's eatin' you? Sho' I'll stay by you. Ain't we pardners?

BOLL-WEEVIL. Yeh, yeh, we is. I's yo' buddy in dis, an' you's mine—huh?

BLUE-GUM. We is to de jumpin' off place. You lay and take a li'l snooze ef you wishes it. I's a reg'lar night-hawk foh watchin' an' listenin'.

BOLL-WEEVIL. [*Sleepily.*] Sho' is a good thing I gut you wid me.

BLUE-GUM. Yeh—be easy—be easy. [*A moment passes and* BOLL-WEEVIL *begins to snore.* BLUE-GUM *cautiously raises his head and listens. He calls softly.*] Boll-Weevil! Boll-Weevil! [*As* BOLL-WEEVIL *makes no reply, he stands up, muttering to himself.*] Dat fool is a hindrance an' a drag on me. 'Spicious, too, worse'n a ol' woman. [*He pulls a long knife from his belt.*] Why I ever git in wid him! Dunno how to use his haid mo'n a clay root . . . Boll-Weevil! [*There is no answer. The window slams shut with a bang.*] God a'mighty!

BOLL-WEEVIL. [*Springing up.*] Whut's dat! Uh-hunh, I sees you wid dat knife out, Blue-Gum? Whut'n de name o' God you doin'!

BLUE-GUM. [*Turning towards him.*] S-ss-h! You crazy! I heahd a racket an' gut out my knife to see whut 'twas. 'Twon't nothin' but de wind shettin' de window. See? [*He points to the closed window.*]

BOLL-WEEVIL. Le's leave dis place! Le's git out!

BLUE-GUM. [*Pricking up his ears and grasping* BOLL-WEEVIL *suddenly by the arm.*] Hush! hush! I heah somethin' sho' 'nough now. [*He runs to the door and stands listening. Then he hurries back.*] Listen, you heah somethin'? [BOLL-WEEVIL *listens. A halloo comes from the swamp.*]

BOLL-WEEVIL. Lawd, dat's de officers! Dey's on our trail!

BLUE-GUM. Listen again. You don' heah no bloodhoun's, does you?

BOLL-WEEVIL. [*Listening.*] Not yit. But le's clear out o' heah right now.

BLUE-GUM. Not on yo' life. 'Tain't dark enough yit, I tell you. You'd run right in deir arms in dat swamp. [*Voices are heard nearer.*]

BOLL-WEEVIL. [*Breathlessly.*] Dey's comin' towa'ds dis house!

BLUE-GUM. [*With a show of bravery.*] Quiet yo'se'f. Breave easy. Crawl under dat bed in de corner.

BOLL-WEEVIL. I's 'fraid o' snakes under dere.

BLUE-GUM. Git under. Hurry. [*He crawls under, with the satchel still in his hand.*] I'll lie behind dis mess o' willows.

[*He secretes himself in the shadows. In a moment the* SHERIFF, *a big burly white man, heavily armed, appears at the door and looks in. Behind him is a small thin man, his* DEPUTY, *armed also.*]

DEPUTY. Lonesome looking place, all right.

SHERIFF. It sure is. Waste of time coming by here. Them niggers is ten miles off by now.

DEPUTY. I dunno, you never can tell. Want to go in?

SHERIFF. You couldn't drag a nigger to this part of the swamp with a two-horse team.

DEPUTY. That Blue-Gum Ed is purty keen.

SHERIFF. But not keen enough to hide in a ha'nted house.

DEPUTY. Hynh, I'm gonna look around a bit.

SHERIFF. And I don't like the looks of this place myself. I'll tell the world. Them two negroes is headed straight for Fayetteville this minute. I've already wired the Sheriff there.

DEPUTY. Wait for me while I look in and see what this old witch place is like. [*He pulls out his pistol and steps over the sill. The* SHERIFF *remains at the door with pistol drawn.*] Here's a pot on the floor—what's that for?

SHERIFF. [*Poking his head in.*] They say old Aunt Mahaly used to have that in her witch business. I remember that old woman, and it was so.

DEPUTY. For God's sake! And here hangs one of her dresses on a nail. Been hynh many a year. Phew! Everything's growed up. And, say, here's a bed. Looks like a fine place for highland moccasins and all sorts of snakes. It sure is ha'nted, or nothing ever was.

SHERIFF. I hear some of the boys hallooing down the creek. Maybe they've struck a trail.

DEPUTY. [*Suddenly shouting.*] Heigh, you two niggers, come out of here! [*A drum of wings follows as some birds fly out through the door.*]

SHERIFF. [*Jumping back.*] Heigh, look out! [*He fires his pistol twice in the air.*]

DEPUTY. [*Running to the door.*] What'n the world you shooting at?

SHERIFF. [*Weakly.*] Something went past me with a whiz— and I took a couple of cracks at it.—[*Embarrassed.*] like a fool.

DEPUTY. [*Quietly.*] Nothing but birds I shooed out of there.

SHERIFF. Mebbe so, but it might have been ol' Nick hisself from the racket they made.

DEPUTY. [*Looking back over the room.*] I guess you're right, they didn't come by here. Got a flashlight?

SHERIFF. No, I haven't.

DEPUTY. Why'n the devil didn't we bring one? Trailing a nigger in the dusk like this you need a light to watch for tracks.

SHERIFF. Let's go. The boys ketch 'em and then another lynching!

DEPUTY. You're right and a sweet message from the governor.

[*They go out and are heard talking as they disappear down the slope.* BLUE-GUM *runs to the door and watches a moment; then he comes back and sits down in the chair.*]

BLUE-GUM. Lawd, I don't lak dat depity! [*He looks at his watch.*] Heigh, Boll-Weevil, come out, you'n me's gut to be leavin' heah soon. [BOLL-WEEVIL *suddenly sets up a kicking and thundering under the bed.*] Whut's de trouble? [*Boll-* WEEVIL *rolls out from under the bed, and begins slapping himself, his eyes turning in fear.*] You havin' a fit, man?

BOLL-WEEVIL. [*With a little moan.*] Lawd, I thought I was a gone sucker! Dey's plumb mergens of old scaly pilots under dat bed, and dey kept passin' at me and blowin' der breaf in my face while dat Sheriff was a-cropin' in dis room. A little mo' an' dey'd uh—et me up. [*Shuddering.*] Oh, Lawd!

[BLUE-GUM *starts towards the bed.* BOLL-WEEVIL *like a streak slides under and out again with the satchel.*] Oh, no, nigger, I totes de satchel yit a-while.

BLUE-GUM. [*Shaking his head.*] Min' how you crosses me, I tells you. [*He goes and lies down on the floor back of the willow clump.*]

BOLL-WEEVIL. [*Sitting down in the chair, and holding the sachel in his lap.*] I ain't gwine cross you no mo'n I has to. But we ain't splittin' up till we gits out o' dis trouble to-gedder. How I know you won't gimme de highball soon's you git yo' half? Jesus dem li'l ol' black snake-eyes, how dey shined at me!

BLUE-GUM. I done gi'n you my word of honor.

BOLL-WEEVIL. Word of honor! Whut you doin' standin' up wid yo' knife a while ago?

BLUE-GUM. You is des' a fool from in to out. I tol' you I was listenin' foh somethin'! An' didn't dem officers come im-mejetly?

BOLL-WEEVIL. Mebbe so, mebbe so. [*He sits pondering.*]

BLUE-GUM. [*Trying to change the subject.*] Ain't dat a Sheriff adder yo' heart! De fat head. He couldn't ketch de itch, no lessen me! He's des' too skeered. [*Apprehensively.*] But I don' lak dat li'l man.

BOLL-WEEVIL. Me nuther. [*He begins feeling among the pile of firewood.* BLUE-GUM *watches him carefully. Finally he selects a club and holds it in his hand.*]

BLUE-GUM. [*Somewhat uneasily.*] Whut you doin' wid dat piece o' wood?

BOLL-WEEVIL. Nothin'. I ain't gut no knife an' thought I'd better be puhpared to die fightin' ef dem officers comes back.

BLUE-GUM. [*Eyeing him straightly.*] Uh-huh. [BOLL-WEEVIL *shivers.*] Whut you shilly-shakin' foh—cold?

BOLL-WEEVIL. Yeh. I run so fas' an' gut so hot. I's cold now since I cooled off.

BLUE-GUM. [*Sitting up.*] You's skeahed, ain't you?

BOLL-WEEVIL. No, I ain't skeahed. But I wants to git out o' dis house, I do. Even dat Sheriff was a-feared to come in heah. Ain't no good gwine come of us stayin'—[*His eyes roam around the room.*] Look yonder—whut's dat?

BLUE-GUM. [*Turning.*] What?

BOLL-WEEVIL. Up above dat do!

BLUE-GUM. [*Standing up.*] Oh, dat's a pair o' hawns Aunt Mahaly used to have when dey was a witch man helpin' her, so dey said. He'd put dem hawns on an' go th'ought de country at night layin' spells on people. [*He sits down again and speaks nervously.*] Heah, you quit looking foh dem quare things. 'Twon't do nuther of us no good. Why de devil you shake so?

BOLL-WEEVIL. I cain't he'p it, I tol' you. I's col'.

BLUE-GUM. [*Roughly.*] Yeh, an' you's gwine be colder'n you is if you don' min' out.

BOLL-WEEVIL. [*Straining forward.*] Whut you mean by dat?

BLUE-GUM. Neveh min'. You'll see. I done tol' you to rest an' git yo' wind back. An' heah you is shiverin' an' shakin', skeahed to de'f oveh bein' in a ha'nted house. How you gwine rest if yo' min' don' rest?

BOLL-WEEVIL. [*Mournfully.*] I's a-feahed I's gut reason to shiver.

BLUE-GUM. Reason! You wouldn't ef you had any sense. De ol' woman's been daid twelve long yeah. She cain't hurt you.

BOLL-WEEVIL. How you know? Some of 'em says yo' pap was brought to his de'f by her long adder she was dead 'cause he crossed her in her ways.

BLUE-GUM. All bull, every bit. Pap died natchel. I heard him say dat onct he stuck a redhot farstick into some milk dat ol' Aunt Mahaly had bewitched. An' when she died heah in dis house, dey foun' all de meat burnt away from her breast bone, an' dey 'lowed she'd come to git him. May be somethin' in it, may not be. Ain't nothin' quare in his dyin' sudden, dough. 'Pose yo' min' an' shet out sich thoughts.

BOLL-WEEVIL. She mought a had somethin' to do wid it adder all.

BLUE-GUM. Why'n de hell don't you lie down an' die ef you's skeahed to de'f!

BOLL-WEEVIL. [*After a pause.*] You talks mighty rough. Is we still pardners?

BLUE-GUM. Sho' God is. Why you ax dat?

BOLL-WEEVIL. [*Wretchedly.*] I des' axed.

BLUE-GUM. [*Leaning his head on his hand.*] Hope you's satisfied?

BOLL-WEEVIL. [*Turning towards him, vehemently.*] Blue-Gum Ed, you knows why I's shakin' an' skeahed out'n my skin.

BLUE-GUM. [*Feigning surprise.*] Me? No suh.

BOLL-WEEVIL. You knows dey's somethin' else I's skeahed of mo'n I is de ol' woman.

BLUE-GUM. Lawd, whut kin it be?

BOLL-WEEVIL. You knows what I mean, don't you?

BLUE-GUM. I ain't gut no idee.

BOLL-WEEVIL. [*Almost sobbing.*] Yeh, you has; yeh, you has.

BLUE-GUM. Well, tell me den, so I'll know whut to do.

BOLL-WEEVIL. [*Looking at him piteously.*] It's you, Blue-Gum, you I's skeahed of an' you knows it.

BLUE-GUM. [*Still lying sprawled out.*] Me? [*Softly.*] You hain't gut no reason to be a-feahd o' me, Boll-Weevil.

BOLL-WEEVIL. Don't try to hoss me now, boy. I seed you when you come steppin' over heah wid yo' knife drawed 'while ago. An' I was gittin' ready to down you wid a stick o' wood.

BLUE-GUM. [*Jumping up.*] You damn worm, whut you mean? [*He reaches for his knife.*]

BOLL-WEEVIL. [*Springing out of his chair and gripping his piece of wood.*] I know whut's in yo' min'! An' you knows I ain't gut no knife. I was makin' out I was 'sleep to see whut you'd do.

BLUE-GUM. [*Subsiding and covering his surprise.*] For crap's sake, stop dat yowlin'! You want dat depity comin' heah ag'in?

BOLL-WEEVIL. I wants to know whut you'n me's gwine do.

BLUE-GUM. *Do?* We's gwine make tracks in about five minutes.

BOLL-WEEVIL. I dunno—mebbe not.

BLUE-GUM. Hunh! Why not?

BOLL-WEEVIL. Listen to me, nigger. I's done gut onto yo' game. Whut proof I gut you won't stob me in de back when we gits out in dat swamp an' take all de money an' scoot? Tell me dat.

BLUE-GUM. [*Looking at him in astonishment.*] You's crazy in de haid.

BOLL-WEEVIL. I ain't nuther. I seed you 'while ago, an' I heahd you say I been a drag on you.

BLUE-GUM. [*Shrugging his shoulders.*] I was des' talkin'.

BOLL-WEEVIL. I ain't a complete fool by no means. An' I ain' gwine step out th'ough dat do' til you th'ows away dat knife, so we kin start even.

BLUE-GUM. Th'ow my knife away! Whut we do in a tight!

BOLL-WEEVIL. You said we won't gwine git in no tight— all easy sailin'. No suh, I ain't riskin' it a step. If you wants to go on an' leave all de cash wid me, go ahead. But I ain't budgin' an' givin' up a cent of it till you gits rid o' dat knife.

BLUE-GUM. [*Making a step towards him, his eyes shining.*] You—you chinchy dog, whut's to hinder my cuttin' yo' th'oat dis minnit?

BOLL-WEEVIL. [*Backing away and whining.*] Don't come tow'ds me lookin' lak dat.

BLUE-GUM. [*Pulling his knife.*] You know whut I's gwine do foh you? Des' dis—strangle yo' guts out an' take dat money an' git away. You 'spicious bastard!

BOLL-WEEVIL. [*Moving farther away from him and holding his club in readiness.*] We's buddies, Blue-Gum! [*Swallowing and choking with fear.*] Foh God's sake, don' come at me wid dat knife.

BLUE-GUM. [*Half-snarling.*] We ain' buddies ner nothin' to each other. I's on to yo' game, yes suh. You huntin' a piece o' wood to brad my haid wid. Well, stid o' you brainin' me an' gittin' it all, I's cuttin' yo' th'oat an' gittin' it all. Won't be no halves.

BOLL-WEEVIL. [*Licking his lips.*] You come one step mo' an' I'll yell so loud dem officers'll come a-runnin'.

BLUE-GUM. Do you no good. Dey's clean out'n heahin'.

BOLL-WEEVIL. [*Casting the satchel behind him and taking his club in both hands.*] Aw right, nigger, come on me den, an' yo' brains'll be smeared all over dis stick o' wood. [*They stand watching each other.*] I axes you now ef you wants yo' ha'f o' dat money.

BLUE-GUM. Ha'f! I wants it all an' I's gwine have it all.

BOLL-WEEVIL. Not long as dis light'ood knot holds out. [*They stand calculating.* BOLL-WEEVIL *suddenly cries out.*] Look, foh God's sake, at dat do' a-shettin'! [*With a start of fear* BLUE-GUM *turns his head. As he does so,* BOLL-WEEVIL *springs forward quick as a cat, and brings his club crashing down on his head. With a deep groan,* BLUE-GUM *sinks to his knees.* BOLL-WEEVIL *searches in the corner and picks up the satchel.*] Now see who's boss o' de proceedin's. Thank you very much foh de plans to git away. [BLUE-GUM *sinks forward on his elbows and knees.*] I'd leave a li'l o' dis kale to bury you wid ef I had time. But I's in a hurry. So long, an' maybe ef you an' de debil ever puts on a scrape o' robbin' in hell, you won't be so greedy. [*He looks around him. The door suddenly closes.*] Dark in heah aw right! Lawd, how come dat do' shet? Nothin' but de win'. Whah's dat do'? Heah she is. [*As his fingers feel the cracks.*] Heah's onct I makes a clean haul. [*He turns and calls.*] Blue-Gum! Blue-Gum! Guess I put his lights out aw right. [*He pulls at the door.*] Whut ails dis damn do'! Mus' be stuck. [*Unseen by him,* BLUE-GUM *rises to his feet, draws his knife, and springs forward.* BOLL-WEEVIL *hears him.*] Whut's dat? [*He turns and sees* BLUE-GUM *upon him. His scream gurgles in his throat as the knife almost severs his head from his shoulders. His body falls in a heap on the ground.*]

BLUE-GUM. [*Gnashing his teeth.*] Now—now—you scrush my haid wid a knot an' I cut yo' damn th'oat! [*He rocks his head in pain.*] Lawd, dat nigger 'bout done foh me. [*Exultantly.*] De money's all mine now. Nigger, you is fixed foh life. Rich! No mo' hidin' in de swamps an' jookin' th'ough de shadows. You goes norf an' rides wid de best. [*He feels on the floor and gets the satchel.*] Heah she is, heavy, too. No wonder dat li'l fool didn't want me to git my han's on it. How my haid hurts! [*He puts his hand to it.*] Mercy! My face is civered wid blood. An' everythin' is dizzy lak. [*In a sudden rage he kicks* BOLL-WEEVIL's *body.*] You—you damn dirty thief, to kill me when I won't lookin'. [*He spits on his dead partner, then dropping the satchel, he seizes the body, lifts it in his hands, and throws it crashing into the briars and creepers at the left front.*] I could cut you into sa'sage meat. [*Feeling in his belt.*] Heah, heah, I's lost my knife. [*He feels on the floor. Failing to find it, he stands up.*] Lemme think. I cain't 'member, my haid th'obs so. Yeh, yeh, it mus' still be stickin' in Boll-Weevil's neck. [*Shuddering.*] Ugh, I don' lak de job of gittin' it out now. But I cain't go off wid nothin' to 'tect me. Git on, git on, don' be 'fraid. [*He urges himself over to* BOLL-WEEVIL's *body and feels for his knife.*] Ugh, he's all wet from his shoulders down.

[*While he is searching for his knife a glow begins to rise under the old pot. It grows and gradually lights up the room.* BLUE-GUM *draws back suddenly from the body.*] Ooh! his haid's des' hangin' by a piece o' bone. I sho' gi'n him a rake. But I was mad! Seems lak dey's a light from somewhah. [*He turns and sees the fire mounting around the pot. With a *choking cry, he springs behind the willow clump and stands trembling. In a throaty whisper he talks to himself.*] Now whut kin dat mean! Huh, is I crazy? Sho' cain't be nothin', but dat lick I gut on de haid makes me see red fi' lak dat. Dat's all. [*With a trembling hand he pulls out his watch.*] Time I was leavin' heah. [*He peers through the willows.*] Golly, dey's steam risin' out o' dat pot. Mus' be r'al fiah. [*He puts his hand to his head. Blood is trickling down his face from a gash above his forehead. He feels it gingerly.*] Lawd, I's hurt bad! [*He looks again through the willows.*] Who built dat fi', I want to know? Hain't been nobody in heah to do dat. [*With sudden terror.*] Ha'nts! De ol' woman's mixed up in it somehow! [*His voice in a whine.*] I gut to git away from heah quick. [*He creeps to the extreme right of the room and then by the bed to the door, keeping his eyes all the time on the fire. Picking up the satchel he rushes to the door.*] Dat's quare! She won't open. Pull harder. [*He sets the satchel down and puts his fingers in the crack of the door, pulling again and again. He wipes the sweat and blood from his face.*] Somethin' wrong. Try ag'in, I gut to leave heah.

[*As he is straining at the door, a great black dog rises up out of the shadow at the left rear of the room, comes near* BLUE-GUM *and begins licking up the blood on the floor. He has an enormous mouth and fiery, set eyes that always look straight before him.*]

[BLUE-GUM *backs away from the door and runs against it with all his might. Then he grabs his head in both hands, shaking himself in pain.*] My po' haid, my po' haid. Too much of a jar! I gut to have a log or somethin' an' break down dat do'. [*He turns to look for a heavy timber and sees the dog. With a shout he flies behind the clump of willows, and stands shaking as if with an ague. The dog then goes and sits on his haunches to the left of the door, his great red tongue hanging motionlessly from his jaws and his eyes staring straight before him.* BLUE-GUM *stands twisting his hands together. After a moment he gets up courage to peep through the willows.*] Dere he sets by dat do' to keep me from gwine out. Whut is he—bloodhoun'? Ain' no r'al dog, I 'spects. [*Pondering a moment.*] Seems lak I 'member heahin Pap say people'd meet a dog lak dat roun' graveyards. Ugh! dat ain't no dog. God a'mighty, dat's a ha'nt.

[*He crouches down on his knees.*] Whah's my knife! [*He feels in his pockets, in his belt.*] Gone—lost. Yeh, I 'member, she's lost. [*He looks around at the pile of wood and reaches to pull three or four sticks towards him. He holds a heavy one in his hand and seems to draw comfort from feeling it.*] I reckons ef dat black devil 'tacks me, he's gwine git de hardest tussle he ever had. [*Almost moaning.*] Oh, if I on'y had my knife! [*He raises his head and looks over the room again and cries out almost jubilantly as he spies it lying a few feet from the dog.*] Yonder she is! [*He makes a move to get it and stops.*] No, I cain't face dat dog—wait'll he moves.

[*He sits down again, shaking his head and rocking to and fro.*]

[*While he is doing this, a little girl dressed in white with long yellow hair rises up from the brambles and vines at the left and comes out into the center of the room, all the time keeping her face towards the rear.* BLUE-GUM *looks at his watch.*] Nigger, time you was leavin' dis burg, I tells you. I's gwine git th'ough dat do' somehow. No other way, I'll clamb up to de rafters an' bust my way th'ough de house top! Mus' be rotten by dis time. [*He staggers to his feet and sees the little girl. Gasping.*] Whah'd dat li'l gal come from! [*He watches her with fascinated eyes as she walks forward and picks up the knife and drops it in the pot. Then she walks backwards to the chair and sits down with her face averted from* BLUE-GUM.] Dere goes de last o' my knife. [*He looks at her perplexedly. Something like joy comes into his voice.*]

Things is lookin' better foh me. Dat's a sho' 'nough li'l white gal. I b'lieves she is. Quare how she gut in, dough. I know, she's lost an' come heah tryin' to fin' her mammy. I'll ax her how come she's heah. An' mebbe I'll take her wid me an' have her sont back to her home. Her folks'll sho' be glad. [*He addresses her in a gentle voice.*] Say, li'l gal, whut you doin' in dis ol' house?—She don' heah me! [*Suddenly afraid.*] Mebbe dey's somethin' 'ceiving 'bout her, too. I didn't lak de way she put dat knife in de pot an' den walk back'ards to dat chur. [*He calls again.*] Is you lost, li'l gal, an' cain't fin' yo' mammy? [*She makes no reply.*] Is you a fur ways f'om de place whah you lives? [*He watches her anxiously.*] I cain't make out why she don' say nothin'. Is she lak dat dog—cain't speak? [*Eyeing her closely.*] Sho' she ain't no ha'nt. Look at her li'l han' hangin' by her side, des' as purty as any li'l baby's—flesh an' blood she is. Wish I could see her face dough. [*Shaking his head mournfully.*] Don' know whut to make o' all dis. I's gwine git closer an' git her to speak to me. [*Suddenly jerking his head up.*] Lawd, I's hear'n tell o' people goin' th'ough swamps an' meetin' a li'l gal in de road an' she leadin' 'em into de quag-mars an' leavin' 'em to die. [*Catching his breath.*] Ooh! she ain't gwine lead me into no place to drownd. Nigger, heah's whah you lights a rag. I's gwine out o' dis house. [*He grasps a log, preparatory to climbing up to the rafters.*]

[*The little girl turns toward him. She has neither ears, eyes, nose, nor mouth.* BLUE-GUM *takes his hand from the log.*] Golly, 'bout to leave my satchel. Dat'll never do. [*He looks longingly towards the door where it sits close to the dog.*] Cain't tempt dat dog wid nothin' in my han'. Git me a stick an' I'll have dat satchel. Take mo'n harmless ha'nts to git de best o' me. [*He turns towards the pile of firewood and sees the little girl facing him. His eyes almost start from his head and he clutches at his throat as if stifling. He yells.*] Turn yo' haid away! Turn yo' haid away! God ha' muhcy, she ain't gut no face! [*He puts his arm over his eyes to *shield him from the sight. The little girl turns towards the rear. After a moment,* BLUE-GUM *dares to raise his eyes. He breathes with great relief when he sees she has turned away. Weakly he sits down on the ground, wipes his face, and rocks back and forth.*] Oh, whut's to happen to me!

[*Out of the right corner near the bed rises* JACK-MUH-LAN-TERN, *a creature about four or five feet high, part boy and part dog. His body is hairy like a dog, he leaps like a grasshopper, and his face is terrible to look upon—thick sausage lips open from ear to ear, great goggle eyes, and a goatish beard that sticks sharply down from his chin. He hops noiselessly to his place to the right of the door.*]

[BLUE-GUM *rouses himself out of his moaning and rocking.*] I tells you, nigger, us mus' be leavin' out'n heah. You'll have flesh an' blood ha'nts to deal wid in another hour. [*He picks up a stick.*] Dog or no dog I's gwine git my li'l satchel, an' beat it. [*He taps the stick softly against the ground.*] Des' hold yo' nerve an' be steady. [*He looks up at the rafters.*] Th'ee jumps an' you is out th'ough de roof. [*Shaking his head.*] Dat dog's whut gits my goat. Ef he'd des' shet his eyes or pull in his tongue or somethin'. But he sets an' des' sets. [*With sudden resolve.*] Whut'n de devil you git groanin' an' moanin' over it! Ef dey is ha'nts you's gut to stand 'em. [*He gets up and grips his club.*] Heah goes. Fightin' is better'n givin' up an' dyin'. If dats a sho' 'nough dog an' tries to stop me from gittin' away wid my money, he's gwine call for de calf-rope an' he'p to git dis chunk o' wood out'n his th'oat. [*He turns quickly and takes a step forward, then stops as if paralyzed at the sight of* JACK-MUH-LANTERN. *The piece of wood falls to the ground. He drops to his knees with a sob, wringing his hands, crying out.*] Who is you, standin' dere grinnin'? Speak to me! Is you de devil come to tote me off? [*He suddenly turns his back and sits panting for breath.*] Lawd, I cain't look at dat sight no mo'. [*He lifts up his hands and pleads.*] Jesus, help me, save me! Keep dat grinnin' critter from me. [*Moaning.*] Oh, somebody he'p me. Heah I is shet in wid ha'nts an' cain't git away. [*He bends over and leans his head on the ground, pulling his hair. Presently he grows calmer and sits up.*] Dese heah is ha'nts. Ain't no doubt of it. Dat last one—I knows him. I seed him one night on de road to Selma. Dat's Jack-muh-Lantern. I knows every one of 'em. Now, so fur, so good. An', nigger, you needn't call for help. You gut to help yo'self. Use yo' haid, work yo' brains, I tells you. I knows whut dese ha'nts does. An' ef I keeps up a strong backbone dey cain't make me do nothin' I don' want to. [*Questioningly.*] Now, I dunno 'bout dat. Mought be so ef I had a charm, mole foot or rabbit foot or somethin'. [*Disgustedly.*] Listen at him! 'Cose dey ain't no power in sech.

[*During his talk* RAW-HEAD-AND-BLOODY-BONES *rises up in the left rear and stands between the dog and the left wall. He is a tall specter with a raw, hairless head, dressed in a loose flowing garment. His hands and feet are long, bony and bloody. His eyes and mouth are close.*]

[*Not seeing him,* BLUE-GUM *goes on with his talk.*] Dis much is certain. Ef I's to git away 'fo' dem blood houn's gits on my trail and chews me into flinders, I better be stirrin'. I cain't git out de do', it seems. I's sho' I kin make it th'ough de roof. But I cain't go off an' leave my money. Den—all to be done is to git dat satchel. An', 'y God, I's gwine git it. [*He grasps the club and turns around. A gasp breaks from him as he sees* RAW-HEAD *standing to the left of the dog. His knees almost sag to the floor.*] Uh-huh, another one! Every time I turns my back, one of you comes. I knows you, ol' Raw-Head-and-Bloody-Bones. [*Moistening his lips.*] Hold yo' peace, I ain't gwine bother you. Yeh, lak all de rest, you don' say nothin'. Whut you all doin' heah so silent lak? [*While he is keeping up this rapid talk, he is cunningly slipping towards his satchel sitting between the dog and* JACK-MUH-LANTERN.] Yeh, you all think you'll come heah

an' skeah a po' nigger to de'f, don' you? Well, you's gut yo'
han's full. You all sees me wid my haid laid wide open, ain't
it so? Well, look over in de fur corner an' you'll fin' de body
of him whut done it.

[*Behind him near the willow bushes the* IRON-FACED-MAN
*rises and waits with arms folded across his breast. His uni-
form is that of a Yankee soldier, without a cap. His head and
face are the color of bronze or dull iron.*]

[BLUE-GUM *moves nearer to his satchel, talking boldly all
the while, although his eyes are rolling in terror.*] Yessuh, over in de corner you'll find de fool whut tried to kill
me in de dark. You ha'nts wouldn't harm a po' nigger, would
you? 'Co'se you wouldn't. You's des' heah on yo' own business. I ain't never gwine tell nobody whut I seed. Go right
on ha'ntin' folkses, I ain' never gwine stop you. No-suh!

[*He suddenly darts down and snatches the satchel from the
floor and backs away from them. He shouts joyfully.*]

Hooray, dey's harmless, dey didn't even bother me!
Now, to clamb to de top. [*He looks up, searching a place to
break through the roof.*] Dere's a good place above de bed.
Looks rotten dere. You's des' in time, my boy. Ef you'd
a-waited much longer, you'd been cotched. Tomorrow you
sleeps in Liza's house, hee! hee! Lemme back back, an' git
a runnin' start an' I goes up lak a squirrel. [*Looking at his
satchel.*] No, I gut to have bofe han's free. [*Calculating the
distance.*] Lemme see, I know, I'll buckle dis li'l money safe
to my belt. [*Suddenly springing up in the air.*] Lawd God,
whah dat fi'ry bre'f come from? [*He turns, sees the* IRON-
FACED-MAN *standing stolidly before him.*] Ugh—who's you!
[*He rubs the back of his neck with a trembling hand and
whines.*] Don' you breave on me no mo'. Oh, don' you move.
Hah, I knows you, I knows you, I'on-Face-Man. [*Laughing
weakly.*] *Hee-hee*. I's de only man whut's ever felt yo' bre'f
an' lived. [*His voice rising high.*] Yeh, yeh, I cain't be killed,

dat's it. I's dea'f-proof. [*Pondering.*] Didn't dat low-down
Boll-Weevil try to spill my brains? Didn't do it. No, couldn't,
dat's it. Den dat—dog come to skeer me to deaf. Couldn't do
it. [*Laughing wildly.*] No, suh. An' den each of you ghosts
come to finish de job. [*Boldly.*] But you couldn't do it. I's
too much man foh you. You cain't skeah me. I's lak de cat
whut cain't be killed. Take heart, nigger, take heart, you's
gwine make it yit. Now lemme fix dis satchel to my waist an'
out I goes. [*He undoes his belt and passes it through the
handle and buckles it.*]

[*While he is thus employed, the* MOONACK, *an old thin beard-
less man in a long nightshirt, carrying a walking-stick, eyes
set in a deathly stare, his white hair rising like writhing
worms above his forehead, a frothy substance on his lips,
comes up out of the shadows at the right and stands between*
JACK-MUH-LANTERN *and the* IRON-FACED-MAN.]

[BLUE-GUM *finishes fastening his satchel.*] Ef any o' you
thinks you'll stop me now, you's mistaken a mighty damn
sight. Heah I goes. [*He sees the old man. Blubbering.*]
Anudder one still. Whah you come from, daid man? [*Drawing back before his stare.*] Look at dem eyes! [*Terrified.*]
Yeh, Lawd in heaben, he's come f'om de grave. He ain't
lak dem udder ghostes. I sees de purgin' on his lips. Make
way, make way, I's gwine rise an' fly. [*With a bound he is
on the bed, and stepping on the edge of it, he springs up,
but the satchel hangs between him and the wall, hindering
his movements. He clings to a log and pants.*] How come I
so heavy, cain't lift myself up. Dat damn satchel in de way.
Christ, I's slipping back. [*His hands slip from the wall and
he crashes down among the briars and debris of the bed.
He stands up.*] I ain't hurt, des' jarred a bit. [*He springs
out of the bed and lunges against the door, then claws at it.
Moaning.*] Cain't make it dere. I know. I'll git rid o' dis
hindrance. [*He unbuckles the satchel.*] I'll put dat long green
in my shirt, den nothin' to git in de way. [*He takes the*

satchel from his waist and buckles his belt tightly about him.]
Whyn't I think o' dat befo'? [*He opens the satchel and with
eager hands pulls out a package wrapped in loose brown
paper.*] She's heavy, must be lot o' gol' an' silver in it, too.
[*He undoes the package and holds up a stone. His eyes almost start from his head.*] Whut's dis, whut's dis! [*He
seizes the satchel and feels in it, then throws it from him.
Screaming.*] Dat Boll-Weevil robbed me! [*Crying out in a
loud voice.*] Whah's my money! whah's my money! He's tuk
it an' hid it! [*Seizing the stone.*] Gimme back my money,
damn you, or I'll beat you into sass. [*He springs across the
room and towers above the dead* BOLL-WEEVIL, *holding the
stone high over him.*] Spit out, spit out, whah is she?
[*Lowering his arm.*] He cain't answer you, nigger. He's
daid, daid as a do' nail. [*Sobbing.*] Oh, you li'l devil! whyn't
I look in dat bag 'fo' I cut yo' haid off? [*He hurls the stone
against the lifeless body and stands beaten and helpless in the
middle of the room. Then he falls down on the pile of firewood, moaning and beating his forehead with his fist. He
lays hold of a small stick of wood and sits thinking. Suddenly he springs up, brandishing the stick.*] Dat li'l v'lise was
conjured. 'Twan't Boll-Weevil done it, 'twas dem ha'nts.
[*Glaring at the motionless specters.*] Gi'me back my money!
[*Threateningly.*] You's gut it hid somewhahs, better tell me,
better tell me! [*They eye him silently.*] Don't move, uh?
'Y God, I'll churn you into butter. [*He moves towards
them.*] Talk to me, cough up dat dough! [*With a yell he
springs forward, and whirling his stick above his head,
brings it down on the* IRON-FACED-MAN. *It passes through
him as if he were smoke, and he fades away. Jubilantly.*] I
tol' you I'd smash you up. One gone. [*He strikes at the*
MOONACK, *who also disappears in the shadows at the right.*]
Two of 'em. [*He rushes from one to the other, fighting
and cursing. In a moment he stands alone in the room, panting and wiping his face.*] I reckon I gut de best o' dem
devils. Dat's somethin' foh one nigger to do. Now I clambs

out th'ough de roof. [*Looking around on the floor.*] But I
cain't leave my money. It's heah somewhah in dis room. I'll
find it. [*Looking at the fire around the pot.*] Dat fi' burn
cu'ious. I'll smash dat pot! [*He starts forward with his stick
raised, then stops.*] I gut to have light to look foh dat bundle
o' greenbacks. I'll put out de fi' when I gits my kale. [*He
falls on his knees and begins crawling among the vines and
brambles, all the while talking to himself.*] Rise, dollars,
show yo'self. You's boun' to be heah. [*While he is searching,
a little old ragged Negro woman, wearing a slat-bonnet
pulled down over her face, appears in the room and begins
stirring the pot. She stops stirring and raises her fleshless
hands above her head in an incantation. As she brings them
down, a low rumble of thunder sounds in the distance.* BLUE-
GUM *raises his head and listens.*] Ha, thunder! Dat's good.
Come a big rain an' I's safe from de bloodhoun's. [*He turns
again to his searching, and the old woman resumes her stirring. After a moment she raises her hands again. A louder
rumble of thunder sounds in answer to her summons.*] Sho'
is a storm rising aw right. Hot enough foh somethin'.
Whah's dat money? [*He wriggles among the briars and
shrubs. The wind moans in the trees outside. He scratches
in the bushes and overturns pieces of plank.*] Dat win' do
soun' lak lost speerits cryin'. [*The old woman raises her
hands again, and a louder roll of thunder responds.*] Dat
storm comin' nigher, thank God! I'll take it easy, mebbe stay
heah till day or git dat money back. [*Sitting on his haunches
and thinking.*] Oh, I cain't think foh my po' haid. Lemme
see. Dat satchel was opened whiles I won't lookin'. Dem
ha'nts ain't flesh an' blood. Dey couldn't tuk it. Yessuh, dat
Boll-Weevil slipped dat money out an' hid it heah, figur'n'
to come back an' git it later. I'll fin' it, an' dey won't be no
splittin' it up. [*He cautiously approaches* BOLL-WEEVIL'*s body
and rolls it over.*] Must be heah somewhah in dis corner,
dat's whah he sot most of de time. Jesus, how his eyes shine,
lak a stuck hog! [*The* OLD WOMAN *picks up the open satchel*

and fastens it to her belt.] Thought I heard a jinglin' sound.
[*He turns and gasps.*] Whah'd dat ol' 'oman come from?
[*Standing up.*] Who's you? [*She makes no response and
goes on with her stirring.*] What's she stirrin' in dat pot?
[*Backing behind the willow clump.*] Dat dress an' bonnet's
gone from de wall yonder. She's gut 'em on. [*Whining.*]
Aunt Mahaly, is dat you, come back to ha'nt po' Blue-Gum
Ed? Is you? [*The only reply she makes is to raise her arms
again above her head. This time there is a flash of lightning
seen through the crack in the door, followed by a heavy crash
of thunder.* BLUE-GUM *stands watching her breathlessly.*]
Muhcy, her han's is nothin' but white bone! Whut's she up
to? Dat thunder an' lightnin' seem to be answerin' her or
somethin'. [*She raises her hands. A nearer crash responds.*]
God a'mighty, she's bringin' a storm down on dis house.
[*The wind begins to roar.*] I cain't leave heah now, dat's a
harrycane comin' th'ough de swamp. Whut kin I do! Whut
kin I do! [*He raises his head.*] Whut's she doin' wid dat
satchel? [*As if in answer to his question, she reaches into
it and pulls out a frog by one leg and throws it into the pot.*]
Aunt Mahaly! Aunt Mahaly! Oh, she's makin' her witch
soup to destroy me wid! [*She pulls out a wriggling lizard
and casts it into the pot and goes on stirring. The wind
blows louder. He shivers and watches her with open mouth.
She pulls out a snake and throws it into the pot. A crash of
thunder jars the ground. He cries out.*] Aunt Mahaly, don'
put no mo' in dat pot. Don't destroy me wid thunder an'
lightnin'! [*She throws a mole in. The storm increases.* BLUE-
GUM *moans and rocks on the ground and a wild glazed look
begins to creep into his eyes. He sits with his back to the
old witch. She throws a rat in. He starts as if a pain had
caught him. His tongue hangs from his mouth, and he gasps
for breath. The storm increases. He cries out in a high quavering voice.*] Don't put dat spell on me, don't conjure me!
[*He falls to sobbing. She pulls out several small bones and
throws them in.* BLUE-GUM *squeals in pain, never once look-*

ing around. The wind and thunder gather in violence.] Lawd
have muhcy! Have muhcy, Lawd. Save me! save me! [*She
pulls out a dead man's hand, hairy and pale, and throws it
in. He springs off the ground as if convulsed in unbearable
pain. The storm grows louder, with thunder and lightning
crashing among the trees. His voice rises into a scream.*]
He'p! he'p, she's witchin' me. She's puttin' a spell on me!
[*He pitches forward on his face, his hand falling on the stick
of wood. His fingers feel it, and gradually close around it.
The* OLD WOMAN *stirs the pot and begins circling it.* BLUE-
GUM *crawls to his knees, holding the stick in his hand. Slowly
he staggers to his feet. His eyes are insane with hate and
fear. He foams at the mouth. Laughing wildly, he starts towards her.*] Hee-hee—I'll beat you into de dirt wid my stick.
[*As he comes across the floor, her face is turned towards
him. He snarls.*] You's a skeletum. I sees you. Hee-hee!

[*At a sign from the old witch woman the* GOBLINS *rise again
out of the shadows and stand around the room.*

[*A moment of enlightenment sets* BLUE-GUM *crazy with fear
and he springs like a cat to the right wall and begins climbing to the roof, all the time champing and foaming at the
mouth like a wild animal.* AUNT MAHALY *makes a movement
as if drawing a circle on the floor with her stick. She points
towards* BLUE-GUM, *and as if struck by sudden paralysis, he
falls with a thud to the floor, and rolls out into the circle.
[With a slow step that gradually increases in time, the* GOB-
LINS *begin to walk around his prostrate form,* AUNT MAHALY
going before and the procession ending with the LITTLE GIRL.
At a movement of the OLD WOMAN'*s stick,* BLUE-GUM *sits up.
He begins mumbling and laughing as they go around him.
The storm grows in intensity as the marchers increase their
time,* BLUE-GUM'*s singing and mumbling, rising with it.*

[*A man dressed in a palm-beach suit, carrying a small
satchel, joins the procession. A wide blood-stain spreads out*

from his heart downward. BLUE-GUM *shouts out in a crazy slobbering voice.*]

BLUE-GUM. Ain't you daid, white man, ain't you daid? Whah's my knife? He's gut money in dat satchel. [*With fascinated eyes he watches them going by him.*] Gimme my knife an' let me git to him. [*He makes a weak movement to rise and then falls back to the floor, clapping his hands in time with the marchers.*]

[BOLL-WEEVIL, *with his head hanging on his shoulder and his throat cut wide across, comes out of the corner and begins marching behind the* WHITE MAN. *The marchers increase their pace, the storm grows louder, and* BLUE-GUM'S *laughing and chanting rise shriller.*]

BLUE-GUM. Hi-yee—hi-yee—hi-yee! Hee—hee—hee—Hi-yee—hi-yee—hi-yee! Hee—hee—hee!

[*By this time the marchers are whirling by. Suddenly the* GOBLINS *stand still and* AUNT MAHALY *raises her hands. The room is filled with a blinding light and a terrific explosion. With a shriek,* BLUE-GUM *springs in the air and falls flat on his back, and lies still. The light dies away from the pot, and the room is filled with darkness. The wind and storm die away.*

[*Presently voices are heard outside. The door is pushed open and two figures are discerned, one holding a flash light. They are dripping wet.*]

DEPUTY. That bolt of lightning struck near here. By Jees, that was a sudden storm!

SHERIFF. It's growing quiet now, no use going in. We're already wet.

DEPUTY. Let's git in from under them trees. A limb blow against us an' our tale'd be told. [*He steps into the room, turning his flash-light about.*] Heigh, looka here!

SHERIFF. What is it? [*The* DEPUTY *pulls his pistol and comes up to* BLUE-GUM'S *body.*]

DEPUTY. Great God! Watch out, here lies Blue-Gum dead as a nit.

SHERIFF. [*Coming gingerly in.*] Well sir, there he is.

DEPUTY. [*Turning his light about.*] Here's something else. [*He discovers* BOLL-WEEVIL'S *body.*] Boll-Weevil over here in the corner dead, too.

SHERIFF. [*With his pistol in his hand.*] The damnedest come-off I've ever heard of.

DEPUTY. [*Picking up the satchel.*] Here's the money, and that's not so bad. [*He opens the satchel, and searches in it.*] Every dollar of it too, from the feel. [*His flash-light reveals a package of bills.*]

SHERIFF. Killed each other fighting over it, I bet. Let's get out and shoot a few times, and holler for the fellows. [*He runs out at the rear and fires his pistol off, yelling, "Hoo-ah!" Answering halloos sound down in the swamp.*]

DEPUTY. It'll be a man's job toting 'em out'n this marsh.

THE GOODBYE

CHARACTERS

A MAN
A WOMAN
A BOY

SCENE—*A Room.*
TIME—*The Present.*

THE GOODBYE

A LITTLE *boy six or seven years old, of somewhat swarthy countenance, is sitting on a box in a rough bare room. A woman, wearing a veil and dressed for travelling, is packing a trunk.*

BOY. How long 'fore we're ready, Mammy?

WOMAN. Purty soon now. [*Her voice is husky and tight as if from weeping.*] In a hurry to go?

BOY. [*Soberly—after a moment.*] No 'm.

WOMAN. We'll go as soon as Sandy comes.

BOY. He ain't come wiv the wagon yit?

WOMAN. He'll come purty soon now. [*She takes three or four photographs from the floor and puts them in the trunk.*]

BOY. You said leave 'em.

WOMAN. I'll take 'em now. [*All the while she talks as if only partly concerned with what she is saying.*]

BOY. [*Staring at one of the photographs.*] Why you take him, Mammy?

WOMAN. I'll tell you some of these days. Wouldn't you like to take him?

BOY. I dunno.

WOMAN. Why, Sonny!

BOY. [*Kicking his heels against the side of the box.*] I dunno.

WOMAN. Think of all the candy and things he's brought you.

BOY. [*Springing from the box into the middle of the room.*] Look at me jump.

WOMAN. My, you're same as a man.

BOY. How far we going, Mammy?

WOMAN. A long way, son.

BOY. On the old train?

WOMAN. And on a steam-boat, and purty water.

BOY. And will they be plenty of bicycles and elevents, like you said?

WOMAN. Elephants.

BOY. Elevunts, Mammy?

WOMAN. We'll see heaps of things.

[*The boy takes two large marbles from his pocket, gets down on the floor and begins to shoot them. Presently he stops and sits on his haunches thinking.*]

BOY. Kin I run down and see Uzzy 'fore we go?

WOMAN. You won't have time.

BOY. Wuh gonna drive his little steer this evening. [*He goes up to his mother and leans his head against her.*]

WOMAN. That's right, you were. Mind, I want to close the trunk.

BOY. We got us a new yoke made from a bay-tree. I holp him scrape it.

WOMAN. [*Abstractedly.*] Helped, sonny.

BOY. And we got a new bow and wire key. [*Suddenly flinging himself against his mother, weeping.*] I don't wanta leave Uzzy. [*She takes him in her arms and buries her veiled face against his head.*]

WOMAN. Maybe you'll get a bicycle when we get there.

BOY. [*Growing quiet after a moment.*] With a tool-bag?

WOMAN. And a new pump in it.

BOY. And wind in the tires.

WOMAN. Yes, and handle-bars.

BOY. And I can ride back sometime and see Uzzy, cain't I?

WOMAN. Maybe, when you grow great big.

BOY. [*Standing away from her and looking at her intently.*] That black thing feeled funny 'ginst my face.

WOMAN. Never mind it.

BOY. Why you got it over your face, Mammy?

WOMAN. It keeps the sun from your eyes, baby. [*He catches hold of it and lifts it quickly back over her hat.*]

BOY. Wanta see you look at me. [*The woman is beautiful, with dark eyes and smooth brown skin.*] Look, you's crying.

WOMAN. [*Hastily replacing the veil.*] Play with your marbles while I fasten up the trunk. [*She closes the trunk down and buckles the straps.*]

BOY. [*Presently.*] You wanta go?

WOMAN. We want to go, don't we?

BOY. I wanta stay with Uzzy.

WOMAN. Oh my, I forgot the tray. [*She reopens the trunk, lifts the tray from the floor and puts it in.*] Look out and see if Sandy's coming.

BOY. [*At the window.*] Can't see him nowhere. There's my bantling rooster by the stable.

WOMAN. You can leave him for Uzzy.

BOY. [*Almost whimpering again.*] Wanta take him.

WOMAN. Can't take him on the train, son.

BOY. How come?

WOMAN. The man there'd wouldn't let him ride.

BOY. Will he let me ride, Mammy?

WOMAN. You can ride. And listen to the train blow.

BOY. [*Jubilantly.*] And see the smoke from the engine?

WOMAN. And hear it choo-chooing.

BOY. Will there be coal-cars and freight-cars?

WOMAN. And passenger-cars and flat cars and all kinds of cars.

BOY. Painted red?

WOMAN. Painted red and yellow and blue—and some of them black. All kinds of colors. [*The boy gazes out of the window, lost in thought.*]

BOY. [*Pensively.*] And it'll go fast like Mr. Ed's car, won't it?

WOMAN. [*Fastening the trunk.*] Faster—much faster. The trees'll go by, zip-zip.

BOY. Yonder do come somebody.

WOMAN. The wagon?

BOY. A man in a' ortymobile.

WOMAN. You run and play in the yard.

BOY. It's Mr. Ed.

WOMAN. You go play.

BOY. I wanta stay with you. He might hurt you.

WOMAN. Good gracious, silly! He won't hurt mother.

BOY. Yes'm, he might.

WOMAN. He wouldn't hurt mother for anything.

BOY. How come last night he make you cry so? [*Coming up to her and putting his hand timidly on her shoulder.*] Mammy, don't cry.

WOMAN. *Raising her veil and dabbing her eyes with her handkerchief.*] Now you see, Mother's not crying. Run along. [*The car is heard stopping before the house. The boy goes out at the right and presently a man is heard speaking to him.*]

MAN. Hello, buster.

BOY. Mammy's been a-crying.

MAN. Here's some peppermint I brought you. [*Soon he comes up the porch and enters the room. The woman is sitting on the trunk. Awkwardly.*] Oh, you're all ready.

WOMAN. Yes. [*The man is tall and well-dressed and about thirty-five years old.*]

MAN. Sleep well?

WOMAN. All right, thank you.

MAN. Is there anything I can do?

WOMAN. We're all packed now. [*Suddenly rising and extending her hand.*] Goodbye.

MAN. I wondered if I might maybe drive you to the station. The boy can ride on the wagon.

WOMAN. [*Softly.*] And all the neighbors out looking, Ed?

MAN. Now—don't. Well, we don't mind.

WOMAN. I don't mind. [*Extending her hand again.*] And so I won't be seeing you any more.

MAN. [*Catching her hand and holding it tight in his.*] I never knew till this day what it would be.

WOMAN. Neither of us did.

BOY. [*Outside as a chicken is heard squawking.*] Mammy, I caught him. [*He rushes in with a bantam rooster under his arm, his jaws crammed full of candy.*]

MAN. [*Brightly.*] Going to take him?

BOY. Mammy, lemme. [*To the man.*] Won't they let him ride on the train, Mr. Ed?

MAN. Sure. We'll get a little box in town and put him in it.

BOY. [*Eyeing them.*] Why you hold Mammy's hand like that?

WOMAN. I'm telling Mr. Ed. goodbye. [*She pulls her hand away.*]

MAN. You run out and get a sack to put him in.

WOMAN. There's a flour-sack left on the nail in the kitchen.

MAN. And cut a little hole so he can get air.

BOY. [*Addressing the chicken as he goes out.*] You going to ride way off on the train and look fro' the windows.

MAN. Please don't cry any more.

WOMAN. [*Coldly.*] I'm not crying. [*An awkward silence comes over them.*]

MAN. [*Bursting out.*] I'll never love anybody like you, Lalie, you know that.

WOMAN. [*Impetuously.*] Then why— [*She stops.*]

MAN. Please say it.

WOMAN. [*Almost sobbing.*] Then why all this? This . . .

MAN. That's it. [*Angrily.*] Why in God's name do it?

WOMAN. We see things different. It has to be.

MAN. [*Bitterly.*] Aye, we do.

WOMAN. After you told me about her, it had to be. She comes and I go. Goodbye now, I hear Sandy. Sonny! [*She starts towards the door at the right.*]

MAN. [*Drawing her back, almost roughly.*] I reckon you despise me, Lalie.

WOMAN. [*Pushing her veil back and staring at him directly.*] No, I don't.

MAN. My Lord, you're sweet and beautiful.

WOMAN. She's sweeter.

MAN. From the beginning we've known how it would be. I'm getting on— [*Breaking off.*] God knows, I've stood a lot for you—people talking, friends looking down on me.

WOMAN. [*Soberly.*] Yes, you have. You've been brave. I ought not to complain. [*With sudden forlornness.*] But I haven't been enough and I thought I would be. You thought so too.

MAN. You've been everything.

WOMAN. But not enough.

MAN. [*Vehemently.*] Ain't it natural for a man to want— [*Earnestly.*] to want a family, children? You've got more education and all and you're purtier, purtier. [*Wretchedly.*] But—well, it's so.

WOMAN. To leave your plantation to?

MAN. To want to take his right place in the neighborhood! And Nancy's a poor girl, but still she's all right.

WOMAN. [*Levelly.*] White sons.

MAN. Well, it can't be any other way, I tell you.

WOMAN. That's what I've said. And she will bear you many a one. [*After a long while.*] And without disgrace.

MAN. [*Starting.*] I stayed here most of last night begging you, and I won't any more.

WOMAN. Goodbye. [*Lightly as her voice breaks.*] Like it says in that book, "Fare thee well, and fare thee well." [*A wagon is heard drawing up outside.*]

MAN. [*Wistfully.*] Kiss me.

WOMAN. Goodbye then. [*She kisses him, and then for a moment clings to him.*]

MAN. [*His arms tight around her.*] Lalie, I'll never feel right any more. [*Passionately.*] Say it and I'll never see her again, not another time.

WOMAN. You love her, and that's the way for it to be.

MAN. I love both of you, but you best. Oh, I do.

WOMAN. [*Her face close against his in sudden weakness.*] Then keep me close, don't ever let me go away so far from you!

MAN. I will, I will. You're true and good. I believe in you. You make me clean, make me want to do something great.

WOMAN. And for these seven years you've wanted to, and they've kept you down because of me.

MAN. [*Exultantly and speaking in the air.*] You can tie me to a tree and beat me till the blood runs down and still I'll keep her before you.

WOMAN. [*Catching his arm with a cry.*] Have they threatened you!

MAN. But I don't care. I want to suffer for you, to be purified for something I believe in and love!

WOMAN. [*Snatching his arms from around her.*] Go away, go away now! We've both been crazy all these years.

MAN. If you were in my place you'd let 'em kill you first.

WOMAN. [*Almost moaning.*] It don't matter about me. [*With a sob.*] Oh, you would be so happy with your friends and all!

MAN. If I could stand up before the world and tell 'em what you are! Let the disgrace come! If they could see it and understand!—then I'd feel like a man.

WOMAN. [*Coldly and drawing away from him.*] Please, please go and leave us. I'm weak as a fool.

BOY. [*Coming in from the left.*] I got him all tied up. [*The bantam's head is poked out through a hole in the sack. Suddenly crying out.*] Don't you hurt her!

MAN. [*After a moment.*] Well, I'll go. [*Smiling at her funnily.*] That's the way these things are, you know.

WOMAN. Won't you tell your father goodbye?

BOY. [*Staring at him.*] He ain't my favver.

WOMAN. Tell him you're coming back a big man someday.

MAN. Goodbye, sonny. [*He tries to take the boy in his arms.*]

BOY. [*Rushing to his mother and crying.*] He ain't my favver. [*Sobbing.*] Mammy, make him turn me a-loose.

MAN. That's all right, buster.

A VOICE. [*Outside.*] I's heah foh de trunk, you-all!

MAN. Let me take you over, Lalie?

WOMAN. I'm sorry but I meant what I said last night.

MAN. Won't you write me where you are so I can send you —can help you and Sonny?

WOMAN. [*Turning away suddenly and sitting down on the box.*] I may—I won't promise.

MAN. Tell me where you're going?

WOMAN. [*Looking up.*] I'm going where he can be something and forget—

MAN. [*Quickly and bitterly.*] His father.

WOMAN. What he's seen and would see. [*She is silent.*]

MAN. And so we come to the conclusion of the whole matter, as the Scriptures put it.

WOMAN. [*Softly.*] The beginning maybe. As we put it. [*The boy comes up and stands close to his mother as if to protect her.*]

MAN. And anything you need, write me. He'll need money for his education.

WOMAN. I can work again.

MAN. [*Sharply.*] Oh God, you're crazy! Goodbye. *He turns quickly and goes out through the door at the right.*]

BOY. [*Throwing his arms around his mother's bowed figure.*] Don't cry, pleas'm, Mammy. [*A car is heard driving away.*]

WOMAN. I'm not, Sonny. [*She bows her head in her hands, her shoulders heaving.*]

VOICE. [*On the porch.*] De trunk in dere? [*The woman takes the boy by the hand and they go out at the right.*]

WOMAN. Bring the box too, Sandy.

SANDY. [*Coming in with a flickering smile hovering on his lips.*] Aw raght, Lalie.